THE NŌ PLAYS
OF JAPAN

by

ARTHUR WALEY

With Letters by
Oswald Sickert

GROVE PRESS, INC.   NEW YORK

Library of Congress Catalog Card Number: 57-7376

Eleventh printing

MANUFACTURED IN THE UNITED STATES OF AMERICA

DISTRIBUTED BY RANDOM HOUSE, INC., NEW YORK

PREFACE

TILL a few years ago very little was known about the authorship and early history of the Japanese Nō Plays. The recent researches of Japanese scholars have almost dissipated this darkness.

Most important of all has been the re-discovery of the lost *Works* of Seami, an actor-author of the fourteenth century. His book has not only removed many misconceptions about the early history of Nō, but is in itself one of the most interesting treatises on drama which exists.

In the Introduction I have summarized the results of these native researches and have translated considerable portions of Seami's *Works*, which, though they were discovered in 1908, have not hitherto been mentioned by any European writer except Péri, who, writing a study of Nō as it exists to-day, had occasion to allude to them only incidentally.

The reader will, I think, find it convenient to glance at some of the translations of plays before he embarks on the Introduction. Though English versions of Nō can at best be little more than makeshifts, I think I have managed, *hone wo orite*, " breaking my bones " (to use Seami's expression), to retain in one or two passages in each play something of the original beauty.

Hagoromo, Ikeniye and *Hachi no Ki* were read before the Japan Society, *Hatsuyuki* appeared in *Poetry* (Chicago), and a passage from *Hōkazō* was printed in the *New Statesman*. I am deeply grateful to Miss Sybil Pye, who read the proofs and made many corrections.

1920.

CONTENTS

CHAPTER I

CHAPTER II

CHAPTER III

CHAPTER IV

7

CHAPTER V

CHAPTER VI

CHAPTER VII

CHAPTER VIII

THE NŌ PLAYS OF JAPAN

KEY TO PLANS

PLAN I

THEATRE SET UP IN THE RIVER-BED AT KYŌTO IN 1464; ONAMI'S TROUPE ACTED ON IT FOR THREE DAYS "WITH IMMENSE SUCCESS."

A   The Shōgun.
B   His attendants.
C   His litter.
D   His wife.
E   Her ladies.
F   Her litter.
G   Auditorium.
H   Stage.
I   Musicians.
J   *Hashigakari.*
K   *Gakuya*, served as actors' dressing-room and musicians' room.

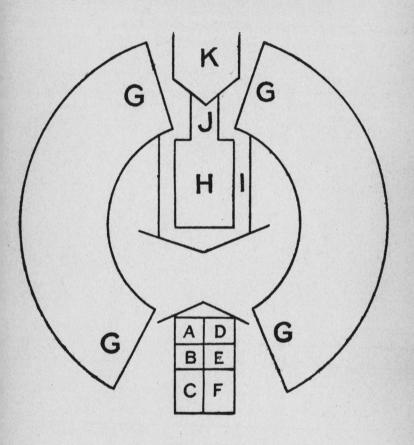

MODERN STAGE

A The Stage.

B The *shite's* Pillar.

C *Shite's* seat, also called "Name-saying seat."

D *Metsuke-bashira*, Pillar on which the actor fixes his eye.

E *Sumi*, the corner.

F *Waki's* Pillar, also called the Prime Minister's Pillar.

G *Waki's* seat.

H *Waki's* direction-point. (The point he faces when in his normal position.)

I Flute-player's Pillar.

J *Atoza*, the Behind-space.

K *Kagami-ita*, the back-wall with the pine-tree painted on it.

L The musicians. (Represented by the four small circles.)

M The stage-attendant's place. (A stage-hand in plain clothes who fetches and carries.)

N *Kirido*, "Hurry-door," also called "Forgetting-door" and "Stomach-ache-door"; used by the chorus and occasionally by actors making a hurried exit. *Vide Hōkazō*, p. 205.

O Chorus, the leader sits near P.

P The Nobles' door (now seldom used).

Q The *Hashigakari*.

R The *kyōgen's* seat.

S The three pine-branches.

T *Shirasu*, a gravel-path.

U *Kizahashi*, steps from stage to auditorium, formerly used by an actor summoned to speak with the Shōgun.

V Actors' dressing-room.

W Curtain between Q and V.

X Dressing-room window.

Y Musicians' room.

see pp. 26ff.

INTRODUCTION

Nō is written with a Chinese character meaning "to
be able." It signifies "talent"; hence "an exhibi-
tion of talent," or "performance."

There flourished in the thirteenth century a performance called *Dengaku no Nō*. The name means
Field-music Performance, and Dengaku seems to have
had its origin in rustic exhibitions of acrobatics and
jugglery.[1] But by the middle of the fourteenth century
it had developed into a kind of opera in which the
performers alternately danced and recited.[2]

About this time another form of Nō came into
prominence. This was the *Sarugaku* or "Monkey-
music," which was originally connected with the
Shintō song-dance or *Kagura*. Its origin is traced
to the occasion when, in order to lure the Sun-god
from his cave, the Goddess Uzume "bared her breasts,
let down her skirt and danced. Then the Gods laughed
till the high plains of Heaven shook." In the reign
of the Emperor Horikawa (1087–1107)[3] on the night
of the holy *Kagura* of the Inner Chamber, the Emperor
sent for the Counsellor Iyetsuna and said to him,
"Let to-night's *Sarugaku* be something remarkable!"
Accordingly, Iyetsuna proposed to his brother that
they should pull up their skirts and, showing their
bare legs in the bright glare of the courtyard fire,
should run round it, singing :

> Later and later grows the night,
> Keener and keener grows the cold ;
> I will lift up my petticoats
> And warm my *fuguri* at the fire.

---

[1] See Seami's *Works*, p. 268.   [2] *Ibid.*, p 201.
[3] Story from the *Uji Shūi*, published *c.* 1215.

When it came to the point, Iyetsuna lost courage ;
but his younger brother Yukitsuna ran twelve or thirteen times round the courtyard fire, warming his bare
legs, "just as though he had really been cold." "The
performance caused a great uproar." Though this
was an admittedly impudent form of *Sarugaku*, the
story enables us to see that the performance consisted
essentially (as the legend of its origin would suggest)
in licentious buffoonery. It was in fact a kind of
indecent charade, an antidote to the solemnity of
the Kagura ceremonies with which it was connected,
and it continued in this state throughout the thirteenth
century.

One of the earliest references to Sarugaku is a passage
in the 24th chapter of the *Romance of Genji* (finished
in 1004 A.D.). Genji holds a great meeting of scholars
and philosophers to celebrate the "naming" of his
daughter. Not possessing Court clothes, they arrive
in oddly assorted garments borrowed from their friends.
Their appearance is so comic that the courtiers cannot
refrain from smiling, a breach of manners which calls
forth a rebuke from one of the philosophers. "Genji
found the sight vastly entertaining, and when, after
the daylight was gone, the fire began to burn up brightly,
the performance took on an even stranger aspect.
In the flickering firelight the garb of the learned men
looked as odd as the disguises of Sarugaku."

The Chinese *Chou Li*[1] speaks of a rustic dance
called Sangaku ("scattered-music") and "Sarugaku"
is often written with characters meaning "scattered-
music," but there is no actual evidence that Sarugaku
came from China ; it must be remembered that the
Japanese liked to give their phrases a Chinese air.

Towards the middle of the fourteenth century the
Sarugaku no Nō had become a serious dramatic performance, the rival of Dengaku, differing from it

---

[1] A book of rites, translated by Biot. Tu Yu (*c.* 800 A.D.) speaks
of Sangaku as "a mixture of masquerade, song and dance" which
certainly sounds very like early Japanese *Sarugaku.*

chiefly in the fact that the actors (instead of sitting in
a row while they recited and then getting up to dance
in silence) sang while they performed the action of
the piece, being aided, after about 1420 A.D., by a
chorus which sang the words for them during the
most energetic parts of their dancing or miming.
During the fourteenth century the term Nō had implied Dengaku ;[1] but from about 1430 onwards it has
meant Sarugaku, and it is with the *Sarugaku no Nō*
that this book deals.

This new kind of performance was a combination
of many elements, such as the *Dengaku* ; the *Kōwaka*,[2]
a recitation accompanied by rhythmical tapping with
the fan ; the *Kuse-mai* or chanted-dance, of which the
portion of a Nō play called *kuse* is the survival ; the
Ko-uta or danced popular-ballad, of which an example
is the song sung by the Hōka-priest in the play *Hōkazō*
(see p. 205) ; and the *Bugaku* or Chinese Court dance.
At its simplest, the Nō play consists of a dance preceded
by a dialogue which explains the significance of the
dance or introduces circumstances which lead naturally
to the dancing of it.

The dancer is called *Shite*, " Doer " or actor ; the
subordinate character who explains is called *Waki*,
" Assistant." Both *Shite* and *Waki* can have *Tsure* or
" Adjuncts."

While Shite dances his principal dance, Waki, as
his name implies, " stands aside " and is for the most
part a silent witness ; the chanting of Shite's part
while he dances falls almost entirely to the chorus,
ten or twelve individuals seated motionless at the side
of the stage. The chanting is accompanied by the

[1] 1250–1350 was the "golden age" of Dengaku. About 1430
it ceased to compete with Sarugaku, though it lingered on till the
middle of the eighteenth century. See five articles on Dengaku by
Prof. Suzuki Chōkō (*Yōkyokukai*, 1916–1917) and *Dengaku in the
Yedo Period*, by Prof. K. Tatsui (*ibid.*, 1918, No. 3).

[2] Supposed to have been invented by Momonoi Tada-aki, aged ten,
in 1403. The words were taken from romances of love and war ;
the Kōwaka survived in Oye (Chikugo Province) till about 1907.

music of a flute, two hand-drums and sometimes a
stick-drum.

I have given a preliminary idea of what the Nō plays
are ; I must now give some account of the farces which
were played as interludes between them. They were
known as *kyōgen* (wild words). This name was applied
to secular entertainments given to relieve the strain
of long religious ceremonies, and implies a prayer that
Buddha may by his magic power turn the mountebank's
"idle chatter" into a hymn of praise. The term is
borrowed from the writings of Po Chü-i,[1] where it
occurs in a passage so popular that it became a *Rōyei* : [2]

> May the vulgar trade of letters that I have plied in this life, all
> the folly of wild words and fine phrases, be transformed into a hymn
> of praise that shall celebrate the Buddha in age on age to come, and
> cause the Great Wheel of Law to turn.

Till a few years ago[3] *kyōgen* were performed in
dumb-show every year at the temple of Mibu-mura in
the province of Aki. These are supposed to have been
instituted to relieve the monotony of the Great Prayer-
meetings *Dai Nembutsu* held by the priest Engaku
Shōnin, *c.* 1300 A.D.

Similarly, comic *kyōgen* were used to relieve the
strain of the elevated Nō performances.[4] They were
acted on the same stage, but musicians and chorus
withdrew. The principal characters are the Daimyō
and the comic servant who hoodwinks him. In the
end the Daimyō usually triumphs and beats the
delinquent violently, reciting the words with which
most *kyōgen* terminate : *Yarumai zo !* "I will not
let you go !" To this type belong most of the farces
which have been translated. There is another class,
fairly numerous and far more entertaining. These
are the *kyōgen* in which Nō plays are parodied. I

[1] Chinese poet, 772–846 A.D. See my *170 Chinese Poems* (Con-
stable, 1918) and *More Translations* (Allen & Unwin, 1919).
[2] A Chinese verse or paragraph set to music and sung.
[3] Still ?
[4] Thus *kyōgen* stands to *Nō* as *sarugaku* had stood to *Kagura*.

have translated the " Bird-catcher in Hell," which is *p. 299.*
a parody of such plays as *Ukai* and *Utō*.

The Nō owes its present form chiefly to the genius
of two men : Kwanami Kiyotsugu (1333–1384 A.D.)
and his son Seami Motokiyo (1363–1444 A.D.).[1] Kwanami
was a priest of the Kasuga Temple near Nara. About
the year 1375 the Shōgun [2] Yoshimitsu saw him performing in a Sarugaku at the New Temple, one of
the three great temples of Kumano in the province of
Kii, and at once took him under his protection.

Ashikaga Yoshimitsu had become ruler of Japan
in 1367, at the age of ten. His family had seized the
Shōgunate in 1338 and wielded absolute power at
Kyōto, while two rival Mikados, one in the north and
one in the south, held impotent and dwindling courts.
The young Shōgun distinguished himself by his patronage
of art and letters, and by his devotion to the religion
of the Zen sect.[3] He gave to Kwanami the fief of
Yūsaki, a small estate in Yamato. The actor left
the priesthood, but soon afterwards died suddenly
in Suruga province at the age of fifty-two.

It is probable that when Yoshimitsu first saw
Kwanami he also became acquainted with his son
Seami, then a boy of twelve. The Shōgun's relations
with this boy seem from the first to have been very
intimate. A diary [4] of the period has the following
entry for the seventh day of the sixth month, 1378 :

For some while Big Tree (i.e. Yoshimitsu) has been making a
favourite of a Sarugaku-boy from Yamato, sharing the same mat
and eating from the same vessels. These Sarugaku people are mere
mendicants, but he treats them with as much esteem as if they were
Privy Counsellors.

The priest Gidō says in his Diary (last day of the
third month, 1386) :

In the course of a conversation which I had with the Shōgun to-day
he asked me how his late uncle Moto-uji had amused himself at

---

[1] I have discussed the question of these dates in No. 5 of *Bulletin
of the School of Oriental Studies.*
[2] Military ruler.   [3] See p. 58.   [4] The *Latter Gumaiki.*

Kamakura. I answered, "He was chiefly occupied with his religious devotions and the cares of government. But in his leisure he delighted in music, and indeed in every other art, except these rustic caperings which are now the fashion. These he never once witnessed during his whole life." The Shōgun asked, "How was that ? " I answered, "He remembered that his uncle Tadayoshi [1] disapproved of places of amusement, thinking that they interfered with good government." At this the Shōgun hung his head and looked very much ashamed.

There is no reason to doubt that this reproof was aimed at Yoshimitsu's patronage of Nō and similar entertainments. [2]

A passage in Seami's own *Works* (p. 271) further illustrates his relations with Yoshimitsu :

The Lord Roku-on-in (i.e. Yoshimitsu) had a mistress named Taka-hashi. She was skilled in ten thousand arts of love and made it her business to please him. This lady died unexpectedly. It was she who had cared for the August Health, forcing her Master to drink when he needed wine and restraining him from drinking at times when abstinence was desirable. By this devoted attention to his welfare she had raised herself to a position of importance.

What I have here recorded is indeed a matter of common knowledge.

After this lady's death every one recommended Seami as one particularly qualified for such a situation.

Seami was not the Shōgun's only boy-favourite. The priest Hekizan records in his Diary for 1460 that at the Jōmyōji he met with a certain ascetic. This ascetic's father had been a boy of great beauty, known as Michichiyo. He was the favourite of the Shōgun Yoshimitsu, who painted for him an image of Kwannon, inscribing it with a mystic poem which bore the colophon " Written for Michichiyo." '" The ascetic," continues the writer of the Diary, " brought out this painting and showed it to me. The inscription convinced me that Michichiyo must indeed have been on intimate terms with the Great."

[1] Brother of the first Ashikaga Shōgun.
[2] Such, at any rate, is the conclusion of a Japanese writer (*Yōkyo-kukai*, September, 1918). It may, of course, be objected that these performances were not exactly what we mean by Nō to-day. But a perusal of Seami's *Works* will show that in all essentials the Nō of to-day already existed in the fourteenth century, under the name *Sarugaku no Nō*.

I have already referred to Seami's *Works*, and as I shall cite them frequently, I must here say something of their history.

About the year 1600 there was printed a book in eight chapters, the *Kwadensho*, purporting to be a treatise by Seami. In 1908, however, a manuscript came to light containing not only a very different version of the *Kwadensho*, but also fifteen other treatises by Seami. The genuineness of these sixteen treatises [1] (which I refer to in this book as Seami's *Works*) has never been questioned, and is indeed beyond doubt. A comparison between the *Kwadensho* of the *Works* and that printed in 1600 shows that the latter, though it reproduces certain passages of Seami's book, is in the main a composition of the sixteenth century. M. Péri calls it the " faux Kwadensho," noting that " néanmoins cet ouvrage garde une certaine valeur, comme témoin de la tradition." I shall refer to it as the *Later Kwadensho*.[2] The name " Kwadensho " means the " Book of the Handing on of the Flower," an allusion to the handing on of Buddha's " flower-thought " to Kāshyapa and from Kāshyapa to the Zen patriarchs in succession.[3]

It is obvious that Seami was deeply imbued with the teachings of Zen, in which cult Yoshimitsu may have been his master. The difficult term *yūgen* which occurs constantly in the *Works* is derived from Zen literature. It means " what lies beneath the surface " ; the subtle, as opposed to the obvious ; the hint, as opposed to the statement. It is applied to the natural grace of a boy's movements, to the gentle restraint of a nobleman's speech and bearing. " When notes fall sweetly and flutter delicately to the ear," that is the *yūgen* of music. The symbol of *yūgen* is " a white bird with a flower in its beak." " To watch the sun sink behind a flower-clad hill, to wander on and on

---

[1] With the possible exception of chapters iv. and v. of the *Kwadensho*.
[2] This is the book which is quoted by Fenollosa.
[3] See note on Buddhism, p. 58.

in a huge forest with no thought of return, to stand
upon the shore and gaze after a boat that goes hid
by far-off islands, to ponder on the journey of wild-
geese seen and lost among the clouds "—such are the
gates to *yūgen*.

In one passage in particular (p. 65) he shows his
Zen training. Gestures and intonations, he says,
which yesterday appeared to be admirable, may
to-day seem insufferable, even though the same actors
be playing in the same play. " If you look deeply
into the ultimate essentials of this art, you will find
that what is called ' the flower ' has no separate existence. Were it not for the spectator who reads into
the performance a thousand excellences, there would
be no ' flower ' at all. The Sūtra says ' Good and ill
are one ; villainy and honesty are of like kind.' Indeed, what standard have we whereby to discern good
from bad ? We can only take what suits the need
of the moment and call it ' good.' "

Seami's treatises were written not for publication,
but for the instruction of his pupils—in particular
of his son Motoyoshi.[1] They contain repeated injunc-
tions of secrecy, for all teaching was regarded as a
form of mystic initiation, however vague the precepts.
There was felt to be a magic in the teacher's words
which lay outside their actual meaning. These " mysteries "—such, for example, as the secret tradition of the
Kanō school of painting—appear extraordinarily meagre
if objectively examined. In the last treatise but
one, written in his seventieth year, Seami sets out
to expound the inner mysteries which he had not
been able to reveal to his short-lived son Motomasa.[2]
The words " Deeply Secret," repeated three times,
occur at the beginning and end of the revelation, but
what lies between seems strangely insignificant.

[1] Retired from the stage and became a priest in 1430. There is
evidence that Seami did not transmit the *Works* to his successor,
Onami, which would account for their long disappearance.
[2] Died in 1431, before the age of forty.

I will now quote a few passages from the *Works*, beginning with those which describe the acting of Kwanami and his predecessors : [1]

ITCHŪ.—Dengaku is generally considered inferior to Sarugaku, but in modern times arose the great master of this art, Itchū, an actor of the Yamato school, who excelled in every kind of rôle; especially in portraying the angry aspect of ghosts and spirits he showed absolute mastery. My late father (Kwanami) constantly said that his own style was based on that of Itchū (p. 42).

In the old style, the Dengaku master Itchū and more recently in our art Kwanami and Inuō of Hiyoshi,—all these made *yūgen* the basis of their singing and movements (p. 167).

KIAMI.—Kiami was the "father of music " . . . When I was twelve years old a *shōzoku-tamawari* [2] Nō was given at the Hō-on-in in the Southern Capital. I went to it very curious to know what I should hear. Kiami was acting the part of the Old Man, with a hemp-wig and bare face.[3] In the passage " Long ago in the great city I lived in splendour . . ." with which the first chant begins, he sang the words quite simply and directly, almost stolidly.

In the Nō of the *Charcoal-Burners* he wore the same hemp-wig pushed back and tied on the top of his head, and had on the old man's mask which Zōami wears to-day. His coloured shirt was of one thickness and his robe was of hackled silk. With sleeves girt up and firewood loaded on his back, thrusting in front of him with his long stick, he halted in the middle of the *hashigakari* [4] and called, " Hie, you mountain-men, is your burden too light, or are you in a hurry to reach your homes, or is it the cold storm-wind that drives you so fast ? . . ."

It is said that soon after this performance at the Southern Capital, Kiami's voice began to lose its power (p. 201 *seq.*).

INUŌ.—Inuō's " flower " was of the " upper-first " rank. It never fell even to the " upper-middle," and the " lower-middle " style was utterly unknown to him. In music, perhaps, he may be said only to have attained to the upper-middle class.

In the Nō of *Aoi no Uye* [5] he appeared as the lady of the chariot, trailing a willow-lined robe. Clutching at the shafts, he stood on the *hashigakari* and sang :

> In the Three Coaches
> That travel on the Road of Law
> I drove out of the Burning House. . . .
> Is there no way to banish the broken coach
> That stands at Yūgao's door ?

---

[1] The reader will perhaps prefer to skip these sections and read them as an appendix to the book. But it seemed better to preserve the chronological order of Seami's account.

[2] A performance acted in costumes lent by noblemen.

[3] I.e. without mask.   [4] See plans, pp. 10–13.

[5] Translated p. 179.

These opening words fell from his lips in a welling stream of sound. And in the crescendo which follows :

> This world is like the wheels of the little ox-cart ;
> Round and round they go . . .

he paused on the last syllable of *kuruma* (" cart ") and marked the beat sharply with his foot.

Later on (when *shite* appears as the phantom of Rokujō), at the words " Then in answer to the Yamabushi's prayers," [1] the way in which he turned his head and manipulated his cloak were inexpressibly beautiful (p. 203).

KWANAMI.—It was in the Nō of *Shizuka's Dance* and the Nō of the mad lady at Saga Prayer-meeting [2] that my father Kwanami won his reputation. In these plays his *yūgen* was unsurpassed.

Though he could take adult male rôles, he played female parts with great delicacy. And when in *Jinen Koji* and other such plays, wearing a black wig, he took his seat on the high daïs, he did not seem much more than twelve years old. And when, beginning with the words " Now the doctrine of our lord Shākyamuni Buddha . . ." he gradually slipped from one chant to another, the Shōgun Roku-on-in (Yoshimitsu), who was opposite Seami, cried in jest, " Though the lad makes good progress, he will never get as far as this." [3] By this pleasantry the Shōgun expressed how deeply he had been moved by Kwanami's acting (p. 207).

My late father, even when acting in the remotest country districts or out-of-the-way mountain villages, was at pains to adapt his performance to local manners and prejudices (p. 47).

The perfect actor is he who can win certain praise alike in palaces, temples or villages, or even at festivals held in the shrines of the remotest provinces (p. 46).

We next come to a few extracts which deal with Seami's own career.

SEAMI.—From my earliest years I had the support of my father, so that the above chapters . . . do not proceed wholly from my own imagination. In the twenty years which have passed since I became a man I have practised his style, drawing on the store of things seen and heard (during his lifetime) (p. 48).

(My) chanting at the beginning of *Ukai* is closely modelled on Kwanami's style,—the words lightly spoken on the ends of the lips. The chanting in this play from beginning to end is all in the vehement mode.

The acting of the ghost in this play is based on the style of the early actor Muma no Shirō, from whom Kwanami learnt to play such parts.

---

[1] These few words do not occur in the play as we now have it.
[2] Now called *Hyakuman*.
[3] The text of the joke is very uncertain and the meaning probably irrecoverable. The " lad " is, of course, Seami.

I never saw Mitsutarō in ghost-rôles. But from what I have been
told by old people I gather that his movements delicately suggested
"disappearing and coming forth." In the Nō *Tōrō* Kwanami took
the secondary part, while I acted *shite*. It was said that my acting
in the "disappearing and coming forth" passages reminded people
of Mitsutarō. This was the first time I had taken a "mad part"
(*kurui*) (p. 209).

In the play *Obasute* (by Seami himself), when she says, "I am
ashamed to be seen even by the moon," some actors of the part stretch
down as though they were snatching up a penny in the road. But
Sarugaku is meant to be seen at a distance; its movements should
be leisurely and deliberate (p. 213).

In the 19th year of Ōyei (1422) (Note in the original : "I am not
sure of this date ; I must verify it ") Oji no Tachibana of the Hōshōji
at Inari met with a serious accident and his life was in danger. The
god of Inari took possession of a girl and said through her mouth,
"If the Kwanze (i.e. Seami) performs some plays for me, the sick
man will recover."

So there was a Sarugaku performance at Inari. The god, speaking
through this girl's mouth, again said, "There must be ten pieces
played, three at the Ise, three at the Kasuga, three at the Hachiman
Temple and one at my shrine." So the ten pieces were played. Seami
went to pay his respects at the (sick man's) house, and as soon as he
got there the servants went in and told their master "The Kwanze
has come !" So he was ushered in and presented with a robe of red
silk, which he still possesses.

In the 29th year of Ōyei (1432) the daughter of a worker in *hinoki*-
bark who lived close to the Shōkoku Temple fell dangerously ill.
Then the god of Kitano sent from his shrine an inspired dream which
said, "Take the words of the poem 'If the east wind blows' [1] and
make progression-poems [2] out of them. Then let the Kwanze 'mark'
them and sealing them up, lay them before the god."

As the message seemed to be without doubt inspired, they made
the poems, "took the affinities" and let Seami do the "marking."
At first the issue was difficult to decide, but when they had performed the ceremony of ablution, they succeeded in arriving at a
"concordance."

At this time I had already retired, so that it was doubtful which
"Kwanze" [3] the divine dream intended. But it was decided that
the god had meant Seami. While I was still called Fujiwaka (Seami's
boy-name), the god sent two dreams bidding them hand over (to
me) an inscription bearing the blessed name of Amida written by the
god of Tabu no Mine in his own hand and preserved from generation
to generation by the people of the place. I still possess it ; the letters
are written in *dei*.[4] Such happenings are strange indeed ; and I

---

[1] A famous poem by Michizane.
[2] I do not know what these "progressions," *susume*, imply ; nor
do I understand what process of divination is referred to in the lines
which follow.
[3] Seami or his nephew Onami.
[4] Gold or silver-dust mixed with glue.

record them only to show what favour our art has found in the sight of the gods.

No such portents have been recorded since long ago (my ancestor) Hata no Ujiyasu received an answer to his prayers from the Dragon-store Divinity of Hatsuse (pp. 266–268).

This anecdote has little to do with Nō, but it acquaints us with the strange mental environment in which Seami lived.

In the paragraphs which follow I shall deal with the various appurtenances of Nō, first quoting Seami's information and then showing to what extent modern practice differs from ancient.

THE STAGE.—The enclosure (auditorium) for a *Kwanjin*[1] perfor-mance should cover an area of about 62 *ken*;[2] in recent times the seats have sometimes covered more than 70 *ken*, the size being in-creased to admit a larger number of spectators on each side. The Dengaku actor Kiami never built an auditorium of more than 50 *ken*. This was because he had not a strong voice and wished his chanting to be properly heard. The Tadasu-ga-hara and Reisei river-beds were the first sites of these performances, and should be carefully studied. (Note by Seami : " I wrote this down from hearsay when I was quite young. It is too vague ; I must make further researches.")

The stage should not stand back or forward, to right or left, but right in the middle of the auditorium, for the voice always travels best in a straight line. Before a performance the stage and " bridge " should be carefully examined and any nails or other dangerous places put to rights.

When the audience is large, the stage-floor may be planed down a little and straw-carpets spread. In certain places, as for example where the *waki*-actor stands to sing, good carpets may be used (p. 247).

Something of the form of the modern Nō stage may be learnt from Plate II and from the plans on pp. 10–13. It is made of very smooth *hinoki*-wood. On the boards of the back wall is painted a pine-tree ; the other sides are open. A "gallery," the *hashigakari*,[3] leads to (V), the green-room, from which it is separated by a curtain (W) which is raised

[1] Performance given by a temple and nobleman in order to collect funds for repairing a temple, bridge or the like.

[2] The *ken* at that date equalled about 5 ft. square.

[3] The *hashigakari* was in early days at right angles to the back of the stage, which was then open. It plays an immensely important part in the spatial conventions of Nō, and is the great " trouvaille " of the Japanese stage-architect.

to admit the actor when he makes his entry. The audience sit either on two or three sides of the stage. The chorus, generally in two rows, sit, or rather squat, in the recess (O). The musicians sit in the recess (J) at the back of the stage, the stick-drum nearest the *hashigakari*, then the two hand-drums and then the flute.

A railing runs round the musicians' recess, as also along the *hashigakari*. To the latter railing three real pine-branches (S) are attached, as seen in Plate II.

The stage is covered by a roof of its own, imitating in form the roof of a Shintō temple.

Performances are now usually given from 9 till 3. In ancient times "day-time Nō" began at dawn; but Seami also speaks of "night-time Nō."

Night-sarugaku is a different thing. . . . At night, even if the people are making a great clatter, so soon as the first chant begins they will immediately become quiet (p. 22).

In everything success depends on a proper harmonization of negative and positive. The day-spirit is positive and the skilful player will make his Nō as quiet as possible in order to balance by negative playing the positive tone of the environment.

At night the playing must be "positive," in order to balance the "negative" of darkness.

But it will sometimes happen even in the day that a gloom settles over the audience and a negative atmosphere is created. The actor must be quick to detect this mood and adapt himself to it. Conversely, at night an outburst of "positivity" will sometimes need to be damped.

These night-performances given by torch-light and in the open-air must have resembled the native plays of India and Java. The modern Nō theatre is fitted with electric light and performances are sometimes given in the evening.

THE PROGRAM (*Bangumi*).—In old times the program consisted of not more than four or five pieces; and to-day (Seami is writing in 1430) in temple and "subscription" performances the program still consists of only three true *Nō-sarugaku* and two *kyōgen*. In recent years, at performances given in the palaces of great men, seven, eight or even ten plays have been acted successively. But this was at the bidding of our patrons, not by our own desire.

The performance should have an introduction, development and climax. The introduction should be a waki-Nō.[1] The 2nd, 3rd and 4th plays should form the "development" of the program; the 5th, the climax. When the number of plays is increased, the proper progression is interfered with (p. 198).

The place which a play should occupy in the program must be judged by its "feeling." A "first Nō" should be based on a simple story and should be easy and dignified, without too much detail. Both the chanting and dancing should be simple and direct in style. Above all, it should contain "words of good wish." It does not matter if a "first Nō" is slightly defective in other ways, so long as it contains "happy wishes." For they form the proper introduction. But in the second and third places really good Nō must be played (p. 24).

In the sixteenth century a fixed order of program came into fashion and to a large extent prevails to-day. I quote it from the *Later Kwadensho*, vol. i, p. 4.

(1) A god-play, or play of prayer.

(2) A battle-play, in which the ghost of a warrior appears.

(3) A "wig"-play, in which the principal character is a woman.

(4) A demon-play.

(5) A play inculcating the virtues of benevolence, justice, politeness and wisdom.

(6) On important occasions a "congratulatory play," or more literally "Nō of happy wishes" (*Shūgen*) was given.

Categories (4) and (5) are in other places differently defined.

Where performances were given on successive days, Seami regarded the whole series of plays as an æsthetic unit.

The "first Nō" on a second day must be different in style from the "first Nō" on the day before. A "weeping-sangaku" must be played in the middle of the program and on a second or later day, the time being carefully selected (p. 24).

COMPETITIONS.[2]—One must give Nō which contrast in style with

---

[1] Technical name for god-plays, such as *Takasago*, *Oimatsu*, etc. "On leur donne aussi le nom de *waki*-Nō pour une raison qui n'a pas encore été élucidée" (M. Péri).

[2] Competitions between Dengaku-troupes are described in the *Taiheiki*, an historical romance dealing chiefly with the thirteenth century.

those of one's opponent. When the play is written by another person, the matter is out of the hands of the actor, however talented he may be; but if he writes the play himself, both the words and action are determined by him, so that if he have knowledge and talent sufficient for the writing of the text, the performance of the Sarugaku should be easy.

The actor who has not a good play at his disposal is like an army without weapons. If the enemy put on a very lively play, you must change the tone and put on a quiet one, making many "cuts" in the text (p. 25).

The practice of competition by rival companies did not, I think, survive the fifteenth century.

MUSIC.—The piercing Nō flute intervenes only at stated intervals, particularly at the beginning, at the climax and at the end of plays.

Before the Sarugaku begins the flute should play for a while in order to quiet the audience and put them in the right mood. When the dancing and singing has begun the flute-player must listen to the actor's voice, follow its rhythm and, as it were, "shadow" it.

There was once a flute-player called Meishō. It was said of him by Dōyo Nyūdō of the Capital, Commissioner of Sado, "The prolongation of the intervals (between the two parts of a play) is always a bad thing, but while I listen to the playing of this Meishō I forget the passage of time" (p. 195).

Seami also tells how, when the voices of two actors did not harmonize, Meishō was able to "bridge" the difference by dexterous flute-playing (p. 193 *seq.*).

Next to the flute-player sit the two hand-drummers, one of whom plays with the bare hand, the other with a thimbled finger. Last (and only in certain plays) comes the big-drum, rested on the ground and played with a stick. The hypnotic effect of drum-taps is well known. The drummers have the nerves of the audience in their hands. By a sudden accelerando they can create an atmosphere of almost unendurable tension.

But they must not go their own way. Their business is to understand the actors' intentions and follow the rhythms of the singing and dancing (p. 193).

The music of Nō has no independent existence as music, but simply supplies a background to the dancing and recitation.

THE ACTORS AND CHORUS.—Not more than four or five actors ought to take part in a play. In old times, even if more actors were at their disposal, in a play which only needed one or two they did not use more than one or two. Nowadays, excusing themselves on the plea that there are some actors " over," they set in rows a number of persons in everyday costume of *eboshi* and *suō* (hat and cloak) and let them sing in unison (*dō-on utau*). This is contrary to the principles of our art. It is an indiscriminate proceeding, and has only been seen in recent years (p. 192).

Seami's advice as to the number of actors has in general been followed, but in some plays as many as nine appear. It will be seen from the above extract that he disapproved of the " chorus," which was introduced towards the close of his career.

It need hardly be said that all the actors are men.

The very essence of *Sarugaku* as opposed to *Dengaku* had been that in the former the actor sang while he danced. The *dō-on* or unison-singers were introduced in order to strengthen his chant by singing in unison with him while he was performing movements which absorbed most of his energy. Later the chorus was employed, as it is to-day, to speak the words for an actor, as a substitute for, not as a complement to, his singing. The modern chorus consists of from eight to twelve persons in ordinary native dress, seated in two rows at the side of the stage. They enter by the side-door (*kirido*) before the play begins and remain seated till it is over. Their sole function is to sing.

MASKS.—The use of masks is confined to the main actor (*shite*) and to his subordinates (*tsure*) or companion (*tomo*). Neither *waki* nor his *tsure* nor any other characters upon the stage ever wear them. *Shite* is always masked if playing the part of a woman or old man. Young men, particularly young warriors, are often not masked. In child-parts (*ko-gata*) also masks are not worn. In order to avoid an irreverent realism the parts of Emperors and Kings are always played as *ko-gata* by boy-actors.

The masks are of wood. Many of those still used

are of great antiquity and rank as important specimens of Japanese sculpture. Seami has a long section on the masks-carvers of his father's time and later. The beauty of the masks cannot be judged from the rough drawings generally reproduced in European works. Exquisite collotype reproductions will be found in an album called *Nōgaku Mandai Kagami*, published by the *Nōgaku Tsūshin Company*.

COSTUMES.—Though almost wholly banishing other extrinsic aids, the Nō relied enormously for its effects on gorgeous and elaborate costume.[1] This has now become stereotyped, but in Seami's time the costumes were constantly varied. He has many passages such as the following :

Sumida-gawa is a play which at the beginning rather lacks colour. It is therefore best to dress the Traveller in an ōguchi.[2]

The wearing of the bamboo kasa (a broad-brimmed hat made of split bamboo), with no mask, at the beginning of Ukai is right, because it suggests country life (p. 253).

It would be tedious to describe the various costumes. They may be studied in the illustrations of *Yōkyokukai* (a magazine of which the British Museum Library possesses some odd numbers, Press Mark 16050. e.) or in the album *Mandai Kagami* mentioned above.

PROPERTIES.—The properties of the Nō stage are of a highly conventionalized kind. An open framework represents a boat ; another, differing little from it, denotes a chariot. Palace, house, cottage, hovel, are all represented by four posts covered with a roof. The fan which the actor usually carries often does duty as a knife, brush or the like. Weapons are more realistically represented. The short-sword, belt-sword, pike, spear, and Chinese broad-sword are carried ; also bows and arrows.

MOVEMENT.—Though the Nō seems to us so little a "realistic performance," it was the development of "imitation" (*mono-mane* or "miming") in the

[1] So did *Dengaku* in the thirteenth century. *Vide* the *Taiheiki*.
[2] A form of loose trousers worn on great occasions : often scarlet.

Yamato school of Sarugaku which differentiated it
from the rival Ōmi school and led it from dance to
drama. But every Nō play (with the sole exception,
I think, of *Hachi no Ki*) includes a *mai*, dance, consist-
ing usually of slow steps and solemn gestures, often
bearing little resemblance to what is in Europe associated with the word " dance." When the *shite*
dances, his dance consists of five " movements," or
parts ; the *tsure's* dance consists of three. Both in
the miming and in the dancing an important element
is the stamping of beats with the shoeless foot. Seami
has pages of minute directions about the stamping
(*hyōshi fumu*) ; whether it should, in a particular passage,
be in syncopation to the main rhythm, or should
coincide with the beat.

In the play *Sano no Funabashi*, at the passage " The willows green,
the flowers crimson," the real beat comes on " flowers," and one
should stamp twice there, but if an additional stamp is inserted at
the *-ri* of *midori* (" green ") the effect is pleasing (p. 217).

Many different kinds of " stamp " and step are distinguished by technical terms which it is now difficult
to identify.

THE TEXTS.—The plays are written partly in prose
(*kotoba*), partly in verse (*utai*). The prose portions serve
much the same purpose as the iambics of a Greek play.
They are in the Court or upper-class colloquial of the
fourteenth century, a language not wholly dead to-day,
as it is still the medium of correspondence. To each
main-verb is appended the honorific auxiliary *sōrō*
and sometimes a string of other weighty auxiliaries.
The effect is to impart great gravity to the very simple
statements and explanations which *kotoba* is called
upon to make. The chanting of these portions is far
removed from singing ; yet they are not " spoken."
The voice falls at each *sōrō*, or its equivalent, in a
monotonous cadence.

No kind of English corresponds to this language,
whose honorific grammatical forms in themselves

build up an impressive weight of sound. Any attempt
to translate these honorific words, *tatematsuru, tamau,
uke-tamawaru, oboshimesu* and the like, is bound to
lead to ludicrous results. *Uke-tamawaru*, for example,
means to " receive as a reward," but it is used simply
as a polite substitute for *kiku*, " to hear." To translate it literally would be as absurd as to translate the
Spanish *usted* by " Your Grace " instead of simply
" you."

The style of *kotoba* did not strike contemporary
audiences as elaborate or long-winded. It was as
familiar to them as the nodding *eboshi* and flowing
suō, or as crinolines to our grandmothers.

" *Kotoba*," says Seami, " should be as brief as is
consistent with clear exposition of the argument, for
such is the ' law of prose ' (*bunshō no hō*) " (p. 244).

The degree of formality differs, of course, according
to the speaker and the situation. Yoshimitsu criti-
cized the play *Hatsuse no Onna* because a girl is made
to use Chinese equivalents for the names of Yamato
and the Hatsuse Temple. He said that the style
was " too stiff " (p. 244). I am afraid that the simple
English into which I have translated the prose speeches
is not nearly " stiff " enough, but the problem of ade-
quately representing *kotoba* in English seems to me
insoluble.

A prose passage often gradually heightens into
verse. The chanting, which has hitherto resembled
the " intoning " of a Roman Catholic priest, takes
on more of the character of " recitativo " in opera,
occasionally attaining to actual " song." The verse
of these portions is sometimes irregular, but on the
whole, tends to that alternation of lines, of seven and
five syllables, which is the standard metre of Japanese
poetry. Regular blank-verse is therefore a bad equivalent. In places I have found that an alternation
between blank-verse and shorter iambic lines best
represented the rhythm of such passages.

The distich of 12 (7+5) syllables is fitted to the eight

3

notes of a common-time bar, or rather to the sixteen
half-notes. It is this fitting of verse to "beats"
(*hyōshi*) which is the characteristic of Nō chanting.

No system of time-notation similar to ours exists.
Each of the different kinds of musical bar which can
result from the fitting of twelve syllables to sixteen
regular notes has its own technical name. The twelve-
syllable distich is the norm ; but shorter and longer
lines have also to be fitted to the common-time bar,
by lengthening of syllables or by "rests."

Pitch is far less elaborately regulated. The intervals
are chiefly of an elementary character, the voice often
rising and falling between the dominant and key-
note. The function of the drums is to maintain the
ground-rhythm which is often syncopated with subtle
effect by the voice, steps or stamping of the foot.
Every syllable chanted, every movement of the feet,
must come at the right moment of the bar.[1]

The verse of the lyric portions is marked by frequent
use of pivot-words and puns, particularly puns on
place-names. Seami insists that pivot-words (*kenyōgen*)
should be used sparingly and with discretion. Many
Nō writers did not follow this advice, but the use of
pivot-words is not in itself a decoration more artificial
than rhyme, and I cannot agree with those European
writers to whom this device appears puerile and
degraded. Each language must use such embellish-
ments as suit its genius. It would be impossible to
render these *kenyōgen* into English. For example,
in the phrase . . . *yuku-ye shira-yuki ni* . . ., *shira* does
duty twice, meaning both "unknown" and "white."
The meaning is "whither-unknown amid the white
snow. . . ." I have never attempted to reproduce
these "pivots" in my version. The elimination of them
often leaves an impression of flatness or incoherence.
It is as though Herbert's poem "The Pulley" (in

---

[1] It is difficult to discuss music lucidly. Those who wish to
know more of Nō music should obtain gramophone records from
Japan.

The meat is bad but the wine is good.

which he puns on " rest," " the rest," " restlessness,"
etc.) were to be literally translated into Russian.

Simple puns, particularly those on the names of
places and persons, which are used much as in Greek
tragedy, though more frequently and perhaps less
felicitously, I have often tried to retain either in the
text or by explanation in a foot-note.

Another characteristic of the texts is the use of
existing literary material. Many of the plays were
adapted from Dengaku or were written round dance-
ballads already existing ; and even new plays made
use of such poems as were associated in the minds of
the audience with the places or persons named in the
play. Often a play is " written round " a poem or
series of poems, as will be seen in the course of this
book. Chinese couplets and Buddhist hymns are
also quoted, a point to which I shall return later. This
use of existing literary material far exceeds the practice
of our own dramatists, but it must be remembered
that if we read Webster, for example, in editions
annotated as minutely as the Nō plays, we should
discover that he was far more addicted to " borrowing "
than we had been aware. It seems to me that in the
finest plays this use of existing material is made with
magnificent effect and fully justifies itself.

Seami's essays on the writing of Nō texts is dated
1423. It is worth quoting at some length :

COMPOSITION.—The writing of Nō consists of three stages : choice
of " seed " (subject), construction and composition. The " seed "
is the story on which the play is based. This story must be well
considered and divided into Introduction, Development and Climax.
. . . Then the words must be put together and the music joined to
them.

Yūgaku [1] expresses itself through dance and song. If the story
on which a play is based contains characters to whom the practice
of dance and song is not natural, however experienced and masterly
the writer may be, his product will lack the essentials of *yūgaku*.

For example, the Angel, Priestess or Witch are all associated with

yūgen

---

[1] A word meaning literally " entertainment-music," used as a
generic term for Nō, Dengaku and the like ; music and dance.

the *kagura* dance and song. Among male characters, Narihira, Kuro-nushi and Genji; among female characters Giō,[1] Gijo,[2] Shizuka[3] and Hyakuman[4] are all persons famous in the arts of dance and song. A play in which such as they are made the principal characters will be completely successful as *yūgaku*.

If a writer wishes to make a new play—one that does not use an existing story—he should bring in some famous place or ancient monument and may thus produce a spectacle which will move his audience.

Such a Nō requires for its composition the highest degree of skill and knowledge.

The Introduction, Development and Climax should be distributed as follows : one part Introduction, three parts Development, and one part Climax.

The first part includes the entrance of the *waki* and everything up to the *shite's* first chant. The development begins with *shite's* entrance. The second part consists of the dialogue between *shite* and *waki*, and the first unison.[5] The third part of the development begins with the *kusemai* (dance) or simple chant (*tada-utai*) which takes its place. The climax consists of the dance, action, quick-dance, or cut-beat ("finale") which follows.

Occasionally the theme of a play may require that it should consist of six parts ; in other cases, of only four. In the composition of a play, the writer must ask himself with regard to each character in the play, "What sort of words ought I to put into this character's mouth ? "

Moreover, he must bear always in mind whether his play be one of prayer, mystery, love, recollection or longing. The poems, both Chinese and Japanese, which he makes use of must be such as are suitable to the particular style of the play. The scene of a Nō should be placed in the locality connected with the original story. If there is a celebrated place or ancient monument in the neighbourhood, use should be made of any poems or Chinese couplets which refer to the subject. These are inserted with the best effect somewhere near the end of the third part of the Development. . . .

If the hero is a famous captain of the wars between the Minanoto and Taira families, the play should be written as far as possible in the actual words of the *Romance of the Taira Family* (p. 153 *seq.*).

An old actor cannot take the part of a girl or of young warriors such as Atsumori. . . . The writer of a play must bear in mind his *shite's* style and write a part for him which will not be inappropriate to his appearance (p. 165).

TEXTS.—The texts of Nō plays are known as *utai-bon*, "chant-books." A series called *Kōyetsu-bon* was

---

[1] A famous dancing-girl, mistress of Kiyomori.
[2] Her sister.   [3] Mistress of Yoshitsune.
[4] Mother of Enkaku Shōnin.
[5] Either of the two actors ; or of actor and chorus, if we may suppose Seami to be referring to an institution of which he so much disapproved.

printed *c*. 1600, each play in a separate fascicule. The
editions which followed generally contained five plays
in each volume. Each of the five official " schools "
of Nō (Kwanze, Komparu, Hōshō, Kita and Kongō),
had its own texts, showing a considerable number of
trivial variations, particularly in the prose passages.

Neither these texts nor the modern editions referred
to in the List of Books (p. 305) give the words of
"everyday characters," such as boatmen, sword-bearers
and the like, rôles known as *kyōgen*, but not to be
confused with the farces of that name. Nor do they
give the "interludes," which in some pieces are
indispensable to a proper understanding of the
play.

Neither these interludes (which occur in the interval
before the second appearance of the *shite*) nor the
kyōgen parts are considered to belong to the "true
Nō." The words were at first improvised by the actors
themselves, but have now, with wide variations, become
traditional.

The impression of incompleteness which Nō plays
have given in some previous translations is partly
due to the fact that neither the *kyōgen* speeches nor
interludes have been taken into account. Moreover,
the texts give no stage-directions, yet are sometimes
unintelligible unless the reader knows what is happening
on the stage. I have therefore supplied this deficiency
by the use of the *Nō no Shiori*, which give *kyōgen*
parts, interludes, and a minute description of the
modus operandi of ninety plays.[1]

There has been considerable controversy in Japan
as to the number of Nō which exist or have existed.
About 250 are now actually played. It is estimated
that, excluding plays posterior to 1868, about 800
texts survive, of which perhaps 300 were written before
the seventeenth century. Those written after the six-

---

[1] I have not translated any interlude in full, for none of the plays
which I have selected seemed to require it. But I have almost always
given the *kyōgen* parts.

teenth century seem to me to be very inferior. Of quite recent plays which have actually been performed the best-known are Yamazaki Gakudō's *Mirror of Oro* and Takahama Kyoshi's *Iron Gate*.

PLACES OF PERFORMANCE.—(1) The "homes" (*honza*) of Nō were the temples at Ise, Kasuga, Hiyoshi and other centres of Shintō worship. Here performances were given as part of the ritual of the temple and on certain occasions, for purposes of propaganda or the like, a wider audience was invited.

(2) Sometimes a great "circus" was erected in a dry river-bed or other convenient place and one of the Nō troupes summoned from its temple to give a "*kwanjin*" or "subscription-collecting" performance.

These performances were usually arranged by the Shōgun or noblemen of his Court and given for the ostensible purpose of collecting money for the repair of a temple, bridge or monument.

Thus in 1464 Seami's successor, Onami, was summoned to the Tadasu river-bed to give a "subscription" performance for the benefit of the Kurama Temple, which was in need of restoration. The earliest of these "popular" performances of which we have any record was one lasting seven days, given by Seami at the Kitano Temple in 1413. "All were admitted, rich and poor, old and young alike." [1]

Kwanjin Nō, attended by mixed audiences, were given throughout the eighteenth century.

An anonymous work of that century, the *Usō Kansetsu* ("Quiet Converse at a Rainy Window") relates that in the Kyōhō period (1716–1735) the Kwanze master (i.e. Seami's remote successor) of those days gave a great *kwanjin* performance in the river-bed at Kyōto. A "circus" and stage were erected.

---

[1] See *Yōkyokukai*, 1916, No. 4. In later times these public performances were given about once a year and lasted four days. In 1702 nearly 30,000 tickets were sold during a four-day *Kwanjin* performance. The box-office account book is still in existence.

When the performance began " the spectators were collected thick as ants." On the first or second day the Nō *Tokusa* was given, a play by Seami in which the *shite* is an old reaper from Shinano. Among the spectators were some actual reapers from Shinano who during the performance whispered together as if in disapproval. After the play was over the Kwanze summoned them to him and asked them how it was that when " all the people high and low, collected together in herds," seemed to be full of admiration, *they* alone whispered together as if dissatisfied. The reapers replied that they too were " reapers of Shinano " and that it had grieved them to see the Kwanze handling his sickle in a manner quite unfamiliar to them. They then showed him how true " Shinano reapers " set to work. Soon afterwards the Kwanze produced *Tokusa* at Yedo and did his reaping as he had been taught to by the Shinano peasants. The performance was a failure, for it " startled the eye " ; art should address itself to the man of average instruction, not to the specialist.

(3) Performances were given in the country. Seami frequently mentions this and boasts, as we have seen, that his father was able to hold the attention of his audiences even in the most remote districts.

(4) I now come to the type of performance which has hitherto been regarded as typical, but did not, I think, become so till the seventeenth century. This was the private performance at a palace or nobleman's house. Before I quote the passages from Seami which deal with such performances and with the relations between patron and actor generally, I must explain how it was that in early days the Nō, contrary to the opinion usually accepted in Europe, was not solely an entertainment of the upper-classes.

During the fourteenth, fifteenth, and sixteenth centuries the " people " had no theatre of their own ; the Dengaku and Sarugaku performances organized by the nobles afforded their only chance of theatre-

going. But during the seventeenth century Ōzaka
developed its puppet-theatres and Yedo its *Kabuki-za*
or Popular Stage. The performances given at the
latter were very varied, but in some cases they were
certainly popular renderings of the Nō plays. The
Kwanjinchō, a turn initiated by the popular actor
Danjūrō the First, *c.* 1700, was taken straight from the
Nō play *Ataka*.

As soon as the populace had its own form of entertainment, it ceased to frequent Nō otherwise than sporadi-
cally. But no kind of anecdote is more frequent in
collections of the eighteenth and early nineteenth
centuries than that of the uncultivated man who
makes naïve comments at a Nō play. Naturally the
performances given at private mansions were inacces-
sible ; it was to " subscription " performances that
people in general were admitted.

When the art of Nō was resurrected after the Restoration of 1868, only private performances were at first
given, for the Shōgunate which had organized the
public performances of old days was now overthrown.
Hence those Europeans who wrote about Nō in the
second half of the nineteenth century have generally
described it not only as being but as always having
been an exclusively aristocratic performance.

The *Later Kwadensho* indeed regards Nō as a means
of teaching Japanese history to the lower-classes :

If Nō were not, how could men and women of humble station learn
what has happened in Japan since the beginning down till to-day ?
(vol. i, f. 3).

But it has further been stated that Nō, owing to
its literary references, cannot ever have been intelligible to any but the learned. This view leaves out of
sight the fact that almost all the Japanese poems
and Chinese couplets quoted were familiar as *songs*.
Nearly all of them will be found in song-books such as
the *Rōyei Shu*, and it is therefore obvious that a quite
illiterate person might, if he had his head full of their

airs, know enough of the words to make the Nō plays
intelligible to him.

The range of quotation is very limited, being confined
almost entirely, as I have said, to poems which we
can prove to have existed as songs. Moreover, many
other classical poems obtained popular currency in
an adapted form as *imayō*, a popular song-form, sung
by the soldiers in *Atsumori* (see p. 72).

The Buddhist quotations are of an even more
restricted character. They consist chiefly of the most
well-worn Amidist tags. In plays where the Buddhist ⋎
references are of a more erudite character (e.g. *Sotoba
Komachi*) a detailed understanding of them is not
necessary to the spectator. The general drift would
have been clear enough to any person of average
intelligence.[1] But it would be going too far to deny
that Nō was, at least after the fifteenth century,
essentially an aristocratic performance. Even during
that century it was shaped by the Daimyōs' tastes and
preferences, as the following extracts will show.
(I quote more than the relevant passage because the
rest is also of some interest.)

When a Sarugaku is performed it is necessary that exactly the right
moment should be chosen for the *sashi* [2] and *issei*.[3] It is bad to
begin them too soon and bad to begin them too late. When the
actor leaves the *gaku-ya* and advances on to the *hashigakari* he should
pause for a moment to scan his audience. He must not begin to
chant till he hears a simultaneous murmur of " Now he is going to
begin ! " arise in every part of the theatre. If he waits thus till he
has secured everyone's attention, his opening will produce the proper
effect. But if he is an instant late, attention will have slackened
and he will fail to move the hearts of the multitude (lit. " 10,000
people "). He ought to begin his first chant standing two-thirds
of the way up the *hashigakari* ; the second phrase should be chanted
at the end of the *hashigakari*, on the edge of the stage itself.

PATRONS.—The actor should not stare straight into the faces of
the audience, but look between them. When he looks in the direction
of the " honourable people " (the Daimyōs) he must not let his eyes
meet theirs, but must slightly avert his gaze.

---

[1] I have fully discussed in *Bulletin of School of Oriental Studies*,
No. 5, the literary materials used by the Nō writers and the degree
of learning required of the audiences.

[2] I think *sashi* must here mean the *waki's* opening words.

[3] *Issei*, the *shite's* first chant.

At Palace-performances or when acting at a banquet, he must
not let his eyes meet those of the Shōgun or stare straight into the
Honourable Face. When playing in a large enclosure he must take
care to keep as close as possible to the side where the Nobles are
sitting ; if in a small enclosure, as far off as possible. But particularly
in Palace-performances and the like he must take the greatest pains
to keep as far away as he possibly can from the August Presence.

Again, when the recitations are given at the Palace it is equally
essential to begin at the right moment. It is bad to begin too soon
and fatal to delay too long.

It sometimes happens that the "noble gentlemen" do not arrive
at the theatre until the play has already reached its Development
and Climax. In such cases the play is at its climax, but the noble
gentlemen's hearts are ripe only for Introduction. If they, ready
only for Introduction, are forced to witness a Climax, they are not
likely to get pleasure from it. Finally even the spectators who were
there before, awed by the entry of the "exalted ones," become so
quiet that you would not know they were there, so that the whole
audience ends by returning to the Introductory mood. At such
a moment the Nō cannot possibly be a success. In such circumstances
it is best to take Development-Nō and give it a slightly "introductory" turn. Then, if it is played gently, it may win the August
Attention.

It also happens that one is suddenly sent for to perform at a
Shōgunal feast or the like. The audience is already in a "climax-
mood"; but "introductory" Nō must be played. This is a great
difficulty. In such circumstances the best plan is to tinge the
introduction with a *nuance* of "development." But this must be
done without "stickiness," with the lightest possible touch, and the
transition to the real Development and Climax must be made as
quickly as possible (p. 82 *seq.*).

In old times there were masters who perfected themselves in Nō
without study. But nowadays the nobles and gentlemen have
become so critical that they will only look with approbation on what
is good and will not give attention to anything bad.

Their honourable eyes have become so keen that they notice the
least defect, so that even a masterpiece that is as pearls many times
polished or flowers choicely culled will not win the applause of our
gentlemen to-day.

At the same time, good actors are becoming few and the Art is
gradually sinking towards its decline. For this reason, if very
strenuous study is not made, it is bound to disappear altogether
(p. 140).

When summoned to play before the noble gentlemen, we are expected to give the regular "words of good-wish" and to divide our
performance into the three parts, Introduction, Development and
Climax, so that the pre-arranged order cannot be varied. . . . But
on less formal occasions, when, for example, one is playing not at
a Shōgunal banquet but on a common, everyday (*yo no tsune*) stage,
it is obviously unnecessary to limit oneself to the set forms of "happy
wish."

One's style should be easy and full of graceful *yūgen*, and the *audience oriented*

piece [1] selected should be suitable to the audience. A ballad (*ko-utai*) or dance-song (*kuse-mai*) of the day will be best. One should have in one's repertory a stock of such pieces and be ready to vary them according to the character of one's audience (pp. 184, 185).

In the words and gestures (of a farce, *kyōgen*) there should be nothing low. The jokes and repartee should be such as suit the august ears of the nobles and gentry. On no account must vulgar words or gestures be introduced, however funny they may be. This advice must be carefully observed (p. 197).

Introduction, Development and Climax must also be strictly adhered to when *dancing* at the Palace. If the chanting proceeds from an "introductory-mood," the dancing must belong to the same mood. . . . When one is suddenly summoned to perform at a riotous banquet, one must take into consideration the state of the noble gentlemen's spirits (p. 211).

In general Seami wrote both words and music for the plays he performed. But not infrequently he was supplied by his patrons with indifferent texts which he patched up as best he could (p. 247) and then furnished with music. Thus " the text of *Ukifune* is by the amateur Yoko-o Mitsuhisa, but Seami added the measures."

He classifies the texts with which he was called upon to deal as follows :

(1) A play founded on a story which is in itself beautiful, the theme subtly handled and embellished with delightful passages ; such a piece, if properly acted, cannot fail.

(2) A play not so well written, but with a tolerably good plot. If well acted, it may be a success.

(3) A bad play which one can yet make something of by taking advantage of its very defects and "breaking one's bones" in the acting of it (p. 25 *seq.*).

Quel métier ! *what craft (skill)!*

I will close my extracts from Seami with a few miscellaneous quotations :

THREE KINDS OF PLAY.—People's tastes differ ; to suit the dispositions of " ten thousand " men is a task of unrivalled difficulty. Yet one's model should be the actor who is successful wherever he

---

[1] The piece to be used as an introduction. Modern performances are not confined to full Nō. Sometimes actors in plain dress recite without the aid of instrumental music, sitting in a row. Or one actor may recite the piece, with music (this is called *Hayashi*) ; or the piece may be mimed without music (this is called *Shimai*).

appears throughout the whole Empire. . . . There are three ways to success, . . . by the eyes, by the ears and by the heart.

A play which appeals successfully to the eye is one to which from the beginning the whole audience succumbs. The style of the dancing and chanting is agreeable to them; the spectators, high and low, burst into applause; the whole theatre wears an air of gaiety. Not only connoisseurs, but even people without knowledge of Nō, are saying to themselves with one accord, "How enjoyable!"

But the actor must beware. If the play is too great a success, everything he does will begin to delight the audience equally. They will be in such a state of exultation and continuous appreciation that the play will begin to fatigue them.

The actor too will exhaust himself in his excitement. . . . In such cases he must hold himself in and restrain his movements in order to give a little repose to the audience. He must, I say, give people time to rest and breathe, and play the exciting passages quietly. Then he will regain his power over the hearts of the audience and the latter part of the play will gain in strength; nor will he progressively lose his power to move as he proceeds from play to play.

The second class of play is that which appeals chiefly to the ear, i.e. to the musical sense. It does not require the highest degree of mastery in the actor.

The third class is that which appeals to the mind.[1] In the hands of a peerless master Sarugaku will move the heart when not only representation, but song, dance, mimic and rapid action are all eliminated, emotion as it were springing out of quiescence. This is called "frozen dance."

Such acting cannot be understood by many spectators of long experience; still less by peasants or the like. This mystic style belongs only to the peerless master-player; and though it is called "Nō that speaks to the mind," yet it is also called "mindless Nō." There are many who have long frequented the theatre, yet do not understand Nō; and many who understand, though they have little experience. For eye-knowledge comes not to all who see, but to him who sees well. . . .

The Book of Criticism says, "Forget the theatre and look at the Nō. Forget the Nō and look at the actor. Forget the actor and look at the "idea" (kokoro). Forget the "idea" and you will understand the Nō" (p. 102 seq.).

THE TRAINING OF ACTORS.—"Venery, gambling and strong wine are strictly forbidden; be resolute in study; avoid disputation" (p. 2).

The training of actors began at seven years old. Until the twelfth year the children are to be put to dancing and recitation, but not praised or blamed.

[1] In this section he speaks in a language compounded of Taoism and Zen.

If they practise " mimic," it must be to amuse themselves ; they should not be instructed.

After twelve the various branches of impersonation are gradually imparted. " There is a natural grace in the boy's form which will be communicated to all his gestures. His faults will be disguised by this charm and his merits enhanced beyond their real value." . . . But this " flower " is not the real flower ; it is only the " flower of youth." At seventeen or eighteen the pupil loses this " first flower " and becomes ungainly in his movements. He must not be discouraged if people point at him and laugh ; but must sit at home and practise such tunes as his changing voice can compass. For if he gives up now, he gives up for ever.

The danger at twenty-four and twenty-five (the time of complete development) is that the actors' friends will overpraise him. " If he gains applause in his own theatre and happens one day to win in a competition with another troupe, people will begin telling him that he is a master. But such persons are doing him a very ill service ; for such temporary success is not the ' true flower.' " Thirty-five is the actor's prime. If he has not then won the approbation of the whole Empire, one may know that he is not an actor who will ever possess the " true flower " in its perfection. And if at this age he has not perfected it, from forty onwards his art is certain to decline.

If at forty-five he still retains his " flower," it is certain that it is the " true flower." But there are some parts which he can no longer play, such as those in which no mask is worn. " For an old man is intolerable in a maskless part, however handsome he may once have been."

After fifty most actors must take " passive parts." For " even Kirin when he grows old is outrun by any nag." But a true master of Nō, though he has lost the varied arts of mimicry and seems capable of little, good or bad, yet retains the " flower." " My late father (Kwanami) died at the age of fifty-two

on the nineteenth day of the fifth month. On the
fourth day of the same month he had given a *Hōgaku*
(religious) performance in the presence of the Sengen
in the province of Suruga. His acting in the *Sarugaku*
on that day was particularly magnificent, and won the
unanimous applause of his spectators, high and low.
At that time he had already resigned the 'character
parts' to his disciples, appearing only in easy rôles,
which he played in the most subdued manner. Yet
his 'flower' was all the more apparent" (p. 2 *seq.*).

Seami makes an important distinction between the
"mastered style" and the "masterless style." A
pupil may have learnt to imitate his teacher exactly;
but if he has not made the movements and intonations
"his own possession" (*waga mono*), "living Nō"
cannot result (p. 133).

IMITATION (*Monomane*).—In imitation there should be a tinge of
the "unlike." For if imitation be pressed too far it impinges on
reality and ceases to give an impression of likeness. If one aims
only at the beautiful, the "flower" is sure to appear. For example,
in acting the part of an old man, the master actor tries to reproduce
in his dance only the refinement and venerability of an old gentleman.[1]
If the actor is old himself, he need not think about producing an
impression of old age. . . .

The appearance of old age will often be best given by making all
movements a little late, so that they come just after the musical
beat. If the actor bears this in mind, he may be as lively and energetic
as he pleases. For in old age the limbs are heavy and the ears
slow; there is the will to move but not the corresponding capacity.
It is in such methods as this that true imitation lies. . . . Youthful
movements made by an old person are, indeed, delightful; they are
like flowers blossoming on an old tree (p. 54 *seq.*).

If, because the actor has noticed that old men walk with bent
knees and back and have shrunken frames, he simply imitates these
characteristics, he may achieve an appearance of decrepitude, but
it will be at the expense of the "flower." And if the "flower" be
lacking there will be no beauty in his impersonation (p. 12).

Women should be impersonated by a young actor. . . . It is very
difficult to play the part of a Princess or lady-in-waiting, for little
opportunity presents itself of studying their august behaviour and
appearance. Great pains must be taken to see that robes and cloaks
are worn in the correct way. These things do not depend on the
actor's fancy but must be carefully ascertained.

The appearance of ordinary ladies such as one is used to see about

---

[1] An old *shiröto*, i.e. person not engaged in trade.

one is easy to imitate. . . . In acting the part of a dancing-girl, mad-woman or the like, whether he carry the fan or some fancy thing (a flowering branch, for instance) the actor must carry it loosely; his skirts must trail low so as to hide his feet; his knees and back must not be bent, his body must be poised gracefully. As regards the way he holds himself—if he bends back, it looks bad when he faces the audience; if he stoops, it looks bad from behind. But he will not look like a woman if he holds his head too stiffly. His sleeves should be as long as possible, so that he never shows his fingers.

APPARITIONS.—Here the outward form is that of a ghost; but within is the heart of a man.

Such plays are generally in two parts. The beginning, in two or three sections, should be as short as possible. In the second half the *shite* (who has hitherto appeared to be a man) becomes definitely the ghost of a dead person (p. 162).

Since no one has ever seen a real ghost [1] from the Nether Regions, the actor may use his fancy, aiming only at the beautiful. To represent real life is far more difficult (p. 214).

If ghosts are terrifying, they cease to be beautiful. For the terrifying and the beautiful are as far apart as black and white (p. 18).

CHILD PLAYS.—In plays where a lost child is found by its parents, the writer should not introduce a scene where they clutch and cling to one another, sobbing and weeping. . . .

Plays in which child-characters occur, even if well done, are always apt to make the audience exclaim in disgust, " Don't harrow our feelings in this way ! "

RESTRAINT.—In representing anger the actor should yet retain some gentleness in his mood, else he will portray not anger but violence.

In representing the mysterious (*yūgen*) he must not forget the principle of energy.

When the body is in violent action, the hands and feet must move as though by stealth. When the feet are in lively motion, the body must be held in quietness. Such things cannot be explained in writing but must be shown to the actor by actual demonstration.

SECRECY.—Seami constantly urges the necessity of secrecy. Secret traditions, he says, exist in all arts and trades. The actor can no more publish his stratagems to the world than can the leader of an army. For Seami has continually in mind the competitions in which troupe vied with troupe. The " flower," he says, consists in forcing upon the audience *an emotion which they do not expect* (p. 60).

The actor must not strain the feelings of the audience; when they cry out " Hold, hold, for pity's sake ! " he must " slacken " his style. . . . These things are secret and must not be known by those who are likely to be spectators (p. 214).

---

[1] This shows that, in Seami's hands, the device of making an apparition the hero of the play was simply a dramatic convention.

My last extracts concern Seami's retirement in favour of his nephew Onami and his subsequent exile in the island of Sado. In the third month of the fifth year of Eikyō (1433) he writes :

I was instructed in the precepts and traditions of this art by my late father, and in my old age I handed them on to my son Motomasa, who received from me the entire mysteries of the art, so that I was left free to wait for the " one great thing " which concerns us in this life.[1]

Then suddenly Motomasa died (in 1431),[2] and with his death has come the end of our School and the final dispersal of our company. For my grandchildren are still in their infancy.

These matchless arts of dance and song have laid too strong, oh all too strong, a hold upon an old man's heart ! They have become a stumbling-block in his path to Salvation.

There are others : yet not one to whom I could entrust the inheritance of either one art or the other. True, there is the Komparu Master ;[3] he has talent and would keep the Art in its true road. But he never saw my sainted father.[4]

As years go by the store of his art will grow ; his talent will ripen and I do not doubt that he will become an accomplished master. But I shall not live to see it, and fear that to-day there is no practicant of this art to whom I can even show the proven bond of my assent.

A few weeks after this was written, Seami's nephew, Onami, was acting with applause as head of the Kwanze troupe at a great " subscription " performance.

A year later Seami was banished. Mr. Yoshida Tōgo has suggested that the aged actor may have resisted the appointment of Onami as his successor and so incurred the displeasure of the Shōgun who desired this appointment. It is at any rate apparent that since Seami did not regard his nephew as a possible successor the choice must have been forced upon him. There is strong evidence that Seami's writings on the art of Nō were never transmitted to Onami. During his exile he wrote a remarkable work, *The Book of the Golden Island*, in which he describes the place of his exile in a style which bears the same relation to his

[1] Salvation : escape from re-birth.
[2] Motomasa seems to have been quasi-head of the troupe from 1429 till 1431.
[3] His son-in-law, Zenchiku.
[4] *Kōshō*, a Zen name for those who have achieved Enlightenment.

plays that Bashō's prose-sketches bear to his *hokku*. The first two sections are in the language of a " song of travel " (*michiyuki*), such as the *waki* sings at the beginning of a Nō. The third section is called " The Place of Exile." The next is called " The Cuckoo " (Hototogisu) which, unlike our cuckoo, sings by night. It begins as follows :

Looking towards the west, I see the waves of the inland sea and its white snow-capped sands both gleaming with a dazzling brightness ; and against them a single clump of pine-trees,—such sights as spring's second month alone provides. Amid the trees stands a little shrine, a holy seat to which the god Hachiman has deigned to carry his abode ; whence it comes that here too the place is called Yawata, the Place of Eight Flags. And going thither on humble pilgrimage that I might do reverence to the god of the shrine, I found a strange portent. For the cuckoo, whose song the men of the Capital must wait for long to hear, in this country of Sado sings not only along every mountain path, but even on the beam-ends of my hut and on the pine-twigs of the eaves, dinning its noise in my ears. But at this shrine not a note is heard. When I asked how this might be, the people of the temples answered, " It was here that long ago the Lord Tamekane lived in exile. And once when he heard the cuckoo's cry, he sang :

> When you sing, I listen ;
> And when I listen, O cuckoo,
> I am sad and long for home.
> Then swiftly pass this village in your journeying,
> O cuckoo of the hill !

So he sang, and afterwards no note of the cuckoo was ever heard in this place."

Then, after allusions to the Preface to the *Kokinshu,* to a Chinese poem and to the *Ise Monogatari* (references in no way pedantic or obscure, but such as would seem tedious if explained in foot-notes) :

But *me*, cuckoo, your voice charms. Cry out, cry once again and weep your woes. For look, I too am weeping ; I that am old am weeping for my native land !

This was written in 1436. He lived till 1444, but whether he died at home or in banishment we do not know. There is a story of his acting with Onami at the Capital in 1443, but as he was then in his eightieth year it is difficult to credit.

Seami has a threefold claim to fame, as an actor,
as a Nō writer and as a writer on the æsthetics of drama.
History attests to his pre-eminence as an actor, but
it is more difficult to judge what place he occupies as
a poet, for we have no means of knowing whether
any given passage of a play attributed to him is in fact
by him or is borrowed from some earlier version of
the play.

The Book of the Golden Island is at any rate an indu-
bitable product of Seami's pen. But it is not a Nō
and is a work of his extreme old age. Still less do his
æsthetic writings provide us with any basis for the
identification of his poetic style. M. Péri speaks of
"la souplesse et la facilité élégante et un peu pré-
cieuse" which characterize Seami's plays, finding in the
Damask Drum and in *Komachi* "une sorte de simplicité
un peu rude et fruste," which he considers to be typical
of Kwanami, the father. But the *Damask Drum* has
always been attributed to Seami and is given in the
list of his plays drawn up by his great-grandson. It
appears, then, that Seami wrote now with "elegant
facility," now with "rude simplicity," a solution by
no means impossible.

But of Seami as a critic we can speak with more
assurance, having before us the well-nigh three hundred
pages of his *Works*. He was not a profound or sys-
tematic thinker. More of a courtier than a philosopher,
he was apt in moments of cynicism to regard the applause
of his audience as the sole end of his art, and even to
be indifferent whence that applause came (see above,
p. 22). But more often we find him assuming (what
we ourselves, whatever may be our philosophy of
æsthetics, do instinctively assume) that the applause
of men "of taste and experience" is worth more than
that of the crowd.

He writes, not as an æsthetician, but as a practical
man, an actor-manager. Yet he constantly amazes
us by the subtlety of his attitude towards the art,
by his capacity for weighing the value of every detail.

There is, indeed, a passive wisdom about him such as one often finds in those who are destined to live in an advanced age. Kwanami, we are sometimes tempted to think, was the genius ; Seami the suave and gifted heir, pious receptacle and transmitter of his father's teachings. We do not, indeed, know of any addition to the art which we can definitely assign to him ; and he opposed the very important development implied in the introduction of a chorus.

Yet in some passages he maintains that the actor's practice must be constantly varied to suit the changing tastes of the day. He indulges, too, in curious outbursts of cynicism, pedantry, superstition, vanity : the placidity of the courtier is suddenly lost. Trivial indications in his writings give one flashes of perception. For example, when one reads that in a certain passage (I have quoted it already) the actor should not " stretch down like a beggar snatching at a penny in the road," the sarcasm brings before one's eyes the picture of a sharp-tongued, elderly *maître de danse*. Can one not imagine M. Cecchetti correcting by some such stinging comparison a laggard member of his ballet ?

The reader will naturally look for some comparison of Nō with other forms of ancient drama.[1] The open-air performances of Nō, with their circular auditorium and round stage in the middle, correspond in a general way to the conditions of Greek drama. The *Gaku-ya* or actor's room (K in Plan I) has its exact counter-part. " On the side away from the spectators was a wooden building to which the performers could retire to change their costume." [2] I gather that *all* the actors in Greek tragedy wore masks, which, as has already been explained, is not true of Nō. Still less does the function of the Nō chorus, who remain seated and

---

[1] Comparison with the almost contemporary mystery-plays would, I think, lead us too far away from our subject. The various types of Chinese drama have not yet, so far as I can discover, been accurately described and distinguished.

[2] J. T. Sheppard, *Greek Tragedy*, 1911.

motionless throughout the play (except for the raising
of their fans when they sing) correspond with that of
the "company of twelve or fifteen persons" who
"stood in the foreground" and danced the choruses
of Greek plays.

"Though much is obscure in the matter of Greek
music and dancing, this at least is certain, that they
were essentially *imitative*";[1] so Seami on page 199,
Yūgaku no michi wa issai monomane ari—"The arts
of music and dancing [the term *yūgaku* comprises both
these] consist entirely in imitation."

The *libretti* of Greek tragedy have won for themselves a separate existence simply as poetic literature.
Yet even of them it has been said that "the words
are only part of the poem." Still less did the words
of Nō constitute the whole "poem," yet if some
cataclysm were to sweep away the Nō theatre, I
think the plays (as literature) would live.

It is above all in "architecture," in the relation
of parts to the whole that these poems are supreme.[2]
The early writers created a "form" or general pattern
which the weakest writing cannot wholly rob of its
beauty. The plays are like those carved lamp-bearing
angels in the churches at Seville ; a type of such beauty
was created by a sculptor of the sixteenth century
that even the most degraded modern descendant of
these masterpieces retains a certain distinction of form.

First comes the *jidai* or opening-couplet, enigmatic,
abrupt. Then in contrast to this vague shadow come
the hard outlines of the *waki's* exposition, the formal
naming of himself, his origin and destination. Then,
shadowy again, the "song of travel," in which picture
after picture dissolves almost before it is seen.

But all this has been mere introduction—the
imagination has been quickened, the attention grasped

---

[1] *Loc. cit.*, p. 24.

[2] This, too, is the only aspect of them that I can here discuss ;
no other kind of criticism being possible without quotation of the
actual words used by the poet.

in preparation for one thing only—the hero's entry. In the "first chant," in the dialogue which follows, in the successive dances and climax, this absolute mastery of construction is what has most struck me in reading the plays.

Again, Nō does not make a frontal attack on the emotions. It creeps at the subject warily. For the action, in the commonest class of play, does not take place before our eyes, but is lived through again in mimic and recital by the ghost of one of the participants in it. Thus we get no possibility of crude realities ; a vision of life indeed, but painted with the colours of memory, longing or regret.

In a paper read before the Japan Society in 1919 I tried to illustrate this point by showing, perhaps in too fragmentary and disjointed a manner, how the theme of Webster's *Duchess of Malfi* would have been treated by a Nō writer. I said then (and the Society kindly allows me to repeat those remarks) :

The plot of the play is thus summarized by Rupert Brooke in his *John Webster and the Elizabethan Drama* : " The Duchess of Malfi is a young widow forbidden by her brothers, Ferdinand and the Cardinal, to marry again. They put a creature of theirs, Bosola, into her service as a spy. The Duchess loves and marries Antonio, her steward, and has three children. Bosola ultimately discovers and reports this. Antonio and the Duchess have to fly. The Duchess is captured, imprisoned and mentally tortured and put to death. Ferdinand goes mad. In the last Act he, the Cardinal, Antonio and Bosola are all killed with various confusions and in various horror."

Just as Webster took his themes from previous works (in this case from Painter's *Palace of Pleasure*), so the Nō plays took theirs from the Romances or *Monogatari*. Let us reconstruct the *Duchess* as a Nō play, using Webster's text as our *Monogatari*.

Great simplification is necessary, for the Nō play corresponds in length to one act of our five-act plays, and has no space for divagations. The comic is altogether excluded, being reserved for the *kyōgen* or farces which are played as interludes between the Nō.

The persons need not be more than two—the Pilgrim, who will act the part of *waki*, and the Duchess, who will be *shite* or Protagonist. The chorus takes no part in the action, but speaks for the *shite* while she is miming the more engrossing parts of her rôle.

The Pilgrim comes on to the stage and first pronounces in his *Jidai* or preliminary couplet, some Buddhist aphorism appropriate to the subject of the play. He then names himself to the audience thus (in prose) :

" I am a pilgrim from Rome. I have visited all the other shrines of Italy, but have never been to Loretto. I will journey once to the shrine of Loretto."

Then follows (in verse) the *Song of Travel* in which the Pilgrim describes the scenes through which he passes on his way to the shrine. While he is kneeling at the shrine, *Shite* (the Protagonist) comes on to the stage. She is a young woman dressed, " contrary to the Italian fashion," in a loose-bodied gown. She carries in her hand an unripe apricot. She calls to the Pilgrim and engages him in conversation. He asks her if it were not at this shrine that the Duchess of Malfi took refuge. The young woman answers with a kind of eager exaltation, her words gradually rising from prose to poetry. She tells the story of the Duchess's flight, adding certain intimate touches which force the priest to ask abruptly, " Who is it that is speaking to me ? "

And the girl shuddering (for it is hateful to a ghost to name itself) answers : " *Hazukashi ya !* I am the soul of the Duke Ferdinand's sister, she that was once called Duchess of Malfi. Love still ties my soul to the earth. *Toburai tabi-tamaye !* Pray for me, oh, pray for my release ! "

Here closes the first part of the play. In the second the young ghost, her memory quickened by the Pilgrim's prayers (and this is part of the medicine of salvation), endures again the memory of her final hours. She mimes the action of kissing the hand (*vide* Act IV, Scene 1), finds it very cold :

> I fear you are not well after your travel.
> Oh ! horrible !
> What witchcraft doth he practise, that he hath left
> A dead man's hand here ?

And each successive scene of the torture is so vividly mimed that though it exists only in the Protagonist's brain, it is as real to the audience as if the figure of dead Antonio lay propped upon the stage, or as if the madmen were actually leaping and screaming before them.

Finally she acts the scene of her own execution :

> Heaven-gates are not so highly arched
> As princes' palaces ; they that enter there
> Must go upon their knees. (*She kneels.*)
> Come, violent death,
> Serve for mandragora to make me sleep !
> Go tell my brothers, when I am laid out,
> They then may feed in quiet.
> > (*She sinks her head and folds her hands.*)

The chorus, taking up the word " quiet," chant a phrase from the Hokkekyō : *Sangai Mu-an*, " In the Three Worlds there is no quietness or rest."

But the Pilgrim's prayers have been answered. Her soul has broken its bonds : is free to depart. The ghost recedes, grows dimmer and dimmer, till at last

> *use-ni-keri*
> *use-ni-keri*

it vanishes from sight.

As has already been stated, I am debarred from criticism of the plays as poetry by the fact that I cannot here quote them in the original. I do not think that any single play is so complete a poem as the tragedies of Sophocles, and perhaps only a dozen rank as supreme literary masterpieces. But Seami knows unfailingly how to gain the reader's attention and how by skilful balancing of quite simple elements quickly to enlist his sympathy and stir his emotions ; in these arts, indeed, not one of Seami's ninety plays seems to me to fall far short of another. And this is equally true of the less numerous plays written by his father and by his immediate successors.

Whether the same impression will be gained from reading these translations I cannot judge. The contrast between the prose and verse (two almost separate languages) has dwindled ; the verbal decorations are lost ; allusions that the mind should seize in its stride are painfully set out in foot-notes. In short, what I have been able to give bears the same relation to the original as the photograph of an oil-painting bears to the painting. One whole element, and this a vital one, is lost. But a clear photograph, which though it omits much, at least adds nothing foreign, is generally preferable to a hand-copy. Sometimes, indeed, physical conditions not unfavourable to the camera may make hand-copying impossible. Analogous, I think, is the case of Nō. I give the reader black-and-whites. He must colour them by the exercise of his own imagination. But I have carried the metaphor too far. For a photograph can never be a work of art. And if I have failed to make these translations in some sense works of art—if they are merely philology, not literature—then I have indeed fallen short of what I hoped and intended.

NOTE ON BUDDHISM

THE Buddhism of the Nō plays is of the kind called the " Greater Vehicle," which prevails in China, Japan and Tibet. Primitive Buddhism (the " Lesser Vehicle "), which survives in Ceylon and Burma, centres round the person of Shākyamuni, the historical Buddha, and uses Pāli as its sacred language. The " Greater Vehicle," which came into being about the same time as Christianity and sprang from the same religious impulses, to a large extent replaces Shākyamuni by a timeless, ideal Buddha named Amida, " Lord of Boundless Light," perhaps originally a sun-god, like Ormuzd of the Zoroastrians. Primitive Buddhism had taught that the souls of the faithful are absorbed into Nirvāna, in other words into Buddha. The " Greater Vehicle " promised to its adherents an after-life in Amida's Western Paradise. It produced scriptures in the Sanskrit language, in which Shākyamuni himself describes this Western Land and recommends the worship of Amida ; it inculcated too the worship of the Bodhisattvas, half-Buddhas, intermediaries between Buddha and man. These Bodhisattvas are beings who, though fit to receive Buddhahood, have of their own free will renounced it, that they may better alleviate the miseries of mankind.

Chief among them is Kwannon, called in India Avalokiteshvara, who appears in the world both in male and female form, but is chiefly thought of as a woman in China and Japan ; Goddess of Mercy, to whom men pray in war, storm, sickness or travail.

The doctrine of Karma and of the transmigration of souls was common both to the earlier and later

forms of Buddhism. Man is born to an endless chain
of re-incarnations, each one of which is, as it were,
the fruit of seed sown in that which precedes.

The only escape from this " Wheel of Life and Death "
lies in *satori*, " Enlightenment," the realization that
material phenomena are thoughts, not facts.

Each of the four chief sects which existed in medieval
Japan had its own method of achieving this Enlightenment.

Pure Land

(1) The Amidists sought to gain *satori* by the study
of the *Hokke Kyō*, called in Sanskrit *Saddharma
Pundarîka Sûtra* or " Scripture of the Lotus of the
True Law," or even by the mere repetition of its
complete title " Myōhō Renge Hokke Kyō." Others
of them maintained that the repetition of the formula
" Praise to Amida Buddha " (*Namu Amida Butsu*) was
in itself a sufficient means of salvation.

Zen

(2) Once when Shākyamuni was preaching before
a great multitude, he picked up a flower and twisted
it in his fingers. The rest of his hearers saw no significance in the act and made no response ; but the
disciple Kāshyapa smiled.

In this brief moment a perception of transcendental
truth had flashed from Buddha's mind to the mind of
his disciple. Thus Kāshyapa became the patriarch
of the Zen Buddhists, who believe that Truth cannot
be communicated by speech or writing, but that it
lies hidden in the heart of each one of us and can be
discovered by " Zen " or contemplative introspection.

At first sight there would not appear to be any possibility of reconciling the religion of the Zen Buddhists
with that of the Amidists. Yet many Zen masters
strove to combine the two faiths, teaching that Amida
and his Western Paradise exist, not in time or space,
but mystically enshrined in men's hearts.

Zen denied the existence of Good and Evil, and was
sometimes regarded as a dangerous sophistry by pious
Buddhists of other sects, as, for example, in the story
of Shunkwan (see p. 271) and in *The Hōka Priests*

(see p. 205), where the murderer's interest in Zen doctrines is, I think, definitely regarded as a discreditable
weakness and is represented as the cause of his undoing.

The only other play, among those I have here translated, which deals much with Zen tenets, is *Sotoba
Komachi.* Here the priests represent the *Shingon
Shū* or Mystic Sect, while Komachi, as becomes a
poetess, defends the doctrines of Zen. For Zen was
the religion of artists ; it had inspired the painters
and poets of the Sung dynasty in China ; it was the
religion of the great art-patrons who ruled Japan in
the fifteenth century.

It was in the language of Zen that poetry and painting
were discussed ; and it was in a style tinged with Zen
that Seami wrote of his own art. But the religion
of the Nō plays is predominantly Amidist ; it is the
common, average Buddhism of medieval Japan.

(3) I have said that the priests in *Sotoba Komachi*
represent the Mystic Sect. The followers of this sect
sought salvation by means of charms and spells, cor-
ruptions of Sanskrit formulæ. Their principal Buddha
was Dainichi, " The Great Sun." To this sect belonged
the Yamabushi, mountain ascetics referred to in
Tanikō and other plays.

(4) Mention must be made of the fusion between
Buddhism and Shintō. The Tendai Sect which
had its headquarters on Mount Hiyei preached
an eclectic doctrine which aimed at becoming the
universal religion of Japan. It combined the cults
of native gods with a Buddhism tolerant in dogma,
but magnificent in outward pomp, with a leaning
towards the magical practices of Shingon.

The Little Saint of Yokawa in the play *Aoi no Uye*
is an example of the Tendai ascetic, with his use of
magical incantations.

CHAPTER I

ATSUMORI
IKUTA
TSUNEMASA

ATSUMORI, IKUTA, AND TSUNEMASA.

In the eleventh century two powerful clans, the Taira and the Minamoto, contended for mastery. In 1181 Kiyomori the chief of the Tairas died, and from that time their fortunes declined. In 1183 they were forced to flee from Kyōto, carrying with them the infant Emperor. After many hardships and wanderings they camped on the shores of Suma, where they were protected by their fleet.

Early in 1184 the Minamotos attacked and utterly routed them at the Battle of Ichi-no-Tani, near the woods of Ikuta. At this battle fell Atsumori, the nephew of Kiyomori, and his brother Tsunemasa.

When Kumagai, who had slain Atsumori, bent over him to examine the body, he found lying beside him a bamboo-flute wrapped in brocade. He took the flute and gave it to his son.

The bay of Suma is associated in the mind of a Japanese reader not only with this battle but also with the stories of Prince Genji and Prince Yukihira. (See p. 268.)

ATSUMORI

By Seami

PERSONS

The Priest Rensei (formerly the warrior Kumagai).
A Young Reaper, who turns out to be the ghost of Atsumori.
His Companion.
Chorus.

PRIEST. (*waki*)

> Life is a lying dream, he only wakes
> Who casts the World aside.

I am Kumagai no Naozane, a man of the country of Musashi. I have left my home and call myself the priest Rensei; this I have done because of my grief at the death of Atsumori, who fell in battle by my hand. Hence it comes that I am dressed in priestly guise.

And now I am going down to Ichi-no-Tani to pray for the salvation of Atsumori's soul.

> (*He walks slowly across the stage, singing a song descriptive of his journey.*)

I have come so fast that here I am already at Ichi-no-Tani, in the country of Tsu.

Truly the past returns to my mind as though it were a thing of to-day.

But listen! I hear the sound of a flute coming from a knoll of rising ground. I will wait here till the flute-player passes, and ask him to tell me the story of this place.

REAPERS (*together*).

> To the music of the reaper's flute
> No song is sung
> But the sighing of wind in the fields.

YOUNG REAPER. (Shite)

They that were reaping,
Reaping on that hill,
Walk now through the fields
Homeward, for it is dusk.

REAPERS (*together*).

Short is the way that leads [1]
From the sea of Suma back to my home.
This little journey, up to the hill
And down to the shore again, and up to the hill,—
This is my life, and the sum of hateful tasks.
If one should ask me
I too [2] would answer
That on the shore of Suma
I live in sadness.
Yet if any guessed my name,
Then might I too have friends.
But now from my deep misery
Even those that were dearest
Are grown estranged.   Here must I dwell abandoned
To one thought's anguish :
That I must dwell here.

PRIEST.

Hey, you reapers ! I have a question to ask you.

YOUNG REAPER.

Is it to us you are speaking ?   What do you wish
to know ?

PRIEST.

Was it one of you who was playing on the flute just
now ?

YOUNG REAPER.

Yes, it was we who were playing.

[1] See p. 268.   [2] Like Yukihira ; see p. 268.

PRIEST.

It was a pleasant sound, and all the pleasanter because one does not look for such music from men of your condition.

YOUNG REAPER.

Unlooked for from men of our condition, you say!
Have you not read :—
" Do not envy what is above you
Nor despise what is below you " ?
Moreover the songs of woodmen and the flute-playing
    of herdsmen,
Flute-playing even of reapers and songs of wood-
    fellers
Through poets' verses are known to all the world.
Wonder not to hear among us
The sound of a bamboo-flute.

PRIEST.

You are right. Indeed it is as you have told me.
Songs of woodmen and flute-playing of herdsmen . . .

REAPER.

Flute-playing of reapers . . .

PRIEST.

Songs of wood-fellers . . .

REAPERS.

Guide us on our passage through this sad world.

PRIEST.

Song . . .

REAPER.

And dance . . .

PRIEST.

And the flute . . .

REAPER.

And music of many instruments . . .

CHORUS.

These are the pastimes that each chooses to his
taste.
Of floating bamboo-wood
Many are the famous flutes that have been
made ;
Little-Branch and Cicada-Cage,
And as for the reaper's flute,
Its name is Green-leaf ;
On the shore of Sumiyoshi
The Corean flute they play.
And here on the shore of Suma
On Stick of the Salt-kilns
The fishers blow their tune.

PRIEST.

How strange it is ! The other reapers have all
gone home, but you alone stay loitering here. How is
that ?

REAPER.

How is it, you ask ? I am seeking for a prayer in
the voice of the evening waves. Perhaps *you* will
pray the Ten Prayers for me ?

PRIEST.

I can easily pray the Ten Prayers for you, if you will
tell me who you are.

REAPER.

To tell you the truth—I am one of the family of Lord
Atsumori.

PRIEST.

One of Atsumori's family ? How glad I am !

Then the priest joined his hands (*he kneels down*) and prayed:—

NAMU AMIDABU.

Praise to Amida Buddha!
  " If I attain to Buddhahood,
  In the whole world and its ten spheres
  Of all that dwell here none shall call on my
      name
  And be rejected or cast aside."

CHORUS.

  " Oh, reject me not!
  One cry suffices for salvation,
  Yet day and night
  Your prayers will rise for me.
  Happy am I, for though you know not my name,
  Yet for my soul's deliverance
  At dawn and dusk henceforward I know that
      you will pray."
So he spoke. Then vanished and was seen no more.

  (*Here follows the Interlude between the two Acts, in
      which a recitation concerning Atsumori's death
      takes place. These interludes are subject to
      variation and are not considered part of the
      literary text of the play.*)

PRIEST.

Since this is so, I will perform all night the rites of prayer for the dead, and calling upon Amida's name will pray again for the salvation of Atsumori.

  (*The ghost of* ATSUMORI *appears, dressed as a young
      warrior.*)

ATSUMORI.

  Would you know who I am
  That like the watchmen at Suma Pass
  Have wakened at the cry of sea-birds roaming
  Upon Awaji shore ?
  Listen, Rensei. I am Atsumori.

PRIEST.

How strange! All this while I have never stopped beating my gong and performing the rites of the Law. I cannot for a moment have dozed, yet I thought that Atsumori was standing before me. Surely it was a dream.

ATSUMORI.

Why need it be a dream? It is to clear the karma of my waking life that I am come here in visible form before you.

PRIEST.

Is it not written that one prayer will wipe away ten thousand sins? Ceaselessly I have performed the ritual of the Holy Name that clears all sin away. After such prayers, what evil can be left? Though you should be sunk in sin as deep . . .

ATSUMORI.

As the sea by a rocky shore,
Yet should I be salved by prayer.

PRIEST.

And that my prayers should save you . . .

ATSUMORI.

This too must spring
From kindness of a former life.[1]

PRIEST.

Once enemies . . .

ATSUMORI.

But now . . .

PRIEST.

In truth may we be named . . .

[1] "Atsumori must have done Kumagai some kindness in a former incarnation." This would account for Kumagai's remorse.

ATSUMORI.

Friends in Buddha's Law.

CHORUS.

There is a saying, " Put away from you a wicked
friend ; summon to your side a virtuous enemy." For
you it was said, and you have proven it true.

And now come tell with us the tale of your con-
fession, while the night is still dark.

CHORUS.

He [1] bids the flowers of Spring
Mount the tree-top that men may raise their eyes
And walk on upward paths ;
He bids the moon in autumn waves be drowned
In token that he visits laggard men
And leads them out from valleys of despair.

ATSUMORI.

Now the clan of Taira, building wall to wall,
Spread over the earth like the leafy branches of a
great tree :

CHORUS.

Yet their prosperity lasted but for a day ;
It was like the flower of the convolvulus.
There was none to tell them [2]
That glory flashes like sparks from flint-stone,
And after,—darkness.
Oh wretched, the life of men !

ATSUMORI.

When they were on high they afflicted the humble ;
When they were rich they were reckless in pride.
And so for twenty years and more
They ruled this land.
But truly a generation passes like the space of a dream.
The leaves of the autumn of Juyei [3]

[1] Buddha.

[2] I have omitted a line the force of which depends upon a play
on words.

[3] The Taira evacuated the Capital in the second year of Juyei, 1188.

Were tossed by the four winds;
Scattered, scattered (like leaves too) floated their
    ships.
And they, asleep on the heaving sea, not even in
    dreams
Went back to home.
Caged birds longing for the clouds,—
Wild geese were they rather, whose ranks are broken
As they fly to southward on their doubtful journey.
So days and months went by; Spring came again
And for a little while
Here dwelt they on the shore of Suma
At the first valley. [1]
From the mountain behind us the winds blew down
Till the fields grew wintry again.
Our ships lay by the shore, where night and day
The sea-gulls cried and salt waves washed on our
    sleeves.
We slept with fishers in their huts
On pillows of sand.
We knew none but the people of Suma.
And when among the pine-trees
The evening smoke was rising,
Brushwood, as they called it,[2]
Brushwood we gathered
And spread for carpet.
Sorrowful we lived
On the wild shore of Suma,
Till the clan Taira and all its princes
Were but villagers of Suma.

ATSUMORI.

But on the night of the sixth day of the second month
My father Tsunemori gathered us together.
" To-morrow," he said, " we shall fight our last fight.
To-night is all that is left us."
We sang songs together, and danced.

---

[1] Ichi-no-Tani means " First Valley."
[2] The name of so humble a thing was unfamiliar to the Taira lords.

PRIEST.

Yes, I remember ; we in our siege-camp
Heard the sound of music
Echoing from your tents that night ;
There was the music of a flute . . .

ATSUMORI.

The bamboo-flute ! I wore it when I died.

PRIEST.

We heard the singing . . .

ATSUMORI.

Songs and ballads . . .

PRIEST.

Many voices

ATSUMORI.

Singing to one measure.

(ATSUMORI *dances*.)

First comes the Royal Boat.

CHORUS.

The whole clan has put its boats to sea.
He [1] will not be left behind ;
He runs to the shore.
But the Royal Boat and the soldiers' boats
Have sailed far away.

ATSUMORI.

What can he do ?
He spurs his horse into the waves.
He is full of perplexity.
And then

---

[1] Atsumori. This passage is mimed throughout.

CHORUS.

He looks behind him and sees
That Kumagai pursues him ;
He cannot escape.
Then Atsumori turns his horse
Knee-deep in the lashing waves,
And draws his sword.
Twice, three times he strikes ; then, still saddled,
In close fight they twine ; roll headlong together
Among the surf of the shore.
So Atsumori fell and was slain, but now the Wheel
    of Fate
Has turned and brought him back.

(ATSUMORI *rises from the ground and advances
    towards the* PRIEST *with uplifted sword.*)

" There is my enemy," he cries, and would strike,
But the other is grown gentle
And calling on Buddha's name
Has obtained salvation for his foe ;
So that they shall be re-born together
On one lotus-seat.
" No, Rensei is not my enemy.
Pray for me' again, oh pray for me again."

IKUTA *The field of life*

By Zembō Motoyasu (1453–1532) *is anicca*

dream.
more prominent

PERSONS

PRIEST (a follower of Hōnen Shōnin).[1]   ATSUMORI'S CHILD. *in Tsunemasa*
ATSUMORI.   CHORUS.

PRIEST.

I am one that serves Hōnen Shōnin of Kurodani ;
and as for this child here,—once when Hōnen was on
a visit to the Temple of Kamo he saw a box lying under
a trailing fir-tree ; and when he raised the lid, what
should he find inside but a lovely man-child one year
old ! It did not seem to be more than a common
foundling, but my master in his compassion took the
infant home with him. Ever since then he has had it
in his care, doing all that was needful for it ; and now
the boy is over ten years old.

But it is a hard thing to have no father or mother,
so one day after his preaching the Shōnin told the child's
story. And sure enough a young woman stepped out
from among the hearers and said it was her child. And
when he took her aside and questioned her, he found
that the child's father was Taira no Atsumori, who
had fallen in battle at Ichi-no-Tani years ago. When the
boy was told of this, he longed earnestly to see his
father's face, were it but in a dream, and the Shōnin
bade him go and pray at the shrine of Kamo. He was
to go every day for a week, and this is the last day.

That is why I have brought him out with me.

But here we are at the Kamo shrine.

Pray well, boy, pray well !

[1] A great preacher; died 1212 A.D.

74

BOY.

How fills my heart with awe
When I behold the crimson palisade
Of this abode of gods !
Oh may my heart be clean
As the River of Ablution ; [1]
And the God's kindness deep
As its unfathomed waters. Show to me,
Though it were but in dream,
My father's face and form.
Is not my heart so ground away with prayer,
So smooth that it will slip
Unfelt into the favour of the gods ?
But thou too, Censor of our prayers,
God of Tadasu,[2] on the gods prevail
That what I crave may be !

How strange ! While I was praying I fell half-asleep
and had a wonderful dream.

PRIEST.

Tell me your wonderful dream.

BOY.

A strange voice spoke to me from within the Treasure
Hall, saying, " If you are wanting, though it were but
in a dream, to see your father's face, go down from
here to the woods of Ikuta in the country of Settsu."
That is the marvellous dream I had.

PRIEST.

It is indeed a wonderful message that the God has
sent you. And why should I go back at once to
Kurodani ? I had best take you straight to the forest
of Ikuta. Let us be going.

[1] The name given to streams which flow through temples. In
this case the River Kamo.

[2] Tadasu means to " straighten," " correct." The shrine of Kamo
lay in the forest of Tadasu.

PRIEST (*describing the journey*).

> From the shrine of Kamo,
> From under the shadow of the hills,
> We set out swiftly;
> Past Yamazaki to the fog-bound
> Shores of Minasé;
> And onward where the gale
> Tears travellers' coats and winds about their
> bones.
> " Autumn has come to woods where yesterday
> We might have plucked the green." [1]
> To Settsu, to those woods of Ikuta
> Lo! we are come.

We have gone so fast that here we are already at the woods of Ikuta in the country of Settsu. I have heard tell in the Capital of the beauty of these woods and the river that runs through them. But what I see now surpasses all that I have heard.

Look! Those meadows must be the Downs of Ikuta. Let us go nearer and admire them.

But while we have been going about looking at one view and another, the day has dusked.

I think I see a light over there. There must be a house. Let us go to it and ask for lodging.

ATSUMORI (*speaking from inside a hut*).

> Beauty, perception, knowledge, motion, conscious-
> ness,—
> The Five Attributes of Being,—
> All are vain mockery.
> How comes it that men prize
> So weak a thing as body?
> For the soul that guards it from corruption
> Suddenly to the night-moon flies,
> And the poor naked ghost wails desolate
> In the autumn wind.

Oh! I am lonely. I am lonely!

[1] Adapted from a poem in the *Shin Kokinshū.*

PRIEST.

How strange ! Inside that grass-hut I see a young
soldier dressed in helmet and breastplate. What can
he be doing there ?

ATSUMORI.

Oh foolish men, was it not to meet me that you came
to this place ? I am—oh ! I am ashamed to say it,—
I am the ghost of what once was . . . Atsumori.

BOY.

Atsumori ? My father . . .

CHORUS.

And lightly he ran,
Plucked at the warrior's sleeve,
And though his tears might seem like the long
  woe
Of nightingales that weep,
Yet were they tears of meeting-joy,
Of happiness too great for human heart.
So think we, yet oh that we might change
This fragile dream of joy
Into the lasting love of waking life !

ATSUMORI.

Oh pitiful !
To see this child, born after me,
Darling that should be gay as a flower,
Walking in tattered coat of old black cloth.
Alas !
Child, when your love of me
Led you to Kamo shrine, praying to the God
That, though but in a dream,
You might behold my face,
The God of Kamo, full of pity, came
To Yama, king of Hell.
King Yama listened and ordained for me
A moment's respite, but hereafter, never.

[handwritten margin note:] But contradicts his statement about 5 attributes 7 being.

[handwritten:] N3

CHORUS.

" The moon is sinking.
Come while the night is dark," he said,
" I will tell my tale."

ATSUMORI.

When the house of Taira was in its pride,
When its glory was young,
Among the flowers we sported,
Among birds, wind and moonlight;
With pipes and strings, with song and verse
We welcomed Springs and Autumns.
Till at last, because our time was come,
Across the bridges of Kiso a host unseen
Swept and devoured us.
Then the whole clan
Our lord leading
Fled from the City of Flowers.
By paths untrodden
To the Western Sea our journey brought us.
Lakes and hills we crossed
Till we ourselves grew to be like wild men.
At last by mountain ways—
We too tossed hither and thither like its waves—
To Suma came we,
To the First Valley and the woods of Ikuta.
And now while all of us,
We children of Taira, were light of heart
Because our homes were near,
Suddenly our foes in great strength appeared.

CHORUS.

Noriyori, Yoshitsune,—their hosts like clouds,
Like mists of spring.
For a little while we fought them,
But the day of our House was ended,
Our hearts weakened
That had been swift as arrows from the bowstring.

We scattered, scattered ; till at last
To the deep waters of the Field of Life [1]
We came, but how we found there Death, not
    Life,
What profit were it to tell ?

ATSUMORI.

Who is that ?

    (*Pointing in terror at a figure which he sees off the
        stage.*)

Can it be Yama's messenger ?   He comes to tell me
that I have outstayed my time.   The Lord of Hell is
angry : he asks why I am late ?

CHORUS.

So he spoke.   But behold
Suddenly black clouds rise,
Earth and sky resound with the clash of arms ;
War-demons innumerable
Flash fierce sparks from brandished spears.

ATSUMORI. *Battle-pieces*

The Shura foes who night and day
Come thick about me !

CHORUS.

He waves his sword and rushes among them,
Hither and thither he runs slashing furiously ;
Fire glints upon the steel.
But in a little while
The dark clouds recede ;
The demons have vanished,
The moon shines unsullied ;
The sky is ready for dawn.

    [1] Ikuta means " Field of Life."

ATSUMORI.

Oh! I am ashamed. . . .
And the child to see me so. . . .

CHORUS.

"To see my misery!
I must go back.
Oh pray for me ; pray for me
When I am gone," he said,
And weeping, weeping,
Dropped the child's hand.
He has faded ; he dwindles
Like the dew from rush-leaves
Of hazy meadows.
His form has vanished.

into a dream

Parallels [g Tsunemad] with western
spiritualist doctrines are more than
interesting. Note the spirit's uncertainty
as to his own success in appearing.
The priest concludes if he really
saw anything. The spirit affirms that
"No body was there if you saw it."
Pound, 264.

[handwritten marginalia: Seasons / dream / music / wind sym. amica p. 300 / lute / Prayer for the salvation of departed souls.]

TSUNEMASA

By Seami

PERSONS

THE PRIEST GYŌKEI.
THE GHOST OF TAIRA NO TSUNEMASA.
CHORUS.

GYŌKEI.

I am Gyōkei, priest of the imperial temple Ninnaji. You must know that there was a certain prince of the House of Taira named Tsunemasa, Lord of Tajima, who since his boyhood had enjoyed beyond all precedent the favour of our master the Emperor. But now he has been killed at the Battle of the Western Seas.

It was to this Tsunemasa in his lifetime that the Emperor had given the lute called Green Hill. And *[handwritten: image]* now my master bids me take it and dedicate it to Buddha, performing a liturgy of flutes and strings for the salvation of Tsunemasa's soul. And that was my purpose in gathering these musicians together.

Truly it is said that strangers who shelter under the same tree or draw water from the same pool will be friends in another life. How much the more must intercourse of many years, kindness and favour so deep . . .[1]

Surely they will be heard,
The prayers that all night long
With due performance of rites
I have reverently repeated in this Palace
For the salvation of Tsunemasa
And for the awakening of his soul.

---

[1] The relation between Tsunemasa and the Emperor is meant.

81

CHORUS.

And, more than all, we dedicate
The lute Green Hill for this dead man;
While pipe and flute are joined to sounds of prayer.
For night and day the Gate of Law   Dharma
Stands open and the Universal Road
Rejects no wayfarer.

TSUNEMASA (*speaking off the stage*).

"The wind blowing through withered trees: rain
    from a cloudless sky.
The moon shining on level sands : frost on a summer's
    night."[1]
Frost lying . . . but I, because I could not lie at rest,
Am come back to the World for a while,
Like a shadow that steals over the grass.
I am like dews that in the morning
Still cling to the grasses. Oh pitiful the longing
That has beset me !

GYŌKEI.

How strange ! Within the flame of our candle
that is burning low because the night is far spent,
suddenly I seemed to see a man's shadow dimly appearing.   Who can be here ?

TSUNEMASA (*his shadow disappearing*).

I am the ghost of Tsunemasa. The sound of your
prayers has brought me in visible shape before you.

GYŌKEI.

"I am the ghost of Tsunemasa," he said, but when I
looked to where the voice had sounded nothing was
there, neither substance nor shadow !

TSUNEMASA.
Only a voice,

---

[1] I.e. the wind sounds like rain; the sands appear to be covered
with frost. A couplet from a poem by Po Chü-i.

GYŌKEI.

A dim voice whispers where the shadow of a man
Visibly lay, but when I looked

TSUNEMASA.

It had vanished—

GYŌKEI.

This flickering form . . .

TSUNEMASA.

Like haze over the fields.

CHORUS.

Only as a tricking magic,
A bodiless vision,
Can he hover in the world of his lifetime,
Swift-changing Tsunemasa.
By this name we call him, yet of the body
That men named so, what is left but longing?
What but the longing to look again, through the
    wall of death,
On one he loved?
"Sooner shall the waters in its gardens cease to
    flow
Than I grow weary of living in the Palace of my
    Lord." [1]
Like a dream he has come,
Like a morning dream.

GYŌKEI.

How strange! When the form of Tsunemasa had
vanished, his voice still lingered and spoke to me!
Am I dreaming or waking? I cannot tell. But this
I know,—that by the power of my incantations I have
had converse with the dead. Oh! marvellous potency
of the Law!

---

[1] Part of the poem which Tsunemasa gave to the Emperor before
he went to battle.

TSUNEMASA.

It was long ago that I came to the Palace. I was but a boy then, but all the world knew me; for I was marked with the love of our Lord, with the favour of an Emperor. And, among many gifts, he gave to me once while I was in the World this lute which you have dedicated. My fingers were ever on its strings.

CHORUS.

Plucking them even as now
This music plucks at your heart;
The sound of the plectrum, then as now
Divine music fulfilling
The vows of Sarasvati.[1]
But this Tsunemasa,
Was he not from the days of his childhood pre-eminent
In faith, wisdom, benevolence,
Honour and courtesy; yet for his pleasure
Ever of birds and flowers,
Of wind and moonlight making
Ballads and songs to join their harmony
To pipes and lutes?
So springs and autumns passed he.
But in a World that is as dew,
As dew on the grasses, as foam upon the waters,
What flower lasteth?

GYŌKEI.

For the dead man's sake we play upon this lute Green Hill that he loved when he was in the World. We follow the lute-music with a concord of many instruments.

(*Music.*)

TSUNEMASA.

And while they played the dead man stole up behind them. Though he could not be seen by the light of the candle, they felt him pluck the lute-strings. . . .

---

[1] Goddess of Music, who vowed that she would lead all souls to salvation by the music of her lute.

GYŌKEI.

It is midnight. He is playing *Yabanraku*, the dance
of midnight-revel. And now that we have shaken
sleep from our eyes . . .

TSUNEMASA.

The sky is clear, yet there is a sound as of sudden
rain. . . .

GYŌKEI.

Rain beating ceaselessly on trees and grasses. What
season's music [1] ought we to play ?

TSUNEMASA.

No. It is not rain. Look ! At the cloud's fringe

CHORUS.

The moon undimmed
Hangs over the pine-woods of Narabi [2] Hills.
It was the wind you heard ;
The wind blowing through the pine-leaves
Pattered, like the falling of winter rain.
O wonderful hour !
" The big strings crashed and sobbed
Like the falling of winter rain.
And the little strings whispered secretly together.
The first and second string
Were like a wind sweeping through pine-woods,
Murmuring disjointedly.
The third and fourth string
Were like the voice of a caged stork
Crying for its little ones at night
In low, dejected notes." [3]

[1] Different tunes were appropriate to different seasons.
[2] A range of hills to the south of the Ninnaji. The name means
the " Row of Hills."
[3] Quotation from Po Chü-i's "Lute Girl's Song"; for paraphrase
see Giles' *Chinese Literature*, p. 166.

The night. must not cease.
The cock shall not crow
And put an end to his wandering.[1]

TSUNEMASA.

" One note of the phœnix-flute [2]

CHORUS.

Shakes the autumn clouds from the mountain-side." [3]
The phœnix and his mate swoop down
Charmed by its music, beat their wings
And dance in rapture, perched upon the swaying
    boughs
Of kiri and bamboo.

(*Dance.*)

TSUNEMASA.

Oh terrible anguish !
For a little while I was back in the World and my
heart set on its music, on revels of midnight. But
now the hate is rising in me. . . .[4]

GYŌKEI.

The shadow that we saw before is still visible.
Can it be Tsunemasa ?

see p. 80

TSUNEMASA.

Oh ! I am ashamed ; I must not let them see me.
Put out your candle.

CHORUS.

" Let us turn away from the candle and watch
    together
The midnight moon."
Lo, he who holds the moon,
The god Indra, in battle appeareth
Warring upon demons.

[1] The ghost must return at dawn.
[2] The *shĕng*.
[3] Quotation from Chinese poem in *Rōyei Shū*.
[4] He had died in battle and was therefore condemned to perpetual
war with the demons of Hell.

Fire leaps from their swords,
The sparks of their own anger fall upon them like
    rain.
To wound another he draws his sword,
But it is from his own flesh
That the red waves flow ;
Like flames they cover him.
" Oh, I am ashamed of the woes that consume me.
No man must see me. I will put out the candle ! "
    he said ;
For a foolish man is like a summer moth that flies
    into the flame.[1]
The wind that blew out the candle
Carried him away. In the darkness his ghost has
    vanished.
The shadow of his ghost has vanished.

---

[1] " The wise man is like the autumn deer crying in the mountains ; the fool is like the moth which flies into the candle " (*Gempei Seisuiki,* chap. viii.).

CHAPTER II

KUMASAKA
EBOSHI-ORI
BENKEI ON THE BRIDGE

THESE three plays deal with the boyhood of the hero Yoshitsune, whose child-name was Ushiwaka.

Eboshi-ori is a *genzai-mono*, that is to say a play which describes events actually in progress. In *Kumasaka* these same events are rehearsed by the ghost of one who participated in them. There are two other well-known Yoshitsune plays, *Funa-Benkei* and *Ataka*. In the former the phantoms of the dead Taira warriors attack the boat in which Yoshitsune and Benkei are riding ; in the latter occurs the famous scene called the *Kwanjinchō*, in which Benkei pretends to read out from a scroll a long document which he is in reality improvising on the spot. (See Mr. Sansom's translations of these two plays in the *Transactions of the Asiatic Society of Japan*, 1911.) The *Kwanjinchō* was borrowed by the popular stage, and became one of the favourite " turns " of the great Danjūrō (1660–1703) and his successors. (See above, p. 40.)

[handwritten marginalia:] footfall clangs / pike / iron crowbar / sword. / note the rythm p.97. / Chorus p.99 / ending p.101. / force action cluster / in shadow? / fenestrees.

KUMASAKA

By Zenchiku Ujinobu (1414–1499?)

PERSONS

A Priest from the Capital.
A Priest of Akasaka (really the ghost of the robber Kumasaka no Chōhan).
Chorus.

[handwritten: Waki] Priest.

> These weary feet that found the World
> Too sad to walk in, whither
> Oh whither shall wandering lead them?

I am a priest from the Capital. I have never seen the East country, and now I am minded to go there on pilgrimage.

> (*He describes the journey, walking slowly round the stage.*)

> Over the mountains, down the Ōmi road by a foam-
>   flecked stream;
> And through the woods of Awazu.
> Over the long bridge of Seta
> Heavily my footfall clangs.
> In the bamboo-woods of Noji I await the dawn.
> There where the morning dew lies thick, over the
>   Greenfield Plain,
> Green in name only—for the leaves are red with
>   autumn—
> In evening sunshine to the village of Akasaka I am
>   come!

[handwritten: Shite] Kumasaka.

> (*It is convenient to call him this, but he is the ghost of Kumasaka, appearing in the guise of a priest.*)

> Hey, you priest, I have something to say to you!

92

PRIEST.

What is it you would say to me ?

KUMASAKA.

To-day is some one's birthday. I beg of you to pray for the salvation of his soul.

PRIEST.

I have left the World, and it is my business now to say such prayers ; but of whom am I to think when I pray ?

KUMASAKA.

There is no need to know his name. He is buried in that tomb over there, among the rushes to this side of the pine-tree. It is because he cannot get free[1] that he needs your prayers.

PRIEST.

No, no ; it will not do. I cannot pray for him unless I know his name.

KUMASAKA.

Pray, none the less. For it is written, " All the creatures of the world shall be profited.
There shall be no distinction."

PRIEST.

From dying and being born

KUMASAKA.

Deliver him, oh deliver him !

CHORUS.

For he that taketh a prayer unto himself
Even though his name be not named, if he receive
    it gladly,
Is the owner of the prayer.

[1] I.e. he is " attached " to earth and cannot get away to the Western Paradise.

Was not promise made to the trees of the field,
To the soil of the land ?   Though the heart that prays
        marks no name upon the prayer,
Yet shall it be heard.

KUMASAKA.

Then come back to my cottage with me and pass
the night there.

PRIEST.

I will come.

> (*They go into the cottage, which is represented by a
> wicker framework open at the front.*)

Listen ! I thought you were taking me to where
there would be a chapel, so that I could begin my prayers.
But here I can see no painted picture nor carven image
that I could put up.   There is nothing on the wall but
a great pike,—no handstaff, but only an iron crowbar ;
and other weapons of war are nailed up.   What is the
reason of this ?

KUMASAKA.

You must know that when I first took the vows of
priesthood I went round from village to village here,
to Tarui, Auhaka and Akasaka—there is no end to them,
but I know all the roads,—through the tall grass at
Aono and the thick woods of Koyasu, night or day,
rain or fine.   For I was a hill-bandit in those days, a
thief of the night, tilting baggage from mules' backs ;
even stripping servant-girls of their clothes, as they
went from farm to farm, and leaving them sobbing.
    Then it was that I used to take with me that pike
there and waving it in their faces, " Stand and deliver ! "
I would cry.
    But at last a time came when it was not so.[1]   And
after that time I was glad enough to find shelter even in
such a place as this.   I yielded my will and was content.

---

[1] I.e. the time of his encounter with Ushiwaka.

For at last I had indeed resolved to leave the hateful
World.

  Oh petty prowess of those days !

CHORUS.

  For hand of priest unfit indeed
  Such deeds and weapons had I thought ;
  Yet among gods
  Hath not the Lord Amida his sharp sword ?
  Doth not the King of Love [1]
  Shoot arrows of salvation from his bow ?
  Tamon with tilted lance
  Outbattled demons and hath swept away
  All perils from the world.

KUMASAKA.

  Thoughts of love and pity
  May be sins fouler

CHORUS.

  Than the Five Faults of Datta ; [2]
  And the taking of life for faith
  Be holiness greater
  Than the six virtues of Bosatsu.[3]
  These things have I seen and heard.
  But for the rest, is it not Thought alone
  That either wanders in the trackless night
  Of Error or awakes to the wide day ?
  "Master thy thoughts, or they will master thee,"
  An ancient proverb [4] says.

(Speaking for Kumasaka.)

" But I must have done, or dawn will find me talking
still. Go to your rest, Sir ; and I too will doze awhile."
So he spoke, and seemed to go into the bedroom. But

---

  [1] Aizen.
  [2] Devadatta, the wicked contemporary of Buddha.
  [3] The six paths to Bodisattva-hood, i.e. Almsgiving, Observance
of Rules, Forbearance, Meditation, Knowledge and Singleness of
Heart.
  [4] Actually from the Nirvāna Sūtra.

suddenly the cottage vanished : nothing was left but the tall grass. It was under the shadow of a pine-tree that he [1] had rested !

> (*There is usually an interlude to occupy the time while Kumasaka is changing his costume. An inhabitant of Akasaka tells stories of Kumasaka's exploits.*)

PRIEST.

I have seen strange things. I cannot sleep, no, not even for a while as little as the space between the antlers of a young stag. Under this autumn-winded pine-tree lying, all night long I will perform a service of chanted prayer.[2]

KUMASAKA.

> (*Reappearing with a scarf tied round his head and a long pike over his shoulder.*)

The wind is rising in the south-east. The clouds of the north-west are shifting ; it is a dark night. A wild wind is sweeping the woods under the hill.

CHORUS.

See how the branches are heaving.

KUMASAKA.

The moon does not rise till dawn to-night ; and even when she rises she will be covered.

Send along the order for an assault !

> (*Recollecting himself.*)

The whole heart divided between bow-hand and rein-hand,—oh the sin of it ! For ever seizing another's treasure ! Look, look on my misery, how my heart clings to the World !

PRIEST.

If you are Kumasaka himself, tell me the story of those days.

---

[1] The Priest.　　　　[2] *Koye-butsuji,* " Voice-service."

KUMASAKA.

There was a merchant, a trafficker in gold, called Kichiji of the Third Ward. Each year he brought together a great store, and loading it in bales carried it up-country. And thinking to waylay him I summoned divers trusty men. . . .

PRIEST.

Tell me the names of those that were chosen by you and the countries they came from.

KUMASAKA.

There was Kakujō of Kawachi, and the brothers Surihari that had no rivals in fencing.

PRIEST.

Well, and from within the City itself among many there were—

KUMASAKA.

There was Emon of the Third Ward and Kozaru of Mibu.

PRIEST.

Skilful torch-throwers; in broken-attack

KUMASAKA.

Their like will never be seen.

PRIEST.

And from the North country, from Echizen

KUMASAKA.

There was Matsuwaka of Asau and Kurō of Mikuni.

PRIEST.

And from the country of Kaga, from Kumasaka

KUMASAKA.

There was this Chōhan, the first of them, a great hand at deeds of villainy ; and with him seventy men of the band.

PRIEST.

On all the roads where Kichiji might be passing, up hill and down dale on every halting-place they spied, till at last

KUMASAKA.

Here at the Inn of Akasaka we found him,—a fine place, with many roads leading from it. We set watch upon the place. The merchants had sent for women. From nightfall they feasted. They roystered the hours away—

PRIEST.

And at last, very late at night,
Kichiji and his brother, with no thought for safety,
Fell into a sodden sleep.

KUMASAKA.

But there was with them a boy of sixteen.[1]
He put his bright eye to a hole in the wall.
He did not make the least noise.

PRIEST.

He did not sleep a wink.

KUMASAKA.

Ushiwaka ! We did not know he was there.

PRIEST.

Then the robbers, whose luck was run out,

KUMASAKA.

Thinking that the hour of fortune was come,

[1] Yoshitsune (Ushiwaka) had run away from the temple where he was being educated and joined the merchant's caravan, see p. 103.

PRIEST.

Waited impatiently.

CHORUS.

Oh how long it seemed till at last the order came.

KUMASAKA.

Dash in !

CHORUS.

And, hurling their firebrands,
In they rushed, each jostling to be first,
More of them and more, in a wild onslaught.
Not even the God of Peril had dared to face them.
But little Ushiwaka showed no fear.
He drew his belt-sword and met them.
The Lion Pounce, The Tiger Leap, The Bird
Pounce . . .[1]
He parried them all. They thrust at him but could
not prevail.
Thirteen there were who attacked him ;
And now, done to death, on the same pillow head to
head they lie.
And others, wounded, have flung down their swords
and slunk back weaponless,
Stripped of all else but life.
Then Kumasaka cried : " What demon or god can
he be
Under whose hand all these have fallen ? For a
man he cannot be !
But even robbers need their lives ! This is no work
for me ; I will withdraw."
And slinging his pike, slowly he turned to go,

KUMASAKA.

I was thinking.

---

[1] Names of strokes in fencing.

CHORUS.

He was thinking as he went,
" Though this stripling slash so bravely,
Yet should Kumasaka employ his secret art,—
Then though the boy be demon or hobgoblin,
Waist-strangled he would be pressed to dust."
" I will avenge the fallen," he cried, and, turning
    back,
He levelled his pike and sheltered behind the wattled
    door,
Waiting for the urchin to come.
Ushiwaka saw him, and drawing his sword held it
    close to his side,
Stood apart and watched.   But Kumasaka too stood
    with his pike ready.
Each was waiting for the other to spring.
Then Kumasaka lost patience.   He lunged with his
    left foot and with his pike
Struck a blow that would have pierced an iron
    wall.
But Ushiwaka parried it lightly and sprang to the
    left.
Kumasaka was after him in a moment, and as he
    sprang nimbly over the pike,[1]
Turned the point towards him.
But as he drew back the pike, Ushiwaka crossed to
    the right.
Then levelling the pike, Kumasaka struck a great
    blow.
This time the boy parried it with a blow that dis-
    engaged them,
And springing into the air leapt hither and thither
    with invisible speed.
And while the robber sought him,
The wonderful boy pranced behind and stuck his
    sword through a chink in his coat of mail.

---

[1] I have thought it better to print these "recitals" as verse,
though in the original (as obviously in my translation) they are
almost prose.

" Hey, what is that ? " cried Kumasaka. " Has
  this urchin touched me ? "
And he was very angry.
But soon Heaven's fatal ordinance was sealed by
  despair :
" This sword-play brings me no advantage," he
  cried ; " I will wrestle with him."
Then he threw away his pike, and spreading out his
  great hands,
Down this corridor and into this corner he chased
  him, but when he would have grasped him,
Like lightning, mist, moonlight on the water,—
The eye could see, but the hand could not touch.

KUMASAKA.

I was wounded again and again.

CHORUS.

He was wounded many times, till the fierce strength
of his spirit weakened and weakened. Like dew upon
the moss that grows.

KUMASAKA.

Round the foot of this pine-tree

CHORUS.

Are vanished the men of this old tale.
" Oh, help me to be born to happiness."

  (KUMASAKA entreats the PRIEST with folded hands.)

The cocks are crowing. A whiteness glimmers over
  the night.
He has hidden under the shadow of the pine-trees of
  Akasaka ;

  (KUMASAKA hides his face with his left sleeve.)

Under the shadow of the pine-trees he has hidden
  himself away.

EBOSHI-ORI
By MIYAMASU (sixteenth century ?)

PERSONS

KICHIJI
HIS BROTHER KICHIROKU } *Gold-merchants.*
USHIWAKA.   MESSENGER.
HATMAKER.   HATMAKER'S WIFE.
INNKEEPER.   KUMASAKA.
BRIGANDS.   CHORUS.

KICHIJI.

We as travellers dressed—
Our weary feet upon the Eastern road
For many days must speed.

I am Sanjō no Kichiji. I have now amassed a great store of treasure and with my brother Kichiroku am going to take it down to the East. Ho! Kichiroku, let us get together our bundles and start now.

KICHIROKU.

I am ready. Let us start at once.

USHIWAKA.

Hie, you travellers! If you are going up-country, please take me with you.

KICHIJI.

That is a small thing to ask. Certainly we would take you with us . . . , but by the look of you, I fancy you must be an apprentice playing truant from your master. If that is so, I cannot take you.

USHIWAKA.

I have neither father nor mother, and my master has turned me adrift. Please let me go with you.

KICHIJI.

If that is so, I cannot any longer refuse to take you with me. (*Describing his own action.*)
Then he offered the boy a broad-brimmed hat.

USHIWAKA.

And Ushiwaka eagerly grasped it.
To-day, he said, begins our troublous journey's toil.

CHORUS (*describing the journey and speaking for* USHI-WAKA).

Past the creek of Awata, to Matsusaka,
To the shore of Shinomiya I travel.
Down the road to the barrier of Ōsaka walking
    behind pack-ponies,
How long shall I serve in sadness these hucksters of
    gold ?
Here where once the blind harper [1] lay sorrowing
On a cottage-bed, far away from the City,
Thinking perhaps some such thoughts as I do now.
We have passed the plain of Awazu. Over the long
    bridge of Seta
The hoofs of our ponies clank.
We cross the hill of Moru, where the evening dew
Lies thick on country paths and, caught in the
    slanting light,
Gleams on the under-leaves till suddenly night
Comes on us and in darkness we approach
The Mirror Inn.

KICHIJI.

We have travelled so fast that we have already reached the Mirror Inn.   Let us rest here for a little while.

MESSENGER.

I am a servant in the Palace of Rokuhara.   I have been sent to fetch back young Ushiwaka, Lord Yoshi-tomo's son, who has escaped from the Temple of Kurama. It is thought that he has taken service with the merchant

[1] Semimaru.

Kichiji and has gone up-country with him; so they sent me to bring him back. Why, I believe that is he! But perhaps he is not alone. I cannot be sure. I had better go home and fetch help, for if I were one against many, how could I hope to take him?

USHIWAKA.

I think it is about me that this messenger is speaking. I must not let him know me. I will cut my hair and wear an *eboshi*,[1] so that people may think I am an Eastern boy.

> (*He goes to the curtain which separates the green-room from the entrance-passage. This represents for the moment the front of the hatmaker's shop.*)

May I come in? (*The curtain is raised.*)

HATMAKER.

Who is it?

USHIWAKA.

I have come to order an *eboshi*.

HATMAKER.

An *eboshi* at this time of night? I will make you one to-morrow, if you like.

USHIWAKA.

Please make it now. I am travelling in a hurry and cannot wait.

HATMAKER.

Very well then; I will make it now. What size do you take?

USHIWAKA.

Please give me an *eboshi* of the third size, folded to the left.

HATMAKER.

I am afraid I cannot do that. They were worn folded to the left in the time of the Minamotos. But now that

---

[1] A tall, nodding hat.

the Tairas rule the whole land it would not be possible to wear one folded so.

USHIWAKA.

In spite of that I beg of you to make me one. There is a good reason for my asking.

HATMAKER.

Well, as you are so young there cannot be much harm in your wearing it. I will make you one.

(*He begins to make the hat.*)

There is a fine story about these left-folded *eboshi* and the luck they bring. Shall I tell it you?

USHIWAKA.

Yes, pray tell me the story.

HATMAKER.

My grandfather lived at Karasu-maru in the Third
　　　Ward.
It was the time when Hachimantarō Yoshi-iye,
　　　having routed[1] the brothers Sadatō and Munetō,
Came home in triumph to the Capital.
And when he was summoned to the Emperor's
　　　Palace, he went first to my grandfather and
　　　ordered from him
A left-folded *eboshi* for the Audience. And when
　　　he was come before the Throne
The Emperor welcomed him gladly
And as a token of great favour made him lord
Of the lands of Outer Mutsu.
Even such an *eboshi* it is that I am making now,
A garment of good omen.
Wear it and when into the world

CHORUS.

When into the world you go, who knows but that
　　　Fate's turn
May not at last bring you to lordship of lands,

[1] 1064 A.D.

Of Dewa or the country of Michi.
And on that day remember,
Oh deign to remember, him that now with words
    of good omen
Folds for you this *eboshi*.
On that day forget not the gift you owe!
But alas!
These things were, but shall not be again.
The time of the left-folded *eboshi* was long ago:
When the houses of Gen and Hei [1] were in their
    pride,
Like the plum-tree and cherry-tree among flowers,
Like Spring and Autumn among the four seasons.
Then, as snow that would outsparkle the moonlight,
Gen strove with Hei; and after the years of Hōgen,[2]
The house of Hei prevailed and the whole land was
    theirs.
So is it now.
But retribution shall come; time shall bring
Its changes to the world and like the cherry-blossom
This *eboshi* that knows its season
Shall bloom again. Wait patiently for that time!

HATMAKER.

And while they prayed

CHORUS.

Lo! The cutting of the *eboshi* was done.
Then he decked it brightly with ribbons of three
    colours,
Tied the strings to it and finished it handsomely.
"Pray deign to wear it," he cried, and set it on
    the boy's head.
Then, stepping back to look,
"Oh admirable skill! Not even the captain of a
    mighty host
Need scorn to wear this hat!"

[1] I.e. Minamoto and Taira.   [2] 1156–1159 A.D.

HATMAKER.

There is not an *eboshi* in the land that fits so well.

USHIWAKA.

You are right ; please take this sword in payment for it.

HATMAKER.

No, no ! I could not take it in return for such a trifle.

USHIWAKA.

I beg you to accept it.

HATMAKER.

Well, I cannot any longer refuse. How glad my wife will be ! (*Calling.*) Are you there ?

WIFE.

What is it ? (*They go aside.*)

HATMAKER.

This young lad asked me to make him an *eboshi*, and when it was made he gave me this sword as a present. Is it not a noble payment ? Here, look at it. (*The wife takes the sword and when she has examined it bursts into tears.*) Why, I thought you would treasure it like a gift from Heaven. And here you are shedding tears over it ! What is the matter ?

WIFE.

Oh ! I am ashamed. When I try to speak, tears come first and choke the words. I am going to tell you something I have never told you before. I am the sister of Kamada Masakiyo who fell at the Battle of Utsumi in the country of Noma. At the time when Tokiwa bore Ushiwaka, her third son, the lord her husband sent her this weapon as a charm-sword, and I was the messenger whom he charged to carry it. Oh were he in the world again ; [1] then would our eyes no longer behold such misery. Oh sorrow, sorrow !

[1] Yoshi-iye.

HATMAKER.

You say that you are the sister of Kamada Masakiyo ?

WIFE.

I am.

HATMAKER.

How strange, how strange ! I have lived with you all these years and months, and never knew till now. But are you sure that you recognize this weapon ?

WIFE.

Yes ; this was the sword they called Konnentō.

HATMAKER.

Ah ! I have heard that name. Then this must be the young Lord Ushiwaka from Kuruma Temple. Come with me. We must go after him and give him back the sword at once. Why, he is still there ! (*To* USHIWAKA.) Sir, this woman tells me she knows the sword ; I beg of you to take it back.

USHIWAKA.

Oh ! strange adventure ; to meet so far from home
With humble folk that show me kindness !

HATMAKER and WIFE.

My Lord, forgive us ! We did not know you ; but now we see in you Lord Ushiwaka, the nursling of Kurama Temple.

USHIWAKA.

I am no other. (*To the* WIFE.) And you, perhaps, are some kinswoman of Masakiyo ? [1]

WIFE.

You have guessed wisely, sir ; I am the Kamada's sister.

---

[1] Ushiwaka had not heard this conversation between the hat-maker and his wife, which takes place as an " aside."

USHIWAKA.

Lady Akoya ?

WIFE.

I am.

USHIWAKA.

Truly I have reason to know. . . . And *I*

CHORUS.

Am Ushiwaka fallen on profitless days.
Of whom no longer you may speak
As master, but as one sunk in strange servitude.
Dawn is in the east ; the pale moon fades from the
    sky, as he sets forth from the Mirror Inn.

HATMAKER and WIFE.

Oh ! it breaks my heart to see him ! A boy of noble
name walking barefoot with merchants, and nothing
on his journey but cloth of Shikama to clothe him.
Oh ! piteous sight !

USHIWAKA.

Change rules the world for ever, and Man but for a
little while. What are fine clothes to me, what life
itself while foemen flaunt ?

HATMAKER.

As a journey-present to speed you on the Eastern
road . . .

CHORUS.

So he spoke and pressed the sword into the young
lord's hands. And the boy could not any longer refuse,
but taking it said, "If ever I come into the World[1]
again, I will not forget." And so saying he turned and
went on his way in company with the merchants his
masters. On they went till at last, weary with travel,
they came to the Inn of Akasaka in the country of
Mino.

[1] *I*.e. into power.

KICHIJI (*the merchant*).

We have come so fast that here we are at the Inn of Akasaka.

(*To his* BROTHER.)

Listen, Kichiroku, you had better take lodging for us here.

KICHIROKU.

I obey. (*Goes towards the hashigakari or actors' entrance-passage.*)
May I come in ?

INNKEEPER.

Who are you ? Ah ! it is Master Kichiroku. I am glad to see you back again so soon.

(*To* KICHIJI.)

Be on your guard, gentleman. For a desperate gang has got wind of your coming and has sworn to set upon you to-night.

KICHIJI.

What are we to do ?

KICHIROKU.

I cannot tell.

USHIWAKA (*comes forward*).

What are you speaking of ?

KICHIJI.

We have heard that robbers may be coming to-night. We were wondering what we should do. . . .

USHIWAKA.

Let them come in what force they will ; yet if one stout soldier go to meet them, they will not stand their ground, though they be fifty mounted men.

KICHIJI.

These are trusty words that you have spoken to us. One and all we look to you. . . .

USHIWAKA.

Then arm yourselves and wait. I will go out to meet them.

CHORUS.

And while he spoke, evening passed to darkness. "Now is the time," he cried, "to show the world those arts of war that for many months and years upon the Mountain of Kurama I have rehearsed."

Then he opened the double-doors and waited there for the slow incoming of the white waves.[1]

BRIGANDS.

Loud the noise of assault. The lashing of white waves against the rocks, even such is the din of our battle-cry.

KUMASAKA.

Ho, my man! Who is there?

BRIGAND.

I stand before you.

KUMASAKA.

How fared those skirmishers I sent to make a sudden breach? Blew the wind briskly within?

BRIGAND.

Briskly indeed; for some are slain and many grievously wounded.

KUMASAKA.

How can that be? I thought that none were within but the merchants, Kichiji and his brother. Who else is there?

---

[1] I.e. robbers. A band of brigands who troubled China in 184 A.D. were known as the White Waves, and the phrase was later applied to robbers in general.

BRIGAND.

By the light of a rocket [1] I saw a lad of twelve or thirteen years slashing about him with a short-sword; and he was nimble as a butterfly or bird.

KUMASAKA.

And the brothers Surihari?

BRIGAND.

Stood foster-fathers [1] to the fire-throwers and were the first to enter.

But soon there meets them this child I tell of and with a blow at each whisks off their heads from their necks.

KUMASAKA.

Ei! Ei! Those two, and the horsemen that were near a hundred strong,—all smitten! The fellow has bewitched them!

BRIGAND.

When Takase saw this, thinking perhaps no good would come of this night-attack, he took some seventy horsemen and galloped away with them.

KUMASAKA.

Ha! It is not the first time that lout has played me false.

How fared the torch-diviners? [1]

BRIGAND.

The first torch was slashed in pieces; the second was trampled on till it went out; the third they caught and threw back at us, but it too went out. There are none left.

---

[1] Torches were thrown among the enemy to discover their number and defences.

KUMASAKA.

Then is all lost. For of these torch-diviners they sing that the first torch is the soul of an army, the second torch is the wheel of Fate, and the third torch—Life itself. All three are out, and there is no hope left for this night's brigandage.

BRIGAND.

It is as you say. Though we were gods, we could not redeem our plight. Deign to give the word of retreat.

KUMASAKA.

Why, even brigands must be spared from slaughter. Come, withdraw my men.

BRIGAND.

I obey.

KUMASAKA.

Stay! Shall Kumasaka Chōhan be worsted in to-night's affray? Never! Where could he then hide his shame? Come, robbers, to the attack!

CHORUS.

So with mighty voice he called them to him, and they, raising their war-cry, leapt to the assault.

(Speaking for USHIWAKA.)

"Hoho! What a to-do! Himself has come, undaunted by the fate of those he sent before him. Now, Hachiman,[1] look down upon me, for no other help is here." So he prayed, and stood waiting at the gap.

(Speaking for KUMASAKA.)

"Sixty-three years has Kumasaka lived, and to-day shall make his last night-assault."[2] So he spoke and kicking off his iron-shoes in a twinkling he levelled his

[1] God of War and clan-god of the Minamotos.
[2] He feels that he is too old for the work.

great battle-sword that measured five foot three, and as he leapt forward like a great bird pouncing on his prey, no god or demon had dared encounter him.

(*Speaking for* USHIWAKA.)

" Ha, bandit ! Be not so confident ! These slinking night-assaults displease me "; and leaving him no leisure, the boy dashed in to the attack.

Then, Kumasaka, deeply versed in use of the battle-sword, lunged with his left foot and in succession he executed The Ten-Side Cut, The Eight-Side Sweep, The Body Wheel, The Hanyū Turn, The Wind Roll, The Blade Drop, The Gnashing Lion, The Maple-Leaf Double, The Flower Double.

Now fire dances at the sword-points ;
Now the sword-backs clash.

At last even the great battle-sword has spent its art. Parried by the little belt-sword of Zōshi,[1] it has become no more than a guard-sword.

(*Speaking for* KUMASAKA.)

" This sword-play brings me no advantage ; I will close with him and try my strength ! "

Then he threw down his battle-sword and spreading out his great hands rushed wildly forward. But Ushiwaka dodged him, and as he passed mowed round at his legs.

The robber fell with a crash, and as he struggled to rise
The belt-sword of Ushiwaka smote him clean through the waist.
And Kumasaka that had been one man
Lay cloven in twain.

[1] I.e. Ushiwaka.

BENKEI ON THE BRIDGE
(HASHI-BENKEI)
By HIYOSHI SA-AMI YASUKIYO
(Date unknown, probably first half of the fifteenth century.)

PERSONS

BENKEI.	FOLLOWER.
USHIWAKA.	CHORUS.

BENKEI.

I am one who lives near the Western Pagoda. My name is Musashi-bō Benkei. In fulfillment of a certain vow I have been going lately by night at the hour of the Ox [1] to worship at the Gojō Temple. To-night is the last time ; I ought soon to be starting.

Hie ! Is any one there ?

FOLLOWER.

Here I am.

BENKEI.

I sent for you to tell you that I shall be going to the Gojō Temple to-night.

FOLLOWER.

I tremble and listen. But there is a matter that I must bring to your notice. I hear that yesterday there was a boy of twelve or thirteen guarding the Gojō Bridge. They say he was slashing round with his short sword as nimble as a bird or butterfly. I beg that you will not make your pilgrimage to-night. Do not court this peril.

[1] 1–3 a.m.

BENKEI.

That's a strange thing to ask ! Why, were he demon
or hobgoblin, he could not stand alone against many.
We will surround him and you shall soon see him on
his knees.

FOLLOWER.

They have tried surrounding him, but he always
escapes as though by magic, and none is able to lay
hands on him.

BENKEI.

When he seems within their grasp

FOLLOWER.

From before their eyes

BENEKI.

Suddenly he vanishes.

CHORUS.

This strange hobgoblin, elfish apparition,
Into great peril may bring
The reverend limbs of my master.
In all this City none can withstand the prowess
Of this unparalleled monster.

BENKEI.

If this is as you say, I will not go to-night; and
yet. . . . No. It is not to be thought of that such a
one as Benkei should be affrighted by a tale. To-night
when it is dark I will go to the bridge and humble this
arrogant elf.

CHORUS.

And while he spoke,
Evening already to the western sky had come ;
Soon the night-wind had shattered and dispersed
The shapes of sunset. Cheerless night
Came swiftly, but with step too slow
For him who waits.

*(A Comic interlude played by a bow-master is some-
times used here to fill in the time while* BENKEI
is arming himself.)

USHIWAKA.

I am Ushiwaka. I must do as my mother told me ;
" Go up to the Temple [1] at daybreak," she said. But
it is still night. I will go to Gojō Bridge and wait there
till suddenly
  Moonlight mingles with the rising waves ;
  No twilight closes
  The autumn day, but swiftly
  The winds of night bring darkness.

CHORUS (*speaking for* USHIWAKA).

  Oh ! beauty of the waves ! High beats my heart,
  High as their scattered pearls !
  Waves white as dewy calabash [2] at dawn,
  By Gojō Bridge.
  Silently the night passes,
  No sound but my own feet upon the wooden planks
  Clanking and clanking ; still I wait
  And still in vain.

BENKEI.

  The night grows late. Eastward the bells of the
      Three Pagodas toll.
  By the moonlight that gleams through leaves of these
      thick cedar-trees
  I gird my armour on ;
  I fasten the black thongs of my coat of mail.
  I adjust its armoured skirts.
  By the middle I grasp firmly
  My great halberd that I have loved so long.
  I lay it across my shoulder ; with leisurely step
      stride forward.

[1] The Kurama Temple.
[2] Flowers of the *yūgao* or calabash. There is a reference to Lady
Yūgao (see p. 180), who lived at Gojō.

Genji

Be he demon or hobgoblin, how shall he stand against
    me ?
Such trust have I in my own prowess.   Oh, how I
    long
For a foeman worthy of my hand !

USHIWAKA.

The river-wind blows keen ;
The night is almost spent,
But none has crossed the Bridge.
I am disconsolate and will lie down to rest.

BENKEI.

Then Benkei, all unknowing,
Came towards the Bridge where white waves lapped.
Heavily his feet clanked on the boards of the Bridge.

USHIWAKA.

And even before he saw him Ushiwaka gave a whoop
    of joy.
" Some one has come," he cried, and hitching his
    cloak over his shoulder
Took his stand at the bridge-side.

BENKEI.

Benkei discerned him and would have spoken. . . .
But when he looked, lo ! it was a woman's form !
Then, because he had left the World,[1] with troubled
    mind he hurried on.

USHIWAKA.

Then Ushiwaka said,
" I will make game of him," and as Benkei passed
Kicked at the button of his halberd so that it jerked
    into the air.

BENKEI (cries out in surprise).

Ah ! fool, I will teach you a lesson !

---

[1] Because he was a priest.

CHORUS.

Then Benkei while he retrieved his halberd
Cried out in anger,
" You shall soon feel the strength of my arm," and
fell fiercely upon him.
But the boy, not a jot alarmed,
Stood his ground and with one hand pulled aside
his cloak,
While with the other he quietly drew his sword from
the scabbard
And parried the thrust of the halberd that threatened
him.
Again and again he parried the halberd's point.
And so they fought, now closing, now breaking.
What shall Benkei do ?   For when he thinks that he
has conquered,
With his little sword the boy thrusts the blow
aside.
Again and again Benkei strikes.
Again and again his blows are parried,
Till at last even he, mighty Benkei,
Can do battle no longer.
Disheartened he steps back the space of a few bridge-
beams.
" Monstrous," he cries, " that this stripling . . .
No, it cannot be.
He shall not outwit my skill."
And holding out his halberd at full length before
him
He rushed forward and dealt a mighty blow.
But Ushiwaka turned and dived swiftly to the left.
Benkei recovered his halberd and slashed at the
boy's skirts ;
But *he*, unfaltering, instantly leapt from the ground.
And when he thrust at the boy's body,
Then Ushiwaka squirmed with head upon the
ground.
Thus a thousand, thousand bouts they fought,
Till the halberd fell from Benkei's weary hands.

He would have wrestled, but the boy's sword
    flashed before him,
And he could get no hold.
Then at his wits' end, " Oh, marvellous youth ! "
Benkei cried, and stood dumbfounded.

CHORUS.

Who are you that, so young and frail, possess such
daring ? Tell us your name and state.

USHIWAKA.

Why should I conceal it from you ? I am Minamoto Ushiwaka.

CHORUS.

Yoshitomo's son ?

USHIWAKA.

I am. And your name . . . ?

CHORUS (*speaking for* BENKEI).

" I am called Musashi Benkei of the Western Pagoda.
And now that we have told our names,
I surrender myself and beg for mercy ;
For you are yet a child, and I a priest.
Such are your rank and lineage, such your prowess
That I will gladly serve you.
Too hastily you took me for an enemy ; but now
    begins
A three lives' bond ; henceforward [1]
As slave I serve you."
So, while the one made vows of homage, the other
    girded up his cloak.
Then Benkei laid his halberd across his shoulder
And together they went on their way
To the Palace of Kujō.[2]

[1] I.e. three incarnations.   [2] Ushiwaka's home.

CHAPTER III

KAGEKIYO
HACHI NO KI
SOTOBA KOMACHI

KAGEKIYO

By Seami

PERSONS

A Girl (Kagekiyo's daughter).   Her Attendant.
Kagekiyo the Passionate.   A Villager.
Chorus.

Girl and Attendant.

Late dewdrops are our lives that only wait
Till the wind blows, the wind of morning blows.

Girl.

I am Hitomaru. I live in the valley of Kamegaye.
My father Kagekiyo the Passionate fought for the House
of Hei [1] and for this was hated by the Genji. [2] I am
told they have banished him to Miyazaki in the country
of Hyūga, and there in changed estate he passes the
months and years. I must not be downcast at the toil
of the journey; [3] for hardship is the lot of all that
travel on unfamiliar roads, and I must bear it for my
father's sake.

Girl and Attendant.

Oh double-wet our sleeves
With the tears of troubled dreaming and the dews
That wet our grassy bed.
We leave Sagami; who shall point the way
To Tōtōmi, far off not only in name? [4]

[1] The Tairas.
[2] The Minamotos, who came into power at the end of the twelfth
century.   [3] The journey to look for her father.
[4] Tōtōmi is written with characters meaning "distant estuary." The
whole passage is full of double-meanings which cannot be rendered.

123

Over the sea we row :
And now the eight-fold Spider Bridge we cross
To Mikawa. How long, O City of the Clouds,[1]
Shall we, inured to travel, see you in our dreams ?

ATTENDANT.
We have journeyed so fast that I think we must
already have come to Miyazaki in the country of Hyūga.
It is here you should ask for your father.

(*The voice of* KAGEKIYO *is heard from within his hut.*)

shike KAGEKIYO.
Behind this gate,
This pine-wood barricade shut in alone
I waste the hours and days ;
By me not numbered, since my eyes no longer
See the clear light of heaven, but in darkness,
Unending darkness, profitlessly sleep
In this low room.
For garment given but one coat to cover
From winter winds or summer's fire
This ruin, this anatomy !

CHORUS (*speaking for* KAGEKIYO).
Oh better had I left the world, to wear
The black-stained sleeve.
Who will now pity me, whose withered frame
Even to myself is hateful ?
Or who shall make a care to search for me
And carry consolation to my woes ?

GIRL.
How strange ! That hut is so old, I cannot think
that anyone can live there. Yet I heard a voice speaking within. Perhaps some beggar lodges there ; I will
not go nearer. (*She steps back.*)

KAGEKIYO.
Though my eyes see not autumn
Yet has the wind brought tiding

---

[1] The Capital,

GIRL.

Of one who wanders
By ways unknown bewildered,
Finding rest nowhere—

KAGEKIYO.

For in the Three Worlds of Being
Nowhere is rest,[1] but only
In the Void Eternal.
None is, and none can answer
Where to thy asking.

sunyata

ATTENDANT (*going up to* KAGEKIYO'S *hut*).

I have come to your cottage to ask you something.

KAGEKIYO.

What is it you want?

ATTENDANT.

Can you tell me where the exile lives?

KAGEKIYO.

The exile? What exile do you mean? Tell me his name.

ATTENDANT.

We are looking for Kagekiyo the Passionate who fought for the Taira.

KAGEKIYO.

I have heard of him indeed. But I am blind, and have not seen him. I have heard such sad tales of his plight that I needs must pity him. Go further; ask elsewhere.

ATTENDANT (*to* GIRL, *who has been waiting*).

It does not seem that we shall find him here. Let us go further and ask again. (*They pass on.*)

KAGEKIYO.

Who can it be that is asking for me? What if it should be the child of this blind man? For long ago

---

[1] Quotation from the Parable Chapter of the *Hokkekyō*.

when I was at Atsuta in Owari I courted a woman and had a child by her. But since the child was a girl, I thought I would get no good of her and left her with the headman of the valley of Kamegaye. But she was not content to stay with her foster-parents and has come all this way to meet her true father.

CHORUS.

> To hear a voice,
> To hear and not to see!
> Oh pity of blind eyes!
> I have let her pass by;
> I have not told my name;
> But it was love that bound me,
> Love's rope that held me.

ATTENDANT (*calling into the side-bridge*).

Hie! Is there any villager about?

VILLAGER (*raising the curtain that divides the side-bridge from the stage*).

What do you want with me?

ATTENDANT.

Do you know where the exile lives?

VILLAGER.

The exile? What exile is it you are asking for?

ATTENDANT.

One called Kagekiyo the Passionate who fought for the Taira.

VILLAGER.

Did you not see some one in a thatched hut under the hillside as you came along?

ATTENDANT.

Why, we saw a blind beggar in a thatched hut.

VILLAGER.

That blind beggar is your man. *He* is Kagekiyo.

(*The* GIRL *starts and trembles.*)

But why does your lady tremble when I tell you
that he is Kagekiyo ?   What is amiss with her ?

ATTENDANT.

No wonder that you ask.   I will tell you at once ;
this lady is Kagekiyo's daughter.   She has borne the
toil of this journey because she longed to meet her
father face to face.   Please take her to him.

VILLAGER.

She is Kagekiyo's daughter ?   How strange, how
strange !   But, lady, calm yourself and listen.

Kagekiyo went blind in both his eyes, and finding
himself helpless, shaved his head and called himself
the beggar of Hyūga.   He begs a little from travellers ;
and we villagers are sorry for him and see to it that he
does not starve.   Perhaps he would not tell you his
name because he was ashamed of what he has become.
But if you will come with me I will shout " Kagekiyo "
at him.   He will surely answer to his own name.   Then
you shall go to him and talk of what you will, old times
or now.   Please come this way.

(*They go towards the hut.*)

Hie, Kagekiyo, Kagekiyo !   Are you there, Kagekiyo
the Passionate ?

KAGEKIYO (*stopping his ears with his hands, irritably*).

Noise, noise !

Silence !   I was vexed already.   For a while ago there
came travellers from my home !   Do you think I let
them stay ?   No, no.   I could not show them my
loathsomeness. . . . It was hard to let them go,—
not tell them my name !

A thousand rivers of tears soften my sleeve !
A thousand, thousand things I do in dream
And wake to idleness !   Oh I am resolved
To be in the world as one who is not in the world.

Let them shout " Kagekiyo, Kagekiyo " :
Need beggars answer ?
Moreover, in this land I have a name.

CHORUS.

" In Hyūga sunward-facing
A fit name found I.
Oh call me not by the name
Of old days that have dropped
Like the bow from a stricken hand !
For I whom passion
Had left for ever
At the sound of that wrathful name
Am angry, angry."

> (*While the* CHORUS *speaks his thought* KAGEKIYO
> *mimes their words, waving his stick and finally
> beating it against his thigh in a crescendo of
> rage.*)

KAGEKIYO (*suddenly lowering his voice, gently*).
But while I dwell here

CHORUS.

" But while I dwell here
To those that tend me
Should I grow hateful
Then were I truly
A blind man staffless.
Oh forgive
Profitless anger, tongue untended,
A cripple's spleen."

KAGEKIYO.

For though my eyes be darkened

CHORUS.

" Though my eyes be darkened
Yet, no word spoken,
Men's thoughts I see.
Listen now to the wind
In the woods upon the hill :

Snow is coming, snow !
Oh bitterness to wake
From dreams of flowers unseen !
And on the shore,
Listen, the waves are lapping
Over rough stones to the cliff.
The evening tide is in.

(KAGEKIYO *fumbles for his staff and rises, coming just outside the hut. The mention of " waves," " shore," " tide," has reminded him of the great shore-battle at Yashima in which the Tairas triumphed.*)

"I was one of them, of those Tairas. If you will listen, I will tell you the tale . . ."

KAGEKIYO (*to the* VILLAGER).

There was a weight on my mind when I spoke to you so harshly.   Pray forgive me.

VILLAGER.

No, no ! you are always so ! I do not heed you. But tell me, did not some one come before, asking for Kagekiyo ?

KAGEKIYO.

No,—you are the only one who has asked.

VILLAGER.

It is not true. Some one came here saying that she was Kagekiyo's daughter. Why did you not tell her ? I was sorry for her and have brought her back with me.
(*To the* GIRL.) Come now, speak with your father.

GIRL (*going to* KAGEKIYO'S *side and touching his sleeve*).

It is I who have come to you.
I have come all the long way,
Through rain, wind, frost and dew.
And now—you have not understood ; it was all for
      nothing.
Am I not worth your love ? Oh cruel, cruel !
(*She weeps.*)

KAGEKIYO.

All that till now I thought to have concealed
Is known ; where can I hide,
I that have no more refuge than the dew
That finds no leaf to lie on ?
Should you, oh flower delicately tended,
Call me your father, then would the World know you
A beggar's daughter. Oh think not ill of me
That I did let you pass !

(*He gropes falteringly with his right hand and touches
her sleeve.*)

CHORUS.

Oh sad, sad !
He that of old gave welcome
To casual strangers and would raise an angry voice
If any passed his door,
Now from his own child gladly
Would hide his wretchedness.
He that once
Among all that in the warships of Taira
Shoulder to shoulder, knee locked with knee,
Dwelt crowded—
Even Kagekiyo keen
As the clear moonlight—
Was ever called on to captain
The Royal Pinnace.
And though among his men
Many were brave and many of wise counsel,
Yet was he even as the helm of the boat.
And of the many who served him
None cavilled, disputed.
But now
He that of all was envied
Is like Kirin [1] grown old,
By every jade outrun.

[1] A Chinese Pegasus. The proverb says, " Even Kirin, when he
was old, was outstripped by hacks." Seami quotes this proverb,
Works, p. 9.

VILLAGER (*seeing the* GIRL *standing sadly apart*).

Poor child, come back again.

(*She comes back to her father's side.*)

Listen, Kagekiyo, there is something your daughter wants of you.

KAGEKIYO.

What is it she wants ?

VILLAGER.

She tells me that she longs to hear the story of your high deeds at Yashima. Could you not tell us the tale ?

KAGEKIYO.

That is a strange thing for a girl to ask. Yet since kind love brought her this long, long way to visit me, I cannot but tell her the tale. Promise me that when it is finished you will send her back again to her home.

VILLAGER.

I will. So soon as your tale is finished, I will send her home.

KAGEKIYO.

It was in the third year of Juyei,[1]
At the close of the third month.
We of Heike were in our ships,
The men of Genji on shore.
Two armies spread along the coast
Eager to bid in battle
For final mastery.
Then said Noritsune, Lord of Noto,
" Last year at Muro Hill in the land of Harima,
At Water Island, even at Jackdaw Pass,
We were beaten again and again ; outwitted
By Yoshitsune's strategy.
Oh that some plan might be found, some counsel
given

---

[1] " Le vieux guerrier aveugle, assis devant sa cabane d'exilé, mime son dernier combat de gestes incertains et tremblants " (Péri).

For the slaying of Kurō." [1] So spoke he.
Then thought Kagekiyo in his heart,
" Though he be called ' Judge,'
Yet is he no god or demon, this Yoshitsune.
An easy task ! Oh easy for one that loves not
His own life chiefly !
So he took leave of Noritsune
And landed upon the beach.
The soldiers of Genji
" Death to him, death to him ! " cried
As they swept towards him.

CHORUS.

And when he saw them,
" What great to-do ! " he cried, then waving
His sword in the evening sunlight
He fell upon them swiftly.
They fled before his sword-point,
They could not withstand him, those soldiers ;
This way, that way, they scuttled wildly, and he
    cried,
" They shall not escape me ! "

KAGEKIYO (*breaking in excitedly*).

Cowards, cowards all of you !

CHORUS.

Cowards, all of you !
Sight shameful alike for Gen and Hei.
Then, thinking that to stop one man
Could not but be easy,
Sword under arm,
" I am Kagekiyo," he cried,
" Kagekiyo the Passionate, a captain of the soldiers
    of Hei."
And swiftly pursued, with naked hand to grasp
The helm that Mionoya wore.
He clutched at the neck-piece,
Twice and again he clutched, but it slipped from him,
    slid through his fingers.

[1] Yoshitsune.

Then crying " He shall not escape me, this foe I have
    chosen,"
Swooped like a bird, seized upon the helmet,
" Eya, eya," he cried, tugging,
Till " Crack "—the neck-piece tore from the helm
    and was left in his hand,
While the master of it, suddenly free, ran till he was
    come
A good way off, then turning,
" O mighty Kagekiyo, how terrible the strength
    of your arm ! "
And the other called back to him, " Nay, say rather
    ' How strong the shaft
Of Mionoya's neck ! ' " So laughed they across the
    battle,
And went off each his way.

    (KAGEKIYO, *who has been miming the battle, breaks
        off abruptly and turns to the* VILLAGER. *The*
        CHORUS *speaks for him.*)

CHORUS.
  " I am old : I have forgotten—things unforgettable !
My thoughts are tangled : I am ashamed.
But little longer shall this world,
This sorrowful world torment me.
The end is near : go to your home ;
Pray for my soul departed, child, candle to my
    darkness,
Bridge to salvation !

    (*He rises to his feet groping with his stick, comes
        to the* GIRL, *and gently pushes her before him
        towards the wing.*)

" I stay," he said ; and she " I go."
The sound of this word
Was all he kept of her,
Nor passed between them
Remembrance other.

HACHI NO KI

By Seami

PERSONS

The Priest (Lord Tokiyori disguised).
Tsuneyo Genzayemon (a former retainer of Tokiyori).
Genzayemon's Wife.
Tokiyori's Minister, and followers.
Chorus.

Priest.

No whence nor whither know I, only onward,
 Onward my way.

I am a holy man of no fixed abode. I have been travelling through the land of Shinano ; but the snow lies thick. I had best go up to Kamakura now and wait there. When Spring comes I will set out upon my pilgrimage.

(*He walks round the stage singing his song of travel.*)

Land of Shinano, Peak of Asama,
Thy red smoke rising far and near ! Yet cold.
Blows the great wind whose breath
From Greatwell Hill is fetched.
On to the Village of Friends—but friendless I,
Whose self is cast aside, go up the path
Of Parting Hill, that from the temporal world
Yet further parts me. Down the river, down
Runs my swift raft plank-nosed to Plank-nose Inn,
And to the Ford of Sano I am come.

I have travelled so fast that I am come to the Ford of Sano in the country of Kōzuke. Ara ! It is snowing again. I must seek shelter here. (*Goes to the wing and knocks.*) Is there anyone in this house ?

TSUNEYO'S WIFE (*raising the curtain that divides the hashigakari from the stage*).

Who is there ?

PRIEST.

I am a pilgrim; pray lodge me here to-night.

WIFE.

That is a small thing to ask. But since the master is away, you cannot lodge in this house.

PRIEST.

Then I will wait here till he comes back.

WIFE.

That must be as you please. I will go to the corner and watch for him. When he comes I will tell him you are here.

(*Enter* TSUNEYO *from the wing, making the gesture of one who shakes snow from his clothes.*)

TSUNEYO.

Ah ! How the snow falls ! Long ago when I was in the World [1] I loved to see it :
" Hither and thither the snow blew like feathers plucked from a goose ;
   Long, long I watched it fall, till it dressed me in a white coat."
So I sang ; and the snow that falls now is the same that I saw then. But I indeed am frost-white [2] that watch it !
Oh how shall this thin dress of Kefu-cloth [3]
Chase from my bones the winter of to-day,
Oh pitiless day of snow !

> (*He sees his* WIFE *standing waiting.*)

What is this ! How comes it that you are waiting here in this great storm of snow ?

---

[1] Po Chü-i's *Works*, iii. 13.

[2] Alluding partly to the fact that he is snow-covered, partly to his grey hairs.

[3] *Kefu,* " to-day."

WIFE.

A pilgrim came this way and begged for a night's lodging. And when I told him you were not in the house, he asked if he might wait till you returned. That is why I am here.

TSUNEYO.

Where is this pilgrim now ?

WIFE.

There he stands !

PRIEST.

I am he. Though the day is not far spent, how can I find my way in this great storm of snow ? Pray give me shelter for the night.

TSUNEYO.

That is a small thing to ask ; but I have no lodging fit for you ; I cannot receive you.

PRIEST.

No, no. I do not care how poor the lodging may be. Pray let me stay here for one night.

TSUNEYO.

I would gladly ask you to stay, but there is scarce space for us two, that are husband and wife. How can we give you lodging ? At the village of Yamamoto yonder, ten furlongs further, you will find a good inn. You had best be on your way before the daylight goes.

PRIEST.

So you are resolved to turn me away ?

TSUNEYO.

I am sorry for it, but I cannot give you lodging.

PRIEST (*turning away*).

Much good I got by waiting for such a fellow *!* I will go my way. (*He goes.*)

WIFE.

Alas, it is because in a former life we neglected the ordinances [1] that we are now come to ruin. And surely it will bring us ill-fortune in our next life, if we give no welcome to such a one as this! If it is by any means possible for him to shelter here, please let him stay.

TSUNEYO.

If you are of that mind, why did you not speak before? (*Looking after the* PRIEST.) No, he cannot have gone far in this great snowstorm. I will go after him and stop him. Hie, traveller, hie! We will give you lodging. Hie! The snow is falling so thick that he cannot hear me. What a sad plight he is in. Old-fallen snow covers the way he came and snow new-fallen hides the path where he should go. Look, look! He is standing still. He is shaking the snow from his clothes; shaking, shaking. It is like that old song:

> "At Sano Ferry
> No shelter found we
> To rest our horses,
> Shake our jackets,
> In the snowy twilight."

That song was made at Sano Ferry,
At the headland of Miwa on the Yamato Way.

CHORUS.

But now at Sano on the Eastern Way
Would you wander weary in the snow of twilight?
Though mean the lodging,
Rest with us, oh rest till day!

(*The* PRIEST *goes with them into the hut.*)

TSUNEYO (*to his* WIFE).

Listen. We have given him lodging, but have not laid the least thing before him. Is there nothing we can give?

---

[1] Buddhist ordinances, such as hospitality to priests.

WIFE.

It happens that we have a little boiled millet;[1] we can give him that if he will take it.

TSUNEYO.

I will tell him. (*To the* PRIEST). I have given you lodging, but I have not yet laid anything before you. It happens that we have a little boiled millet. It is coarse food, but pray eat it if you can.

PRIEST.

Why, that's a famous dish! Please give it me.

TSUNEYO (*to* WIFE).

He says he will take some; make haste and give it to him.

WIFE.

I will do so.

TSUNEYO.

Long ago when I was in the World I knew nothing of this stuff called millet but what I read of it in poems and songs. But now it is the prop of my life.
    Truly Rosei's dream of fifty years' glory
    That he dreamed at Kántán on lent pillow propped
    Was dreamed while millet cooked, as yonder dish
        now.
    Oh if I might but sleep as he slept, and see in my
        dream
    Times that have passed away, then should I have
        comfort;
    But now through battered walls

CHORUS.

    Cold wind from the woods
    Blows sleep away and the dreams of recollection.

    (*While the* CHORUS *sings these words an* ATTENDANT
        brings on to the stage the three dwarf trees.)

---

[1] Food of the poorest peasants.

TSUNEYO.

How cold it is ! And as the night passes, each hour the frost grows keener. If I had but fuel to light a fire with, that you might sit by it and warm yourself ! Ah ! I have thought of something. I have some dwarf trees. I will cut them down and make a fire of them.

PRIEST.

Have you indeed dwarf trees ?

TSUNEYO.

Yes, when I was in the World I had a fine show of them ; but when my trouble came I had no more heart for tree-fancying, and gave them away. But three of them, I kept,—plum, cherry and pine. Look, there they are, covered with snow. They are precious to me ; yet for this night's entertainment I will gladly set light to them.

PRIEST.

No, no, that must not be. I thank you for your kindness, but it is likely that one day you will go back to the World again and need them for your pleasure. Indeed it is not to be thought of.

TSUNEYO.

My life is like a tree the earth has covered ;
I shoot no blossoms upward to the world.

WIFE.

And should we burn for you
These shrubs, these profitless toys,

TSUNEYO.

Think them the faggots of our Master's servitude.[1]

WIFE.

For snow falls now upon them, as it fell

---

[1] After Shākyamuni left the palace, he served the Rishi of the mountains.

TSUNEYO.

When he to hermits of the cold
Himalayan Hills was carrier of wood.

WIFE.

So let it be.

CHORUS.

" Shall I from one who has cast life aside,
    Dear life itself, withhold these trivial trees ? "

(TSUNEYO *goes and stands by the dwarf trees.*)

Then he brushed the snow from off them, and when
    he looked,
" I cannot, cannot," he cried, " O beautiful trees,
Must I begin ?
You, plum-tree, among bare boughs blossoming
Hard by the window, still on northward face
Snow-sealed, yet first to scent
Cold air with flowers, earliest of Spring ;
' You first shall fall.'
You by whose boughs on mountain hedge entwined
Dull country folk have paused and caught their
    breath,[1]
Hewn down for firewood.   Little had I thought
My hand so pitiless ! "

(*He cuts down the plum-tree.*)

" You, cherry (for each Spring your blossom comes
Behind the rest), I thought a lonely tree
And reared you tenderly, but now
I, I am lonely left, and you, cut down,
Shall flower but with flame."

TSUNEYO.

You now, O pine, whose branches I had thought
One day when you were old to lop and trim,
Standing you in the field, a football-post,[2]

[1] Using words from a poem by Michizane (845-903 A.D.).
[2] For Japanese football, see p. 291.   A different interpretation has
lately been suggested by Mr. Suzuki.   *more related to Buddhist faith.*

Such use shall never know.
Tree, whom the winds have ever wreathed
With quaking mists, now shimmering in the flame
Shall burn and burn.
Now like a beacon, sentinels at night
Kindle by palace gate to guard a king,
Your fire burns brightly.
Come, warm yourself.

PRIEST.

Now we have a good fire and can forget the cold.

TSUNEYO.

It is because you lodged with us that we too have
a fire to sit by.

PRIEST.

There is something I must ask you: I would gladly
know to what clan my host belongs.

TSUNEYO.

I am not of such birth; I have no clan-name.

PRIEST.

Say what you will, I cannot think you a commoner.
The times may change; what harm will you get by
telling me your clan?

TSUNEYO.

Indeed I have no reason to conceal it. Know then
that Tsuneyo Genzayemon, Lord of Sano, is sunk to
this!

PRIEST.

How came it, sir, that you fell to such misery?

TSUNEYO.

Thus it was: kinsmen usurped my lands, and so I
became what I am.

PRIEST.

Why do you not go up to the Capital and lay your
case before the Shikken's court?

TSUNEYO.

By further mischance it happens that Lord Saimyōji[1] himself is absent upon pilgrimage. And yet not all is lost ; for on the wall a tall spear still hangs, and armour with it ; while in the stall a steed is tied. And if at any time there came from the City news of peril to our master—

> Then, broken though it be I would gird this armour on,
> And rusty though it be I would hold this tall spear,
> And lean-ribbed though he be I would mount my horse and ride
> Neck by neck with the swiftest,
> To write my name on the roll.
> And when the fight began
> Though the foe were many, yet would I be the first
> To cleave their ranks, to choose an adversary
> To fight with him and die.

> (*He covers his face with his hands ; his voice sinks again.*)

> But now, another fate, worn out with hunger
> To die useless. Oh despair, despair !

PRIEST.

Take courage ; you shall not end so. If I live, I will come to you again. Now I go.

TSUNEYO and WIFE.

We cannot let you go. At first we were ashamed that you should see the misery of our dwelling ; but now we ask you to stay with us awhile.

PRIEST.

Were I to follow my desire, think you I would soon go forth into the snow ?

TSUNEYO and WIFE.

After a day of snow even the clear sky is cold, and to-night—

---

[1] i.e. Tokiyori.

PRIEST.

Where shall I lodge ?

WIFE.

Stay with us this one day.

PRIEST.

Though my longing bides with you—

TSUNEYO and WIFE.

You leave us ?

PRIEST.

Farewell, Tsuneyo !

BOTH.

Come back to us again.

CHORUS (*speaking for* PRIEST).

"And should you one day come up to the City, seek for me there. A humble priest can give you no public furtherance, yet can he find ways to bring you into the presence of Authority. Do not give up your suit." He said no more. He went his way,—he sad to leave them and they to lose him from their sight.

(*Interval of Six Months.*)

TSUNEYO (*standing outside his hut and seeming to watch travellers on the road*).

Hie, you travellers ! Is it true that the levies are marching to Kamakura ? They are marching in great force, you say ? So it is true. Barons and knights from the Eight Counties of the East all riding to Kamakura ! A fine sight it will be. Tasselled breastplates of beaten silver ; swords and daggers fretted with gold. On horses fat with fodder they ride ; even the grooms of the relay-horses are magnificently apparelled. And along with them (*miming the action of leading a horse*) goes Tsuneyo, with horse, armour and sword that

scarce seem worthy of such names. They may laugh,
yet I am not, I think, a worse man than they ; and
had I but a steed to match my heart, then valiantly—
(*making the gesture of cracking a whip*) you laggard !

CHORUS.

The horse is old, palsied as a willow-bough ; it cannot hasten. It is lean and twisted. Not whip or
spur can move it. It sticks like a coach in a bog. He
follows far behind the rest.

PRIEST (*again ruler* [1] *of Japan, seated on a throne*).
Are you there ?

ATTENDANT.

I stand before you.

PRIEST.

Have the levies of all the lands arrived ?

ATTENDANT.

They are all come.

PRIEST.

Among them should be a knight in broken armour,
carrying a rusty sword, and leading his own lean horse.
Find him, and bring him to me.

ATTENDANT.

I tremble and obey. (*Going to* TSUNEYO.) I must
speak with you.

TSUNEYO.

What is it ?

ATTENDANT.

You are to appear immediately before my lord.

---

[1] Hōjō no Tokiyori ruled at Kamakura from 1246 till 1256. He
then became a priest and travelled through the country incognito
in order to acquaint himself with the needs of his subjects.

TSUNEYO.

Is it I whom you are bidding appear before his lordship ?

ATTENDANT.

Yes, you indeed.

TSUNEYO.

How can it be I ?   You have mistaken me for some other.

ATTENDANT.

Oh no, it is you. I was told to fetch the most ill-conditioned of all the soldiers ; and I am sure you are he. Come at once.

TSUNEYO.

The most ill-conditioned of all the soldiers ?

ATTENDANT.

Yes, truly.

TSUNEYO.

Then I am surely he.
Tell your lord that I obey.

ATTENDANT.

I will do so.

TSUNEYO.

I understand ; too well I understand. Some enemy of mine has called me traitor, and it is to execution that I am summoned before the Throne. Well, there is no help for it. Bring me into the Presence.

CHORUS.

He was led to where on a great daïs
All the warriors of this levy were assembled
Like a bright bevy of stars.

Row on row they were ranged,
Samurai and soldiers ;
Swift scornful glances, fingers pointed
And the noise of laughter met his entering.

TSUNEYO.

Stuck through his tattered, his old side-sewn sash,
His rusty sword sags and trails,—yet he undaunted,
" My Lord, I have come."

(*He bows before the Throne.*)

PRIEST.

Ha ! He has come, Tsuneyo of Sano !
Have you forgotten the priest whom once you shel-
tered from the snowstorm ? You have been true to
the words that you spoke that night at Sano :
　" If at any time there came news from the City of
　　　peril to our master
　Then broken though it be, I would gird this armour
　　　on,
　And rusty though it be, I would hold this tall spear,
　And bony though he be, I would mount my horse
　　　and ride
　Neck by neck with the swiftest."
These were not vain words ; you have come valiantly.
But know that this levy of men was made to this purpose : to test the issue of your words whether they
were spoken false or true ; and to hear the suits of
all those that have obeyed my summons, that if any
among them have suffered injury, his wrongs may
be righted.

　And first in the case of Tsuneyo I make judgment.
To him shall be returned his lawful estate, thirty
parishes in the land of Sano.

　But above all else one thing shall never be forgotten,
that in the great snowstorm he cut down his trees,
his treasure, and burnt them for firewood. And now
in gratitude for the three trees of that time,—plum,

cherry and pine,—we grant to him three fiefs, Plum-
field in Kaga, Cherrywell in Etchū and Pine-branch
in Kōzuke.

He shall hold them as a perpetual inheritance for
himself and for his heirs ; in testimony whereof we
give this title-deed, by our own hand signed and sealed,
together with the safe possession of his former lands.

TSUNEYO.

Then Tsuneyo took the deeds.

CHORUS.

He took the deeds, thrice bowing his head.

(*Speaking for* TSUNEYO.)

" Look, all you barons ! (TSUNEYO *holds up the docu-
ments.*)
Look upon this sight
And scorn to envy turn ! "
Then the levies of all the lands
Took leave of their Lord
And went their homeward way.

TSUNEYO.

And among them Tsuneyo

CHORUS.

Among them Tsuneyo,
Joy breaking on his brow,
Rides now on splendid steed
To the Boat-bridge of Sano, to his lands once torn
Pitiless from him as the torrent tears
That Bridge of Boats at Sano now his own.

*consider the hold of the
actor over the feelings of
his audience   see pp. 41ff. !!*

theme of restoration

THE legend of Komachi is that she had many lovers when she was young, but was cruel and mocked at their pain. Among them was one, Shii no Shōshō, who came a long way to court her. She told him that she would not listen to him till he had come on a hundred nights from his house to hers and cut a hundred notches on the shaft-bench of his chariot. And so he came a hundred nights all but one, through rain, hail, snow, and wind. But on the last night he died.

Once, when she was growing old, the poet Yasuhide asked her to go with him to Mikawa. She answered with the poem :

> " I that am lonely,
> Like a reed root-cut,
> Should a stream entice me,
> Would go, I think."

When she grew quite old, both her friends and her wits forsook her. She wandered about in destitution, a tattered, crazy beggar-woman.

As is shown in this play, her madness was a " possession " by the spirit of the lover whom she had tormented. She was released from this " possession " by the virtue of a sacred Stūpa[1] or log carved into five parts, symbolic of the Five Elements, on which she sat down to rest.

In the disputation between Komachi and the priests, she upholds the doctrines of the Zen Sect, which uses neither scriptures nor idols ; the priests defend the

---

[1] Sanskrit ; Jap. *sotoba*.

doctrines of the Shingon Sect, which promises salvation by the use of incantations and the worship of holy images.[1]

There is no doubt about the authorship of this play. Seami (*Works*, p. 246) gives it as the work of his father, Kwanami Kiyotsugu. Kwanami wrote another play, *Shii no Shōshō*,[2] in which Shōshō is the principal character and Komachi the *tsure* or subordinate.

Seami also used the Komachi legend. In his *Sekidera Komachi* he tells how when she was very old the priests of *Sekidera* invited her to dance at the festival of Tanabata. She dances, and in rehearsing the splendours of her youth for a moment becomes young again.

[1] See p. 59.
[2] Now generally called *Kayoi Komachi*.

Umewaka Minoru acted Ono in this play on March 8, 1899. It is quite usual for an old actor, wearing a mask, to take the part of a young woman. Pound, 225.

SOTOBA KOMACHI

By Kwanami

PERSONS

A Priest of the Kōyasan.   Second Priest.
Ono no Komachi.   Chorus.

Priest.

> We who on shallow hills [1] have built our home
> In the heart's deep recess seek solitude.
>> *(Turning to the audience.)*

I am a priest of the Kōyasan. I am minded to go up
to the Capital to visit the shrines and sanctuaries there.

> The Buddha of the Past is gone,
> And he that shall be Buddha has not yet come into
>> the world.

Second Priest.

> In a dream-lull our lives are passed ; all, all
> That round us lies
> Is visionary, void.
> Yet got we by rare fortune at our birth
> Man's shape, that is hard to get ;
> And dearer gift was given us, harder to win,
> The doctrine of Buddha, seed of our Salvation.
> And me this only thought possessed,
> How I might bring that seed to blossom, till at last
> I drew this sombre cassock across my back.
> And knowing now the lives before my birth,
> No love I owe
> To those that to this life engendered me,
> Nor seek a care (have I not disavowed
> Such hollow bonds ?) from child by me begot.

---

[1] The Kōyasan is not so remote as most mountain temples.

A thousand leagues
Is little road
To the pilgrim's feet.
The fields his bed,
The hills his home
Till the travel's close.

PRIEST.
We have come so fast that we have reached the
pine-woods of Abeno, in the country of Tsu. Let us
rest in this place.

(*They sit down by the Waki's pillar.*)

KOMACHI.
Like a root-cut reed,[1]
Should the tide entice,
I would come, I think ; but now
No wave asks ; no stream stirs.
Long ago I was full of pride ;
Crowned with nodding tresses, halcyon locks,
I walked like a young willow delicately wafted
By the winds of Spring.
I spoke with the voice of a nightingale that has
    sipped the dew.
I was lovelier than the petals of the wild-rose open-
    stretched
In the hour before its fall.
But now I am grown loathsome even to sluts,
Poor girls of the people, and they and all men
Turn scornful from me.
Unhappy months and days pile up their score ;
I am old ; old by a hundred years.
In the City I fear men's eyes,
And at dusk, lest they should cry " Is it she ? "
Westward with the moon I creep
From the cloud-high City of the Hundred Towers.
No guard will question, none challenge
Pilgrim so wretched : yet must I be walking
Hid ever in shadow of the trees.

[1] See p. 148.

Past the Lovers' Tomb,
And the Hill of Autumn
To the River of Katsura, the boats, the moonlight.

(*She shrinks back and covers her face, frightened of
being known.*)

Who are those rowing in the boats ? [1]
Oh, I am weary. I will sit on this tree-stump
and rest awhile.

PRIEST.

Come ! The sun is sinking ; we must hasten on
our way. Look, look at that beggar there ! It is a
holy Stūpa that she is sitting on ! I must tell her to
come off it.

Now then, what is that you are sitting on ? Is it
not a holy Stūpa, the worshipful Body of Buddha ?
Come off it and rest in some other place.

KOMACHI.

Buddha's worshipful body, you say ? But I could
see no writing on it, nor any figure carved. I thought
it was only a tree-stump.

PRIEST.

Even the little black tree on the hillside
When it has put its blossoms on
Cannot be hid ;
And think you that this tree
Cut fivefold in the fashion of Buddha's holy form
Shall not make manifest its power ?

KOMACHI.

I too am a poor withered bough.
But there are flowers at my heart, [2]
Good enough, maybe, for an offering.
But why is this called Buddha's body ?

[1] Seami, writing c. 1430, says : " *Komachi* was once a long play.
After the words ' Who are those,' etc., there used to be a long lyric
passage " (*Works*, p. 240).

[2] " Heart flowers," *kokoro no hana*, is a synonym for " poetry."

PRIEST.

Hear then ! This Stūpa is the Body of the Diamond Lord.[1] It is the symbol of his incarnation.

KOMACHI.

And in what elements did he choose to manifest his body ?

PRIEST.

Earth, water, wind, fire and space.

KOMACHI.

Of these five man also is compounded. Where then is the difference ?

PRIEST.

The forms are the same, but not the virtue.

KOMACHI.

And what is the virtue of the Stūpa ?

PRIEST.

" He that has looked once upon the Stūpa, shall escape for ever from the Three Paths of Evil." [2]

KOMACHI.

" One thought can sow salvation in the heart." [3] Is that of less price ?

SECOND PRIEST.

If your heart has seen salvation, how comes it that you linger in the World ?

KOMACHI.

It is my body that lingers, for my heart left it long ago.

PRIEST.

You have no heart at all, or you would have known the Body of Buddha.

[1] Vajrasattva, himself an emanation of Vairochana, the principal Buddha of the Shingon Sect.
[2] From the Nirvāna Sūtra. [3] From the Avatamsaka Sūtra.

KOMACHI.

It was because I knew it that I came to see it!

SECOND PRIEST.

And knowing what you know, you sprawled upon it without a word of prayer?

KOMACHI.

It was on the ground already. What harm could it get by my resting on it?

PRIEST.

It was an act of discord.[1]

KOMACHI.

Sometimes from discord salvation springs.

SECOND PRIEST.

From the malice of Daiba . . .[2]

KOMACHI.

As from the mercy of Kwannon.[3]

PRIEST.

From the folly of Handoku . . .[4]

KOMACHI.

As from the wisdom of Monju.[5]

SECOND PRIEST.

That which is called Evil

KOMACHI.

Is Good.

PRIEST.

That which is called Illusion

---

[1] Lit. "discordant karma."
[2] A wicked disciple who in the end attained to Illumination. Also called Datta; cp. *Kumasaka*, p. 95.
[3] The Goddess of Mercy.
[4] A disciple so witless that he could not recite a single verse of Scripture.   [5] God of Wisdom.

KOMACHI.
  Is Salvation.[1]

SECOND PRIEST.
  For Salvation

KOMACHI.
  Cannot be planted like a tree.

PRIEST.
  And the Heart's Mirror

KOMACHI.
  Hangs in the void.

CHORUS (*speaking for* KOMACHI).
  " Nothing is real.
  Between Buddha and Man
  Is no distinction, but a seeming of difference planned
  For the welfare of the humble, the ill-instructed,
  Whom he has vowed to save.
  Sin itself may be the ladder of salvation."
  So she spoke, eagerly ; and the priests,
  " A saint, a saint is this decrepit, outcast soul."
  And bending their heads to the ground,
  Three times did homage before her.

KOMACHI.
  I now emboldened
  Recite a riddle, a jesting song.
  " Were I in Heaven
  The Stūpa were an ill seat ;
  But here, in the world without,
  What harm is done ? " [2]

CHORUS.
  The priests would have rebuked her ;
  But they have found their match.

  [1] From the Nirvāna Sūtra.
  [2] The riddle depends on a pun between *sotoba* and *soto wa,* " without,"
." outside."

PRIEST.

Who are you ? Pray tell us the name you had,
and we will pray for you when you are dead.

KOMACHI.

Shame covers me when I speak my name ; but if
you will pray for me, I will try to tell you. This is
my name ; write it down in your prayer-list : I am
the ruins of Komachi, daughter of Ono no Yoshizane,
Governor of the land of Dewa.

PRIESTS.

Oh piteous, piteous ! Is this
Komachi that once
Was a bright flower,
Komachi the beautiful, whose dark brows
Linked like young moons ;
Her face white-farded ever ;
Whose many, many damask robes
Filled cedar-scented halls ?

KOMACHI.

I made verses in our speech
And in the speech of the foreign Court.

CHORUS.

The cup she held at the feast
Like gentle moonlight dropped its glint on her sleeve.
Oh how fell she from splendour,
How came the white of winter
To crown her head ?
Where are gone the lovely locks, double-twined,
The coils of jet ?
Lank wisps, scant curls wither now
On wilted flesh ;
And twin-arches, moth-brows tinge no more
With the hue of far hills. " Oh cover, cover
From the creeping light of dawn

Silted seaweed locks that of a hundred years
Lack now but one.
Oh hide me from my shame."

(KOMACHI *hides her face.*)

CHORUS (*speaking for the* PRIEST).
What is it you carry in the wallet strung at your
neck ?

KOMACHI.
Death may come to-day—or hunger to-morrow.
A few beans and a cake of millet :
That is what I carry in my bag.

CHORUS.
And in the wallet on your back ?

KOMACHI.
A garment stained with dust and sweat.

CHORUS.
And in the basket on your arm ?

KOMACHI.
Sagittaries white and black.

CHORUS.
Tattered cloak,[1]

KOMACHI.
Broken hat . . .

CHORUS.
She cannot hide her face from our eyes ;
And how her limbs

KOMACHI.
From rain and dew, hoar-frost and snow ?

[1] The words which follow suggest the plight of her lover Shōshō
when he travelled to her house " a hundred nights all but one," to
cut his notch on the bench.

CHORUS (*speaking for* KOMACHI *while she mimes the actions they describe*).

Not rags enough to wipe the tears from my eyes!
Now, wandering along the roads
I beg an alms of those that pass.
And when they will not give,
An evil rage, a very madness possesses me.
My voice changes.
Oh terrible!

KOMACHI (*thrusting her hat under the* PRIESTS' *noses and shrieking at them menacingly*).

Grr! You priests, give me something: give me something . . . Ah!

PRIEST.

What do you want?

KOMACHI.

Let me go to Komachi.[1]

PRIEST.

But you told us you were Komachi. What folly is this you are talking?

KOMACHI.

No, no. . . . Komachi was very beautiful.
Many letters came to her, many messages,—
Thick as raindrops out of a black summer sky.
But she sent no answer, not even an empty word.
And now in punishment she has grown old:
She has lived a hundred years—
I love her, oh I love her!

PRIEST.

You love Komachi? Say then, whose spirit has possessed you?

[1] The spirit of her lover Shōshō has now entirely possessed her: this "possession-scene" lasts very much longer on the stage than the brief words would suggest.

KOMACHI.

There were many who set their hearts on her,
But among them all
It was Shōshō who loved her best,
Shii no Shōshō of the Deep Grass.[1]

CHORUS (*speaking for* KOMACHI, *i.e. for the spirit of Shōshō*).

The wheel goes back; I live again through the
    cycle of my woes.
Again I travel to the shaft-bench.
The sun . . . what hour does he show?
Dusk. . . . Alone in the moonlight
I must go my way.
Though the watchmen of the barriers
Stand across my path,
They shall not stop me!

(*Attendants robe* KOMACHI *in the Court hat and travelling-cloak of Shōshō.*)

Look, I go!

KOMACHI.

Lifting the white skirts of my trailing dress,

CHORUS (*speaking for* KOMACHI, *while she, dressed as her lover Shōshō, mimes the night-journey*).

Pulling down over my ears the tall, nodding hat,
Tying over my head the long sleeves of my hunting
    cloak,
Hidden from the eyes of men,
In moonlight, in darkness,
On rainy nights I travelled; on windy nights,
Under a shower of leaves; when the snow was deep,

KOMACHI.

And when water dripped at the roof-eaves,—tok,
    tok . . .

[1] Fukagusa, the name of his native place, means " deep grass."

CHORUS.

> Swiftly, swiftly coming and going, coming and
>   going . . .
> One night, two nights, three nights,
> Ten nights (and this was harvest night) . . .
> I never saw her, yet I travelled ;
> Faithful as the cock who marks each day the dawn,
> I carved my marks on the bench.
> I was to come a hundred times ;
> There lacked but one . . .

KOMACHI (*feeling the death-agony of Shōshō*).

> My eyes dazzle. Oh the pain, the pain !

CHORUS.

> Oh the pain ! and desperate,
> Before the last night had come,
> He died,—Shii no Shōshō the Captain.

> (*Speaking for* KOMACHI, *who is now no longer
>   possessed by Shōshō's spirit.*)

> Was it his spirit that possessed me,
> Was it his anger that broke my wits ?
> If this be so, let me pray for the life hereafter,
> Where alone is comfort ;
> Piling high the sands [1]
> Till I be burnished as gold. [2]
> See, I offer my flower [3] to Buddha,
> I hold it in both hands.
> Oh may He lead me into the Path of Truth,
> Into the Path of Truth.

---

[1] See *Hokkekyō*, II. 18.
[2] The colour of the saints in heaven.
[3] Her " heart-flower," i.e. poetic talent.

CHAPTER IV

UKAI
AYA NO TSUZUMI
AOI NO UYE

Note on Ukai.

Seami tell us (*Works*, p. 246) that this play was written by Enami no Sayemon. " But as I removed bad passages and added good ones, I consider the play to be really my work " (p. 247).

On p. 245 he points out that the same play on words occurs in *Ukai* three times, and suggests how one passage might be amended. The text of the play which we possess to-day still contains the passages which Seami ridiculed, so that it must be Enami no Sayemon's version which has survived, while Seami's amended text is lost.

It is well known that Buddhism forbids the taking of life, especially by cruel means or for sport. The cormorant-fisher's trade had long been considered particularly wicked, as is shown by an early folk-song : [1]

" Woe to the cormorant-fisher
Who binds the heads of his cormorants
And slays the tortoise whose span is ten thousand
 æons !
In this life he may do well enough,
But what will become of him at his next birth ? "

This song, which is at least as old as the twelfth century, and may be much earlier, seems to be the seed from which the Nō play *Ukai* grew.

[1] *Ryōjin Hisshō*, p. 135.

UKAI

(The Cormorant-Fisher)

By Enami no Sayemon (c. 1400)

PERSONS

Priest.	Fisher.
Second Priest.	Yama, King of Hell.
	Chorus.

Priest.

I am a priest from Kiyosumi in Awa. I have never yet seen the country of Kai, so now I am minded to go there on pilgrimage.

(Describing the journey.)

On the foam of white waves
From Kiyosumi in the land of Awa riding
To Mutsura I come; to the Hill of Kamakura,
Lamentably tattered, yet because the World
Is mine no longer, unashamed on borrowed bed,
Mattress of straw, to lie till the bell swings
Above my pillow. Away, away! For dawn
Is on the hemp-fields of Tsuru. Now the noonday sun
Hangs high above us as we cross the hills.
Now to the village of Isawa we come.
Let us lie down and rest awhile in the shelter of this shrine.

(The Fisher comes along the hashigakari towards the stage, carrying a lighted torch.)

Fisher.

When the fisher's torch is quenched
What lamp shall guide him on the dark road that lies before?

Truly, if the World had tasked me hardly
I might be minded to leave it, but this bird-fishing,
Cruel though it be in the wanton taking of life away,
Is a pleasant trade to ply
Afloat on summer streams.

I have heard it told that Yūshi and Hakuyō vowed
their love-vows by the moon, and were changed to
wedded stars of heaven. And even to-day the high
ones of the earth are grieved by moonless nights.
Only *I* grow weary of her shining and welcome nights
of darkness. But when the torches on the boats burn
low,

Then, in the dreadful darkness comes repentance
Of the crime that is my trade,
My sinful sustenance ; and life thus lived
Is loathsome then.

     Yet I would live, and soon
Bent on my oar I push between the waves
To ply my hateful trade.

I will go up to the chapel as I am wont to do, and
give my cormorants rest. (*Seeing the* PRIESTS.) What,
have travellers entered here ?

PRIEST.

We are pilgrim-priests. We asked for lodging in
the village. But they told us it was not lawful for
them to receive us, so we lay down in the shelter of
this shrine.

FISHER.

Truly, truly : I know of none in the village that
could give you lodging.

PRIEST.

Pray tell me, sir, what brings you here ?

FISHER.

Gladly. I am a cormorant-fisher. While the moon
is shining I rest at this shrine ; but when the moon
sinks, I go to ply my trade.

PRIEST.

Then you will not mind our lodging here. But, sir, this work of slaughter ill becomes you ; for I see that the years lie heavy on you. Pray leave this trade and find yourself another means of sustenance.

FISHER.

You say well. But this trade has kept me since I was a child. I cannot leave it now.

SECOND PRIEST.

Listen. The sight of this man has brought back something to my mind. Down this river there is a place they call Rock-tumble. And there, when I passed that way three years ago, I met just such a fisherman as this. And when I told him this cormorant-fishing was reckoned a sin against life, I think he listened ; for he brought me back to his house and lodged me with uncommon care.

FISHER.

And you are the priest that came then ?

SECOND PRIEST.

Yes, I am he.

FISHER.

That cormorant-fisher died.

PRIEST.

How came he to die ?

FISHER.

Following his trade, more shame to him. Listen to his story and give his soul your prayers.

PRIEST.

Gladly we will.

FISHER (*seats himself facing the audience and puts down his torch*)

You must know that on this river of Isawa, for a stretch of three leagues up stream and down, the killing of any living creature is forbidden. Now at that Rock-tumble you spoke of there were many cormorant-fishers who every night went secretly to their fishing. And the people of the place, hating the vile trade, made plans to catch them at their task. But he knew nothing of this; and one night he went there secretly and let his cormorants loose.

There was an ambush set for him; in a moment they were upon him. "Kill him!" they cried; "one life for many," was their plea. Then he pressed palm to palm. "Is the taking of life forbidden in this place? Had I but known it! But now, never again . . ." So with clasped hands he prayed and wept; but none helped him; and as fishers set their stakes they planted him deep in the stream. He cried, but no sound came. (*Turning to the* PRIEST *suddenly.*) I am the ghost of that fisherman.

PRIEST.

Oh strange! If that be so, act out before me the tale of your repentance. Show me your sin and I will pray for you tenderly.

FISHER.

I will act before your eyes the sin that binds me, the cormorant-fishing of·those days. Oh give my soul your prayer!

PRIEST.

I will.

FISHER (*rising and taking up his torch*).

The night is passing. It is fishing-time.
I must rehearse the sin that binds me.

PRIEST.

 I have read in tales of a foreign land [1]
 How sin-laden the souls of the dead
 Have toiled at bitter tasks ;
 But strange, before my eyes
 To see such penance done !

FISHER (*describing his own action*).

 He waved the smeared torches.

PRIEST (*describing the* FISHER'S *action*).

 Girt up his coarse-spun skirts.

FISHER (*going to the " flute-pillar " and bending over as if opening a basket*).

 Then he opened the basket,

PRIEST.

 And those fierce island-birds

FISHER.

 Over the river-waves suddenly he loosed . . .

CHORUS.

 See them, see them clear in the torches' light
 Hither and thither darting,
 Those frightened fishes. [2]
 Swift pounce the diving birds,
 Plunging, scooping,
 Ceaselessly clutch their prey :
 In the joy of capture
 Forgotten sin and forfeit
 Of the life hereafter !
 Oh if these boiling waters would be still,
 Then would the carp rise thick
 As goldfinch in a bowl.

 [1] Or, according to another reading, " tales of Hell."
 [2] The Fisher holds up his torch and looks down as though peering into the water.

Look how the little *ayu* leap [1]
Playing in the shallow stream.
Hem them in : give them no rest !
Oh strange !
The torches burn still, but their light grows dim ;
And I remember suddenly and am sad.
It is the hated moon !

(*He throws down the torch.*)

The lights of the fishing-boat are quenched ;
Homeward on the Way of Darkness [2]
In anguish I depart,

(*He leaves the stage.*)

PRIEST (*sings his " machi-utai " or waiting-song, while the
actor who has taken the part of the* FISHER *changes
into the mask and costume of the* KING OF HELL.)

I dip my hand in the shallows,
I gather pebbles in the stream.
I write Scripture upon them,
Upon each stone a letter of the Holy Law.
Now I cast them back into the waves and their
   drowned spell
Shall raise from its abyss a foundered soul.

(*Enter* YAMA, KING OF HELL ; *he remains on the
hashigakari.*)

YAMA.

Hell is not far away :
All that your eyes look out on in the world
Is the Fiend's home.
I am come to proclaim that the sins of this man, who
from the days of his boyhood long ago has fished in
rivers and streams, were grown so many that they filled
the pages of the Iron Book ; [3] while on the Golden

---

[1] I have omitted the line " Though this be not the river of Tamashima," a reference to the Empress Jingō, who caught an *ayu* at
Tamashima when on her way to fight the Coreans.

[2] A name for Hades.

[3] Good deeds were recorded in a golden book, evil deeds in an
iron one.

Leaves there was not a mark to his name. And he
was like to have been thrown down into the Deepest
Pit ; but now, because he once gave lodging to a priest,
I am commanded to carry him quickly to Buddha's
Place.

> The Demon's rage is stilled,
> The fisher's boat is changed
> To the ship of Buddha's vow,[1]
> Lifeboat of the Lotus Law.[2]

[1] He vowed that he would come as a ship to those drowning in the
Sea of Delusion.

[2] Here follow the twelve concluding lines, too full of Buddhist
technicalities to interest a general reader.

now read pp. 299 ff.

AYA NO TSUZUMI

(THE DAMASK DRUM)

Attributed to SEAMI, but perhaps earlier.

water

PERSONS

A COURTIER.   AN OLD GARDENER.

THE PRINCESS.

COURTIER.

I am a courtier at the Palace of Kinomaru in the country of Chikuzen. You must know that in this place there is a famous pond called the Laurel Pond, where the royal ones often take their walks; so it happened that one day the old man who sweeps the garden here caught sight of the Princess. And from that time he has loved her with a love that gives his heart no rest.

Some one told her of this, and she said, "Love's equal realm knows no divisions,"[1] and in her pity she said, "By that pond there stands a laurel-tree, and on its branches there hangs a drum. Let him beat the drum, and if the sound is heard in the Palace, he shall see my face again."

I must tell him of this.

Listen, old Gardener! The worshipful lady has heard of your love and sends you this message: "Go and beat the drum that hangs on the tree by the pond, and if the sound is heard in the Palace, you shall see my face again." Go quickly now and beat the drum!

---

[1] A twelfth-century folk-song (*Ryōjin Hisshō*, p. 126), speaks of "The Way of Love which knows no castes of 'high' and 'low'."

GARDENER.

With trembling I receive her words. I will go and beat the drum.

COURTIER.

Look, here is the drum she spoke of. Make haste and beat it ! (*He leaves the* GARDENER *standing by the tree and seats himself at the foot of the " Waki's pillar."*)

GARDENER.

They talk of the moon-tree, the laurel that grows in the Garden of the Moon. . . . But for me there is but one true tree, this laurel by the lake. Oh, may the drum that hangs on its branches give forth a mighty note, a music to bind up my bursting heart.
Listen ! the evening bell to help me chimes ;
But then tolls in
A heavy tale of day linked on to day,

CHORUS (*speaking for the* GARDENER).

And hope stretched out from dusk to dusk.
But now, a watchman of the hours, I beat
The longed-for stroke.

GARDENER.

I was old, I shunned the daylight,
I was gaunt as an aged crane ;
And upon all that misery
Suddenly a sorrow was heaped,
The new sorrow of love.
The days had left their marks,
Coming and coming, like waves that beat on a sandy
    shore . . .

CHORUS.

Oh, with a thunder of white waves
The echo of the drum shall roll.

GARDENER.

> The after-world draws near me,
> Yet even now I wake not
> From this autumn of love that closes
> In sadness the sequence of my years.

CHORUS.

> And slow as the autumn dew
> Tears gather in my eyes, to fall
> Scattered like dewdrops from a shaken flower
> On my coarse-woven dress.
> See here the marks, imprint of tangled love,
> That all the world will read.

GARDENER.

> I said " I will forget,"

CHORUS.

> And got worse torment so
> Than by remembrance. But all in this world
> Is as the horse of the aged man of the land of Sai ; [1]
> And as a white colt flashes
> Past a gap in the hedge, even so our days pass. [2]
> And though the time be come,
> Yet can none know the road that he at last must
>   tread,
> Goal of his dewdrop-life.
> All this I knew ; yet knowing,
> Was blind with folly.

GARDENER.

> " Wake, wake," he cries,—

[1] A story from *Huai-nan Tzŭ*. What looks like disaster turns out to be good fortune and *vice versa*. The horse broke away and was lost. A revolution occurred during which the Government seized all horses. When the revolution was over the man of Sai's horse was rediscovered. If he had not lost it the Government would have taken it.

[2] This simile, which passed into a proverb in China and Japan, occurs first in *Chuang Tzŭ*, chap. xxii.

CHORUS.

The watchman of the hours,—
" Wake from the sleep of dawn ! "
And batters on the drum.
For if its sound be heard, soon shall he see
Her face, the damask of her dress . . .
Aye, damask ! He does not know
That on a damask drum he beats,
Beats with all the strength of his hands, his aged
     hands,
But hears no sound.
" Am I grown deaf ? " he cries, and listens, listens :
Rain on the windows, lapping of waves on the pool—
Both these he hears, and silent only
The drum, strange damask drum.
Oh, will it never sound ?
I thought to beat the sorrow from my heart,
Wake music in a damask drum ; an echo of love
From the voiceless fabric of pride !

GARDENER.

Longed for as the moon that hides
In the obstinate clouds of a rainy night
Is the sound of the watchman's drum,
To roll the darkness from my heart.

CHORUS.

I beat the drum. The days pass and the hours.
It was yesterday, and it is to-day.

GARDENER.

But she for whom I wait

CHORUS.

Comes not even in dream. At dawn and dusk

GARDENER.

No drum sounds.

CHORUS.

> She has not come. Is it not sung that those
> Whom love has joined
> Not even the God of Thunder can divide ?
> Of lovers, I alone
> Am guideless, comfortless.
> Then weary of himself and calling her to witness
> of his woe,
> " Why should I endure," he cried,
> " Such life as this ? " and in the waters of the pond
> He cast himself and died.

> (GARDENER *leaves the stage.*)
>
> *Enter the* PRINCESS.

COURTIER.

> I would speak with you, madam.
>
> The drum made no sound, and the aged Gardener in despair has flung himself into the pond by the laurel-tree, and died. The soul of such a one may cling to you and do you injury. Go out and look upon him.

PRINCESS (*speaking wildly, already possessed by the* GARDENER'S *angry ghost, which speaks through her*).[1]

> Listen, people, listen !
> In the noise of the beating waves
> I hear the rolling of a drum.
> Oh, joyful sound, oh joyful !
> The music of a drum.

COURTIER.

> Strange, strange !
> This lady speaks as one
> By phantasy possessed.
> What is amiss, what ails her ?

PRINCESS.

> Truly, by phantasy I am possessed.
> Can a damask drum give sound ?
> √ When I bad him beat what could not ring,
> Then tottered first my wits.

---

[1] Compare the " possession " in *Sotoba Komachi.*

COURTIER.

> She spoke, and on the face of the evening pool
> A wave stirred.

PRINCESS.

> And out of the wave

COURTIER.

> A voice spoke.

> (*The voice of the* GARDENER *is heard ; as he gradually
> advances along the hashigakari it is seen that
> he wears a " demon mask," leans on a staff
> and carries the " demon mallet " at his girdle.*)

GARDENER'S GHOST.

> I was driftwood in the pool, but the waves of
> bitterness

CHORUS.

> Have washed me back to the shore.

GHOST.

> Anger clings to my heart,
> Clings even now when neither wrath nor weeping
> Are aught but folly.

CHORUS.

> One thought consumes me,
> The anger of lust denied
> Covers me like darkness.
> I am become a demon dwelling
> In the hell of my dark thoughts,
> Storm-cloud of my desires.

GHOST.

> " Though the waters parch in the fields
> Though the brooks run dry,
> Never shall the place be shown
> Of the spring that feeds my heart." [1]

[1] Adapted from a poem in the *Gosenshū*.

So I had resolved. Oh, why so cruelly
Set they me to win
Voice from a voiceless drum,
Spending my heart in vain ?
And I spent my heart on the glimpse of a moon
    that slipped
Through the boughs of an autumn tree.[1]

CHORUS.

This damask drum that hangs on the laurel-tree

GHOST.

Will it sound, will it sound ?

    (*He seizes the* PRINCESS *and drags her towards the
        drum.*)

Try !   Strike it !

CHORUS.

" Strike ! " he cries ;
" The quick beat, the battle-charge !
Loud, loud ! Strike, strike," he rails,
And brandishing his demon-stick
Gives her no rest.
" Oh woe ! " the lady weeps,
" No sound, no sound. Oh misery ! " she wails.
And he, at the mallet stroke, " Repent, repent ! "
Such torments in the world of night
Abōrasetsu, chief of demons, wields,
Who on the Wheel of Fire
Sears sinful flesh and shatters bones to dust.
Not less her torture now !
" Oh, agony ! " she cries, " What have I done,
By what dire seed this harvest sown ? "

GHOST.

Clear stands the cause before you.

        [1] Adapted from a poem in the *Kokinshū*.

CHORUS.

> Clear stands the cause before my eyes ;
> > I know it now.
> By the pool's white waters, upon the laurel's bough
> The drum was hung.
> He did not know his hour, but struck and struck
> Till all the will had ebbed from his heart's core ;
> Then leapt into the lake and died.
> And while his body rocked
> Like driftwood on the waves,
> His soul, an angry ghost,
> Possessed the lady's wits, haunted her heart with
> > woe.
> The mallet lashed, as these waves lash the shore,
> Lash on the ice of the eastern shore.
> The wind passes ; the rain falls
> On the Red Lotus, the Lesser and the Greater.[1]
> The hair stands up on my head.
> " The fish that leaps the falls
> To a fell snake is turned," [2]
> I have learned to know them ;
> Such, such are the demons of the World of Night.
> " O hateful lady, hateful ! " he cried, and sank
> > again
> Into the whirlpool of desire.

In the Kwanze School this play is replaced by another called *The Burden of Love*, also attributed to Seami, who writes (*Works*, p. 166) : " *The Burden of Love* was formerly *The Damask Drum*." The task set in the later play is the carrying of a burden a thousand times round the garden. The Gardener seizes the burden joyfully and begins to run with it, but it grows heavier and heavier, till he sinks crushed to death beneath it.

---

[1] The names of two of the Cold Hells in the Buddhist Inferno.
[2] There is a legend that the fish who succeed in leaping a certain waterfall turn into dragons. So the Gardener's attempt to raise himself to the level of the Princess has changed him into an evil demon. See *Bulletin* No. 5.

Note on Aoi no Uye.

At the age of twelve Prince Genji went through. the ceremony of marriage with Aoi no Uye (Princess Hollyhock), the Prime Minister's daughter. She continued to live at her father's house and Genji at his palace. When he was about sixteen he fell in love with Princess Rokujō, the widow of the Emperor's brother ; she was about eight years older than himself. He was not long faithful to her. The lady Yūgao next engaged his affections. He carried her one night to a deserted mansion on the outskirts of the City. " The night was far advanced and they had both fallen asleep. Suddenly the figure of a woman appeared at the bedside. " I have found you ! " it cried. " What stranger is this that lies beside you ? What treachery is this that you flaunt before my eyes ? " And with these words the apparition stooped over the bed, and made as though to drag away the sleeping girl from Genji's side." [1]

Before dawn Yūgao was dead, stricken by the " living phantom " of Rokujō, embodiment of her baleful jealousy.

Soon after this, Genji became reconciled with his wife Aoi, but continued to visit Rokujō. One day, at the Kamo Festival, Aoi's way was blocked by another carriage. She ordered her attendants to drag it aside. A scuffle ensued between her servants and those of Rokujō (for she was the occupant of the second carriage) in which Aoi's side prevailed. Rokujō's carriage was broken and Aoi's pushed into the front

[1] *Genji Monogatari* (Romance of Genji), chap. iii., Hakubunkwan Edition, p. 87.

place. After the festival was over Aoi returned to the Prime Minister's house in high spirits.

Soon afterwards she fell ill, and it is at this point that the play begins.

There is nothing obscure or ambiguous in the situation. Fenollosa seems to have misunderstood the play and read into it complications and confusions which do not exist. He also changes the sex of the Witch, though the Japanese word, *miko*, always has a feminine meaning. The " Romance of Genji " (*Genji Monogatari*) was written by Lady Murasaki Shikibu and was finished in the year 1004 A.D. Of its fifty-four chapters only seventeen have been translated.[1] It furnished the plots of many Nō plays, of which *Suma Genji* (Genji's exile at Suma), *No no Miya* (his visit to Rokujō after she became a nun), *Tamakatsura* (the story of Yūgao's daughter), and *Hajitomi* (in which Yūgao's ghost appears) are the best known.

There is some doubt about the authorship of the play. Seami saw it acted as a Dengaku by his father's contemporary Inuō. He describes Inuō's entry on to the stage in the rôle of Rokujō and quotes the first six lines of her opening speech. These lines correspond exactly with the modern text, and it is probable that the play existed in something like its present form in the middle of the fourteenth century. Kwanze Nagatoshi, the great-grandson of Seami, includes it in a list of Seami's works ; while popular tradition ascribes it to Seami's son-in-law Zenchiku.

[1] By Baron Suyematsu in 1881.

AOI NO UYE

(Princess Hollyhock)

Revised by Zenchiku Ujinobu (1414–1499 ?)

PERSONS

Courtier.	The Saint of Yokawa.
Witch.	Messenger.
Princess Rokujō.	Chorus.

wheel coach

(A folded cloak laid in front of the stage symbolizes the sick-bed of Aoi.)

COURTIER.

I am a courtier in the service of the Emperor Shujaku. You must know that the Prime Minister's daughter, Princess Aoi, has fallen sick. We have sent for abbots and high-priests of the Greater School and of the Secret School, but they could not cure her.

And now, here at my side, stands the witch of Teruhi,[1] a famous diviner with the bow-string. My lord has been told that by twanging her bow-string she can make visible an evil spirit and tell if it be the spirit of a living man or a dead. So he bad me send for her and let her pluck her string. *(Turning to the Witch, who has been waiting motionless.)* Come, sorceress, we are ready!

WITCH *(comes forward beating a little drum and reciting a mystic formula).*

Ten shōjō; chi shōjō.
Naige shōjō; rokon shōjō.

[1] A *miko* or witch called Teruhi is the subject of the play *Sanja Takusen.*

Pure above ; pure below.
Pure without ; pure within.
Pure in eyes, ears, heart and tongue.

(*She plucks her bow-string, reciting the spell.*)

You whom I call
Hold loose the reins
On your grey colt's neck
As you gallop to me
Over the long sands !

(*The living phantasm of* ROKUJŌ *appears at the back of the stage.*)

ROKUJŌ.

In the Three Coaches
That travel on the Road of Law
I drove out of the Burning House . . [1]
Is there no way to banish the broken coach
That stands at Yūgao's door ? [2]
                              This world
Is like the wheels of the little ox-cart ;
Round and round they go . . . till vengeance comes.
The Wheel of Life turns like the wheel of a coach ;
There is no escape from the Six Paths and Four
    Births.
We are brittle as the leaves of the *bashō* ;
As fleeting as foam upon the sea.
Yesterday's flower, to-day's dream.
From such a dream were it not wiser to wake ?

[1] Rokujō has left the " Burning House," i.e. her material body. The " Three Coaches " are those of the famous " Burning House " parable in the *Hokkekyō*. Some children were in a burning house. Intent on their play, they could not be induced to leave the building ; till their father lured them out by the promise that they would find those little toy coaches awaiting them. So Buddha, by partial truth, lures men from the " burning house " of their material lives. Owing to the episode at the Kamo Festival, Rokujō is obsessed by the idea of " carriages," " wheels " and the like.

[2] One day Rokujō saw a coach from which all badges and distinctive decorations had been purposely stripped (hence, in a sense, a " broken coach ") standing before Yūgao's door. She found out that it was Genji's. For Yūgao, see p. 179.

And when to this is added another's scorn
How can the heart have rest ?
So when I heard the twanging of your bow
For a little while, I thought, I will take my pleasure ;
And as an angry ghost appeared.
Oh ! I am ashamed !

(She veils her face.)

This time too I have come secretly [1]
In a closed coach.
Though I sat till dawn and watched the moon,
Till dawn and watched,
How could I show myself,
That am no more than the mists that tremble over
    the fields ?
I am come, I am come to the notch of your bow
To tell my sorrow.
Whence came the noise of the bow-string ?

WITCH.

Though she should stand at the wife-door of the
mother-house of the square court . . . [2]

ROKUJŌ.

Yet would none come to me, that am not in the
flesh.[3]

WITCH.

How strange ! I see a fine lady whom I do not
know riding in a broken coach. She clutches at the
shafts of another coach from which the oxen have
been unyoked. And in the second coach sits one
who seems a new wife.[4] The lady of the broken coach
is weeping, weeping. It is a piteous sight.
    Can this be she ?

[1] Rokujō went secretly to the Kamo Festival in a closed carriage.
[2] Words from an old dance-song or " *saibara*."
[3] " That am a ghost," but also " that have lost my beauty."
[4] Alluding to Aoi's pregnancy.

COURTIER.

It would not be hard to guess who such a one might be. Come, spirit, tell us your name !

ROKUJŌ.

In this Sahā World [1] where days fly like the light-
     ning's flash
None is worth hating and none worth pitying.
This I knew. Oh when did folly master me ?
You would know who I am that have come drawn by
the twanging of your bow ? I am the angry ghost
of Rokujō, Lady of the Chamber.
Long ago I lived in the world.
I sat at flower-feasts among the clouds.[2]
On spring mornings I rode out
In royal retinue and on autumn nights
Among the red leaves of the Rishis' Cave
I sported with moonbeams,
With colours and perfumes
My senses sated.
I had splendour then ;
But now I wither like the Morning Glory
Whose span endures not from dawn to midday.
I have come to clear my hate.

> (*She then quotes the Buddhist saying, " Our sorrows
>   in this world are not caused by others ; for even
>   when others wrong us we are suffering the
>   retribution of our own deeds in a previous
>   existence."*
>
> *But while singing these words she turns towards
>   Aoi's bed ; passion again seizes her and she
>   cries :*)

I am full of hatred.
I must strike ; I must strike.

> (*She creeps towards the bed.*)

[1] A Sanskrit name for the " world of appearances."
[2] I.e. at the Palace.

WITCH.

You, Lady Rokujō, you a Lady of the Chamber!
Would you lay wait and strike as peasant women do ? [1]
How can this be ?   Think and forbear !

ROKUJŌ.

Say what you will, I must strike. I must strike
now. (*Describing her own action.*) "And as she said
this, she went over to the pillow and struck at it."
(*She strikes at the head of the bed with her fan.*)

WITCH.

She is going to strike again. (*To* ROKUJŌ.) You
shall pay for this !

ROKUJŌ.

And this hate too is payment for past hate.

WITCH.

"The flame of anger

ROKUJŌ.

Consumes itself only." [2]

WITCH.

Did you not know ?

ROKUJŌ.

Know it then now.

CHORUS.

O Hate, Hate !
Her [3] hate so deep that on her bed
Our lady [4] moans.
Yet, should she live in the world again,[5]

---

[1] It was the custom for wives who had been put away to ambush
the new wife and strike her "to clear their hate."

[2] From the Sūtrālankāra Shāstra (Cat. No. 1182).

[3] Rokujō's.   [4] Aoi.   [5] I.e. recover.

He would call her to him, her Lord
The Shining One, whose light
Is brighter than fire-fly hovering
Over the slime of an inky pool.

ROKUJŌ.
But for me
There is no way back to what I was,
No more than to the heart of a bramble-thicket.
The dew that dries on the bramble-leaf
Comes back again ;
But love (and this is worst)
That not even in dream returns,—
That is grown to be an old tale,—
Now, even now waxes,
So that standing at the bright mirror
I tremble and am ashamed.
I am come in my broken coach. (*She throws down her
fan and begins to slip off her embroidered robe.*) I will
hide you in it and carry you away !

> (*She stands right over the bed, then turns away and
> at the back of the stage throws off her robe, which
> is held by two attendants in such a way that
> she cannot be seen. She changes her "deigan"
> mask for a female demon's mask and now carries
> a mallet in her hand.*)

> (*Meanwhile the* COURTIER, *who has been standing
> near the bed :*)

COURTIER.
Come quickly, some one ! Princess Aoi is worse.
Every minute she is worse. Go and fetch the Little
Saint of Yokawa.[1]

MESSENGER.
I tremble and obey.
> (*He goes to the wing and speaks to some one off
> the stage.*)
May I come in ?

[1] The hero of the "Finding of Ukifune," a later episode in the
Genji Monogatari.

SAINT (*speaking from the wing*).

Who is it that seeks admittance to a room washed
by the moonlight of the Three Mysteries, sprinkled
with the holy water of Yoga ? Who would draw near
to a couch of the Ten Vehicles, a window of the Eight
Perceptions ?

MESSENGER.

I am come from the Court. Princess Aoi is ill.
They would have you come to her.

SAINT.

It happens that at this time I am practising particular austerities and go nowhere abroad. But if
you are a messenger from the Court, I will follow you.

(*He comes on the stage.*)

COURTIER.

We thank you for coming.

SAINT.

I wait upon you. Where is the sick person ?

COURTIER.

On the bed here.

SAINT.

Then I will begin my incantations at once.

COURTIER.

Pray do so.

SAINT.

He said : " I will say my incantations."
Following in the steps of En no Gyōja,[1]
Clad in skirts that have trailed the Peak of the Two
    Spheres,[2]

[1] Founder of the sect of ascetics called Yamabushi Mountaineers.
[2] Mount Ōmine, near Yoshino, ritual ascents of which were made
by Yamabushi.

That have brushed the dew of the Seven Precious
     Trees,
Clad in the cope of endurance
That shields from the world's defilement,
" Sarari, sarari," with such sound
I shake the red wooden beads of my rosary
And say the first spell :
Namaku Samanda Basarada
Namaku Samanda Basarada.[1]

ROKUJŌ (*during the incantation she has cowered at the
     back of the stage wrapped in her Chinese robe,
     which she has picked up again.*)

Go back, Gyōja, go back to your home ; do not
stay and be vanquished !

SAINT.

Be you what demon you will, do not hope to over-
come the Gyōja's subtle power. I will pray again.

     (*He shakes his rosary whilst the* CHORUS, *speaking
          for him, invokes the first of the Five Kings.*)

CHORUS.

In the east Gō Sanze, Subduer of the Three Worlds.

ROKUJŌ (*counter-invoking*).

In the south Gundari Yasha.

CHORUS.

In the west Dai-itoku.

ROKUJŌ.

In the north Kongō

CHORUS.

Yasha, the Diamond King.

---

[1] Known as the Lesser Spell of Fudō. The longer one which follows
is the Middle Spell. They consist of corrupt Sanskrit mixed with
meaningless magic syllables.

Rokujō.

In the centre the Great Holy

Chorus.

Fudō Immutable.
Namaku Samanda Basarada
Senda Makaroshana
Sohataya Untaratakarman.
" They that hear my name shall get Great Enlighten-
ment ;
They that see my body shall attain to Buddhahood." [1]

Rokujō (*suddenly dropping her mallet and pressing
her hands to her ears.*)

The voice of the Hannya Book ! I am afraid. Never
again will I come as an angry ghost.

Ghost.

When she heard the sound of Scripture
The demon's raging heart was stilled ;
Shapes of Pity and Sufferance,
The Bodhisats descend.
Her soul casts off its bonds,
She walks in Buddha's Way.

---

[1] From the Buddhist Sūtra known in Japan as the Hannya Kyō.
It was supposed to have a particular influence over female demons,
who are also called " Hannyas."

CHAPTER V

KANTAN

THE HŌKA PRIESTS

HAGOROMO

NOTE ON KANTAN.

A YOUNG man, going into the world to make his fortune, stops at an inn on the road and there meets with a sage, who lends him a pillow. While the inn-servant is heating up the millet, the young man dozes on the pillow and dreams that he enters public life, is promoted, degraded, recalled to office, endures the hardship of distant campaigns, is accused of treason, condemned to death, saved at the last moment and finally dies at a great old age. Awaking from his dream, the young man discovers that the millet is not yet cooked. In a moment's sleep he has lived through the vicissitudes of a long public career. Convinced that in the great world "honour is soon followed by disgrace, and promotion by calumny," he turns back again towards the village from which he came.

Such, in outline, is the most usual version of the story of Rosei's dream at Kantan. The earliest form in which we know it is the "Pillow Tale" of the Chinese writer Li Pi, who lived from 722 to 789 A.D.

It is interesting to see how Seami deals with a subject which seems at first sight so impossible to shape into a Nō play. The "sage" is eliminated, and in the dream Rosei immediately becomes Emperor of Central China. This affords an excuse for the Court dances which form the central "ballet" of the piece. In the second half, as in *Hagoromo* and other plays, the words are merely an accompaniment to the dancing.

Chamberlain's version loses by the fact that it is made from the ordinary printed text which omits the prologue and all the speeches of the hostess.

The play is usually attributed to Seami, but it is

not mentioned in his *Works*, nor in the list of plays
by him drawn up by his great-grandson in 1524.

It is discussed at considerable length in the *Later
Kwadensho*, which was printed *c.* 1600. The writer of
that book must therefore have regarded the play as
a work of Seami's period. It should be mentioned
that the geography of the play is absurd. Though
both his starting-point and goal lie in the south-western
province of Ssechuan, he passes through Hantan,[1] which
lay in the northern province of Chih-li.

[1] In Japanese, Kantan.

KANTAN

HOSTESS.

I who now stand before you am a woman of the village of Kantan in China. A long while ago I gave lodging to one who practised the arts of wizardry ; and as payment he left here a famous pillow, called the Pillow of Kantan. He who sleeps on this pillow sees in a moment's dream the past or future spread out before him, and so awakes illumined. If it should chance that any worshipful travellers arrive to-day, pray send for me.

(*She takes the pillow and lays it on the covered "daïs" which represents at first the bed and afterwards the palace.*)

ROSEI (*enters*).

Lost on the journey of life, shall I learn at last
That I trod but a path of dreams ?
My name is Rosei, and I have come from the land of Shoku. Though born to man's estate, I have not sought Buddha's Way, but have drifted from dusk to dawn and dawn to dusk.

They tell me that on the Hill of the Flying Sheep in the land of So [1] there lives a mighty sage ; and now I am hastening to visit him that he may tell by what rule I should conduct my life.

---

[1] Corresponds to the modern province Hupeh.

(*Song of Travel.*)

Deep hid behind the alleys of the sky
Lie the far lands where I was wont to dwell.
Over the hills I trail
A tattered cloak ; over the hills again :
Fen-dusk and mountain-dusk and village-dusk
Closed many times about me, till to-day
At the village of Kantan,
Strange to me save in name, my journey ends.

I have travelled so fast that I am already come to the
village of Kantan.   Though the sun is still high, I will
lodge here to-night.   (*Knocking.*)   May I come in ?

HOSTESS.

Who is it ?

ROSEI.

I am a traveller ; pray give me lodging for the night.

HOSTESS.

Yes, I can give you lodging ; pray come this way.
. . . You seem to be travelling all alone. Tell me
where you have come from and where you are going.

ROSEI.

I come from the land of Shoku.   They tell me that
on the Hill of the Flying Sheep there lives a sage ; and
I am visiting him that he may tell me by what rule I
should conduct my life.

HOSTESS.

It is a long way to the Hill of the Flying Sheep.
Listen !   A wizard once lodged here and gave us a
marvellous pillow called the Pillow of Kantan : he who
sleeps on it sees all his future in a moment's dream.

ROSEI.

Where is this pillow ?

HOSTESS.

It is on the bed.

Rosei.

I will go and sleep upon it.

Hostess.

And I meanwhile will heat you some millet at the fire.

Rosei (*going to the bed*).

So this is the pillow, the Pillow of Kantan that I have heard such strange tales of ?   Heaven has guided me to it, that I who came out to learn the secret of life may taste the world in a dream.

As one whose course swift summer-rain has stayed,
Unthrifty of the noon he turned aside
To seek a wayside dream ;
Upon the borrowed Pillow of Kantan
He laid his head and slept.

> (*While* Rosei *is still chanting these words, the* Envoy *enters, followed by two* Attendants *who carry a litter.   The* Envoy *raps on the post of the bed.*)

Envoy.

Rosei, Rosei !   I must speak with you.

> (Rosei, *who has been lying with his fan over his face, rises when the* Envoy *begins to speak.*)

Rosei.

But who are you ?

Envoy.

I am come as a messenger to tell you that the Emperor of the Land of So[1] resigns his throne and commands that Rosei shall reign in his stead.

---

[1] So, Chinese " Ch'u," was formerly an independent feudal State. The name means " thorn," as does the Japanese " ibara."   Chamberlain calls it " The Country of Ibara," but in this case the reading " So " is indicated by both Ōwada and Haga.

Rosei.

Unthinkable ! I a king ? But for what reason. am I assigned this task ?

Envoy.

I cannot venture to determine. Doubtless there were found in your Majesty's countenance auspicious tokens, signs that you must rule the land. Let us lose no time ; pray deign to enter this palanquin.

Rosei (*looking at the palanquin in astonishment*).

What thing is this ?
A litter spangled with a dew of shining stones ?
I am not wont to ride. Such splendour ! Oh, little
     thought I
When first my weary feet trod unfamiliar roads
In kingly state to be borne to my journey's end.
Is it to Heaven I ride ?

Chorus.

In jewelled palanquin
On the Way of Wisdom you are borne ; here shall
     you learn
That the flower of glory fades like a moment's dream.
See, you are become a cloud-man of the sky.[1]
The palaces of ancient kings
Rise up before you, Abō's Hall, the Dragon's Tower ; [2]
High over the tall clouds their moonlit gables gleam.
The light wells and wells like a rising tide.[3]
Oh splendid vision ! A courtyard strewn
With golden and silver sand ;
And they that at the four sides
Pass through the jewelled door are canopied
With a crown of woven light.

---

[1] Kings and princes are often called "thou above the clouds."
[2] Palaces of the First Emperor. An attendant has removed the pillow from the "bed." From this moment the bed becomes a magnificent palace, as described in the verses which follow.
[3] At this point the Boy Dancer enters.

In the Cities of Heaven, in the home of Gods, I had
    thought,
Shine such still beams on walls of stone ;
Never on palace reared by hands of men.
Treasures, a thousand kinds, ten thousand kinds,
Tribute to tribute joined, a myriad vassal-kings
Cast down before the Throne.
Flags of a thousand lords, ten thousand lords
Shine many-coloured in the sky,
And the noise of their wind-flapping
Rolls round the echoing earth.

ROSEI.

And in the east

CHORUS.

Over a silver hill of thirty cubits height
A golden sun-wheel rose.

ROSEI.

And in the west
Over a golden hill of thirty cubits height
A silver moon-wheel rose,
To prove his words who sang
" In the Palace of Long Life [1]
The Springs and Autumns cease.
Before the Gate of Endless Youth [2]
The days and months pass slow." [3]

COURTIER.

I would address your Majesty. Your Majesty has
reigned for fifty years. Deign but to drink this drink
and you shall live a thousand years. See ! I bring
you the nectar and the grail.

ROSEI.

The nectar ?

[1] Name of a famous Chinese palace.
[2] Famous Gate in the palace of the T'ang Emperors.
[3] These lines are from a poem by Yasutane, d. 997 A.D. (Chamberain attributes them to Po Chü-i.)

COURTIER.

It is the wine that Immortals drink.

ROSEI.

The grail ?

COURTIER.

It is the cup from which they drink.

ROSEI.

The magic wine !   A thousand generations shall pass

COURTIER.

Or ever the springtime of your glory fade.

ROSEI.

I bountiful . . .

COURTIER.

Your people prosperous.

CHORUS.

For ever and ever
The land secure ;
The flower of glory waxing ;
The " herb of increase," joy-increasing
Into the cup we pour.
See ! from hand to hand it goes.
" I will drink," he cries.

ROSEI.

Go circling, magic cup,

CHORUS.

Circling from hand to hand ; [1]
As at the Feast of Floating Cups [2]

[1] Here the Boy Dancer begins to dance the Dream-dance.
[2] On the third day of the third month people floated cups in the stream.   Each person as the cup passed in front of him, had to com pose a poem and drink the contents of the cup.

Hands thrust from damask sleeves detain
The goblet whirling in the eager stream ;
Now launched, now landed ! [1]
Oh merry flashing light, that shall endure
Long as the Silver Chalice [2] circles space.

BOY DANCER.

The white chrysanthem-dew,

CHORUS.

" The dew of the flowers dripping day by day
In how many thousand thousand years
Will it have grown into a pool ? " [3]
It shall not fail, it shall not fail,
The fountain of our Immortality ;
He draws, and yet it wells ;
He drinks, and to his taste it is as sweet
As the Gods' deathless food.
His heart grows airy ; day and night
In unimagined revel, incomparable pride and glory
Eternally shall pass.

(*End of the* BOY DANCER's *dance.* ROSEI, *who has
been watching this dance, now springs up in
ecstasy to dance the Gaku or Court Dance.*)

ROSEI.

The spring-time of my glory fades not . . .

CHORUS.

Many times shall you behold
The pale moon of dawn . . .

ROSEI.

This is the moon-men's dance ;
Cloud-like the feathery sleeves pile up ; the song
of joy
From dusk to dawn I sing.

---

[1] These words also describe the dancer's movements.
[2] The Moon.   [3] See Waley, *Japanese Poetry*, p. 77.

CHORUS.
  All night we sing.
  The sun shines forth again,
  Sinks down, and it is night . . .

ROSEI.
  Nay, dawn has come !

CHORUS.
  We thought the morning young, and lo ! the
    moon

ROSEI.
  Again is bright.

CHORUS.
  Spring scarce has opened her fresh flowers,

ROSEI.
  When leaves are crimson-dyed.

CHORUS.
  Summer is with us yet ;

ROSEI.
  Nay, the snow falls.

CHORUS (*speaking for* ROSEI).
  " I watched the seasons pass :
  Spring, summer, autumn, winter ; a thousand trees,
  A thousand flowers were strange and lovely in their
    pride.
  So the time sped, and now
  Fifty years of glory have passed by me,
  And because they were a dream,

    (*At this point an* ATTENDANT *brings back the pillow,
      and places it in the " palace," which becomes
      a bed again.*)

All, all has vanished and I wake
On the pillow where I laid my head,
The Pillow of Kantan.

(*The* BOY DANCER *and the two* COURTIERS *slip out
by the side-door " kirido " ;* ROSEI *has mounted
the bed and is asleep.*)

HOSTESS (*tapping twice with her fan*).
Listen, traveller ! Your millet is ready. Come
quickly and eat your dinner.

ROSEI (*rising slowly from the bed*).
Rosei has woken from his dream . . .

CHORUS.
Woken from his dream ! The springs and autumns of
fifty years
Vanished with all their glory ; dazed he rises from
the bed.

ROSEI.
Whither are they gone that were so many . . .

CHORUS.
" The queens and waiting-ladies ? What I thought
their voices "

ROSEI.
Were but the whisperings of wind in the trees.

CHORUS.
The palaces and towers

ROSEI.
Were but the baiting-house of Kantan.

CHORUS.
The time of my glory,

ROSEI.
Those fifty years,

CHORUS.

Were but the space of a dream,

ROSEI.

Dreamed while a bowl of millet cooked!

CHORUS.

It is the Inscrutable, the Mystery.

ROSEI.

Yet when I well consider
Man's life in the world of men . . .

CHORUS.

Then shall you find that a hundred years of gladness
Fade as a dream when Death their sequence closes.
Thus too has ended
This monarch's fifty years of state.
Ambition, length of days,
Revels and kingly rule,
All, all has ended thus, all was a dream
Dreamed while the millet cooked.

ROSEI.

Glory be to the Trinity,[1]
Glory to the Trinity!

CHORUS.

Seek you a sage to loose
The bonds that bound you to life's woes?
This pillow is the oracle you sought.
Now shall the wayfarer, content to learn
What here he learnt, that Life is but a dream,
Turn homeward from the village of Kantan.

[1] I.e. Buddha, the Law and the Priesthood. A pious exclamation
of astonishment like the Spanish " Jesù, Maria, José ! "

See p. 59, 13, 17

THE HŌKA PRIESTS
(HŌKAZŌ)

By ZENCHIKU UJINOBU (1414–1499)

PERSONS

MAKINO.	NOBUTOSHI (their father's murderer).
HIS BROTHER.	NOBUTOSHI'S SERVANT.

MAKINO.

MY name is Kojirō; I am the son of one Makino no Sayemon who lived in the land of Shimotsuke. You must know that my father had a quarrel with Nobutoshi, a man of Sagami, and was done to death by him. So this man was my father's murderer and I ought to kill him. But he has many bold fellows to stand by him, while I am all alone. So the days and months slip by with nothing done.

A brother indeed I have, but he left home when he was a child, made himself into a priest, and lives at the seminary near by.

I am much puzzled how to act. I think I will go across and speak to my brother of this matter. (*He goes to the curtain at the end of the hashigakari.*) May I come in ?

(*The curtain is raised and the* BROTHER *appears.*)

BROTHER.

Who is it ?

MAKINO.

It is I.

BROTHER.

Come in, brother. What has brought you hither ?

MAKINO.

I will tell you. It is this matter of our father's murder that has brought me. I have been thinking that I ought to kill his enemy, and would have done so but he has many bold fellows to stand by him and I am all alone. So the days and months slip by and nothing is done.

For pity's sake, decide with me what course we must pursue.

BROTHER.

Brother, what you have said is true enough. But have you forgotten that I left my home when I was but a child and made myself a priest ? Since that is so, I cannot help you.

MAKINO.

So you are pleased to think ; but men say he is a bad son who does not kill his father's foe.

BROTHER.

Can you tell me of any that have ministered to piety by slaying a parent's foe ?

MAKINO.

Why, yes. It was in China, I think. There was one whose mother had been taken by a savage tiger. " I will take vengeance," he cried, and for a hundred days he lay ambushed in the fields waiting for the tiger to come. And once when he was walking on the hillside at dusk, he thought he saw his enemy, and having an arrow already on his bow-string, he shot with all his might. It was nothing but a great rock that he had seen, shaped like a tiger. But his arrow stuck so deep in the stone that blood gushed out from it. If then the strength of piety is such that it can drive an arrow deep into the heart of a stone, take thought, I beseech you, whether you will not resolve to come with me.

BROTHER.

You have cited me a notable instance. I am persuaded to resolve with you how this thing may be effected.

Come now, by what strategy may we get access to our foe ?

MAKINO.

A plan has suddenly come into my head. You know that these *hōka* plays are become the fashion of the day. Why should not I dress up as a *hōka* and you as a *hōka* priest ? They say that our man is a great lover of the Zen doctrine ; so you may talk to him of Zen.

BROTHER.

That is indeed a pretty notion ; let me lose no time in effecting it.

I am resolved ; in a pilgrim guise
I mask my limbs.

MAKINO.

And I, glad-thoughted,
In a minstrel's garb go forth.

BROTHER.

Secretly

MAKINO.

We steal from a home

CHORUS.

" Where fain ·we would stay, but now
Long as life lasts,
Life fickle as the moon of dawn,
No refuge know we
But the haven of our intent.

(*The* BROTHERS *leave the stage. Enter their enemy*
NOBUTOSHI, *followed by his Servant.*)

NOBUTOSHI.

> To the home of gods my footsteps turn
> To the Sacred Fence that bars
> No suppliant's desire.

I am called Tone no Nobutoshi. My home is in the
land of Sagami. Because for much time past I have
been troubled with evil dreams, I have resolved to
visit the Three Isles of Seto.

> (*Re-enter the Brothers:* MAKINO *with bow and
> arrow in his hand and bamboo sprigs stuck in
> his belt behind; the* BROTHER *carrying a long
> staff to which a round fan is attached.*)

BROTHER.

> A fine sight are we now!
> From priest and laic way alike removed,
> Scarce men in speech or form!

MAKINO.

> This antic garb shall hide us from the World
> More safe than hermit cell;
> All earthly thoughts shut out here might we bide
> Cloistered in ease. Oh why,
> Why back to the bitter World
> Are we borne by our intent?

MAKINO and BROTHER.

> The flower that has fallen dreams that Spring is
>   done,
> There are white clouds to cover
> The green hillside . . .

MAKINO.

> To match the scarlet
> Of the autumn leaves
> Red sunlight glitters
> On the flowing stream.

CHORUS.

Wind at morning, rain at night ;
To-day and to-morrow
Shall be part of long ago.
We who pass through a world
Changeful as the dews of evening,
Uncertain as the skies of Spring,
We that are as foam upon the stream,—
Can *any* be our foe ?

SERVANT (*seeing them and going towards the hashi-gakari*).

You're a merry pair of guys ! What may your
names be ?

BROTHER.

Floating Cloud ; Running Water.

SERVANT.

And what is your friend's name ?

MAKINO.

Floating Cloud ; Running Water.

SERVANT.

Have you then but one name between you ?

BROTHER.

I am Floating Cloud and he is Running Water. And
now, pray, tell us your master's name.

SERVANT.

Why, he comes from the land of Sagami, and Nobutoshi . . . (*here the* SERVANT *suddenly remembers that
he is being indiscreet and stuffs his hand into his mouth*)
. . . is *not* his name.

BROTHER.

That's no matter. Whoever he is, tell him that we
are only two *hōka* come to speak with him.

SERVANT.

I will tell him. Do you wait here.

(*He goes over to* NOBUTOSHI *and whispers with him, then comes back to the* BROTHERS.)

Come this way.

(NOBUTOSHI *comes to meet them, covering his face with a fan.*)

NOBUTOSHI.

Listen, gentlemen, I desire an explanation from you.

BROTHER.

What would you know ?

NOBUTOSHI.

It is this. They alone can be called priests round whose fingers is twisted the rosary of Tenfold Power, who are clad in cloak of Forbearance, round whose shoulders hangs the stole of Penitence. Such is everywhere the garb of Buddha's priests. I know no other habit. But you, I see, carry a round fan tied to your pillar-staff. By what verse do you justify the wearing of a fan ?

BROTHER.

" In motion, a wind ;
    In stillness, a bright moon."
And even as in this one substance
Both wind and moon inhere,
So Thought alone is Truth, and from the mind
Spring all component things.
Such is the sermon of the fan, as a sign we bear it
Of the heart's omnipotence. It is an emblem
Fools only would decry !

NOBUTOSHI.

The fan indeed teaches an agreeable lesson ; but one of you carries a bow and arrow at his side. Are these too reckoned fit gear for men of your profession ?

MAKINO.

The bow ?   Why, surely !
Are not its two horns fashioned
In likeness of the Hare and Crow,
Symbols of the Moon and Sun, of Night and Day ?
Here is the primal mystery displayed
Of fair and foul conjoined.[1]
Bears not the God of Love, unsullied king,
A magical bow ?   Does he not stretch upon its string
Arrows of grace whereby
The armies of the Four Fiends [2] know no rest ?

CHORUS.

And thus we two are armed,
For though the bow be not bent nor the arrow loosed,
Yet falls the prey unmasked.

> (MAKINO *draws his bow as though about to shoot ;
> his* BROTHER *checks him with his staff.*)

So says the song. Now speak no more
Of things you know not of.

NOBUTOSHI.

Tell me, pray, from which patriarch do the *hōka*
priests derive their doctrine ?   To what sect do you
adhere ?

BROTHER.

We are of no sect ; our doctrine stands apart. It
cannot be spoken nor expounded. To frame it in
sentences is to degrade our faith ; to set it down
in writing is to be untrue to our Order ; but by the
bending of a leaf is the wind's journey known.

NOBUTOSHI.

I thank you ; your exposition delights me. Pray
tell me now, what is the meaning of this word " Zen " ?

[1] The Sun is male, i.e. fair. The Moon female, i.e. foul.
[2] The demons of Delusion, of the Senses, of the Air and of Death

MAKINO.

> Within, to sound to their depths the waters of
> Mystery ;
> Without, to wander at will through the portals of
> Concentration.

NOBUTOSHI.

> And of the doctrine that Buddha is in the bones of
> each one of us . . . ?

BROTHER.

> He lurks unseen ; like the golden dragon [1] when he
> leaps behind the clouds.

NOBUTOSHI.

> If we believe that life and death are real . . .

BROTHER.

> Then are we caught in the wheel of sorrow.

NOBUTOSHI.

> But if we deny them . . .

BROTHER.

> We are listed to a heresy.[2]

NOBUTOSHI.

> And the straight path to knowledge . . .

MAKINO (*rushing forward sword in hand*).

> " With the triple stroke is carved." [3]

BROTHER.

> Hold ! (*turning to* NOBUTOSHI *who has recoiled and
> drawn his sword.*)
> " To carve a way to knowledge by the triple
> stroke " . . .

---

[1] The sun.
[2] The heresy of Nihilism. To say that phenomena do not exist
is as untrue as to say that they exist.
[3] He quotes a Zen text.

These are Zen words ; he was but quoting a text.
This perturbation does little honour to your wits.

CHORUS.

Thus do men ever
Blurt out or blazen on the cheek
Red as rock-rose [1] the thing they would not speak.
Now by the Trinity, how foolish are men's hearts !

SERVANT (*aside*).

While my masters are fooling, I'll to my folly too.

(*He slips out by the side door.*)

BROTHER (*embarking upon a religious discourse in order to allay* NOBUTOSHI'S *suspicions*).

It matters not whether faith and words be great or
small,
Whether the law be kept or broken.

CHORUS.

Neither in " Yea " nor " Nay " is the Truth found ;
There is none but may be saved at last.

BROTHER.

Not man alone ; the woods and fields
Show happy striving.

CHORUS.

The willow in his green, the peony
In crimson dressed.

(*The* BROTHER *here begins his first dance ; like that which follows, it is a " shimai," or dance without instrumental music.*)

On mornings of green spring
When at the valley's shining gate
First melt the hawthorn-warbler's frozen tears,
Or when by singing foam

---

[1] *Iwa*, " rock," also means "not speak."

Of snow-fed waters echoes the discourse
Of neighbourly frogs ;—then speaks
The voice of Buddha's heart.
Autumn, by eyes unseen,
Is heard in the wind's anger ;
And the clash of river-reeds, the clamorous descent
Of wild-geese searching
The home-field's face,
Clouds shaped like leaves of rice,—all these
To watchful eyes foretell the evening storm.
He who has seen upon a mountain-side
Stock-still beneath the moon
The young deer stand in longing for his mate,
That man may read the writing, and forget
The finger on the page.

BROTHER.

Even so the fisher's boats that ride
The harbour of the creek,

CHORUS.

Chuang Tzu √ Bring back the fish, but leave the net behind.
These things you have heard and seen ;
In the wind of the hill-top, in the valley's song,
In the film of night, in the mist of morning
Is it proclaimed that Thought alone
Was, Is and Shall be.

BROTHER.

Conceive this truth and wake !
As a cloud that hides the moon, so Matter veils

CHORUS.

The face of Thought.

BROTHER (*begins his second dance, while the* CHORUS
sings the ballad used by the " hōka " players).
Oh, a pleasant place is the City of Flowers ;

CHORUS.
No pen could write its wonders.[1]
In the east, Gion and the Temple of Clear Waters
Where torrents tumble with a noise of many wings ;
In the storm-wind flutter, flutter
The blossoms of the Earth-lord's tree.[2]
In the west, the Temple of the Wheel of Law,
The Shrine of Saga (Turn, if thou wilt,
Wheel of the Water Mill !),
Where river-waves dance on the weir
And river-willows by the waves are chafed ;
Oxen of the City by the wheels are chafed ;
And the tea-mortar by the pestle is chafed.
Why, and I'd forgot ! In the *hōka's* hands
The *kokiriko*[3] is chafed.
Now long may our Lord rule
Age notched on age, like the notches
Of these gnarled sticks !

MAKINO and BROTHER.
Enough ! Why longer hide our plot ?
(*They draw their swords and rush upon* NOBUTOSHI,
*who places his hat upon the ground and slips
out at . the side-door. The hat henceforward
symbolically represents* NOBUTOSHI, *an actual
representation of slaughter being thus avoided.*)

CHORUS.
Then the brothers drew their swords and rushed upon
him,
The foe of their desire.

(MAKINO *gets behind the hat, to signify that* NOBU-
TOSHI *is surrounded.*)
They have scaled the summit of their hate,
The rancour of many months and years.
The way is open to the bourne of their intent.
(*They strike.*)

[1] Some actors, says Ōwada, here write in the air with their fan ;
but such detailed miming is vulgar.
[2] An allusion to the cherry-trees at the Kiyomizu-dera.
[3] Bamboo-strips rubbed together to produce a squeaking sound.

They have laid their enemy low.
So when the hour was come
Did these two brothers
By sudden resolution
Destroy their father's foe.
For valour and piety are their names remembered
Even in this aftertime.

Note on Hagoromo. Stith Thompson

The story of the mortal who stole an angel's cloak and so prevented her return to heaven is very widely spread. It exists, with variations and complications, in India, China, Japan, the Liu Chiu Islands and Sweden. The story of Hasan in the *Arabian Nights* is an elaboration of the same theme. ✳

The Nō play is said to have been written by Seami, but a version of it existed long before. The last half consists merely of chants sung to the dancing. Some of these (e.g. the words to the Suruga Dance) have no relevance to the play, which is chiefly a framework or excuse for the dances. It is thus a Nō of the primitive type, and perhaps belongs, at any rate in its conception, to an earlier period than such unified dramas as *Atsumori* or *Kagekiyo*. The words of the dances in *Maiguruma* are just as irrelevant to the play as those of the Suruga Dance in *Hagoromo*, but there the plot explains and even demands their intrusion.

The libretto of the second part lends itself very ill to translation, but I have thought it best to give the play in full.

HAGOROMO

By Seami

PERSONS

HAKURYŌ (a Fisherman).   ANOTHER FISHERMAN
ANGEL.   CHORUS.

FISHERMAN.

Loud the rowers' cry
Who through the storm-swept paths of Mio. Bay
Ride to the rising sea.

HAKURYŌ.

I am Hakuryō, a fisherman whose home is by the
pine-woods of Mio.

BOTH.

" On a thousand leagues of lovely hill clouds sud-
  denly close ;
But by one tower the bright moon shines in a clear
  sky." [1]
A pleasant season, truly : on the pine-wood shore
The countenance of Spring ;
Early mist close-clasped to the swell of the sea ;
In the plains of the sky a dim, loitering moon.
Sweet sight, to gaze enticing
Eyes even of us earth-cumbered
Low souls, least for attaining
Of high beauty nurtured.
Oh unforgettable ! By mountain paths

[1] A Chinese couplet quoted from the *Shih Jēn Yü Hsieh* (" Jade-
dust of the Poets "), a Sung Dynasty work on poetry which was popular
in Japan.

Down to the sea of Kiyomi I come
And on far woodlands look,
Pine-woods of Mio, thither
Come, thither guide we our course.

Fishers, why put you back your boats to shore,
No fishing done ?
Thought you them rising waves, those billowy clouds
Wind-blown across sea ?
Wait, for the time is Spring and in the trees
The early wind his everlasting song
Sings low ; and in the bay
Silent in morning calm the little ships,
Ships of a thousand fishers, ride the sea.

(*The second* FISHERMAN *retires to a position near
the leader of the* CHORUS *and takes no further
part in the action.*)

HAKURYŌ.

Now I have landed at the pine-wood of Mio and
am viewing the beauty of the shore. Suddenly there is
music in the sky, a rain of flowers, unearthly fragrance
wafted on all sides. These are no common things ; nor
is this beautiful cloak that hangs upon the pine-tree.
I come near to it. It is marvellous in form and fragrance.
This surely is no common dress. I will take it back
with me and show it to the people of my home. It
shall be a treasure in my house.

(*He walks four steps towards the* Waki's *pillar
carrying the feather robe.*)

ANGEL (*entering through the curtain at the end of the
gallery*).

Stop ! That cloak is mine. Where are you going
with it ?

HAKURYŌ.

This is a cloak I found here. I am taking it home.

ANGEL.

It is an angel's robe of feathers, a cloak no mortal man may wear. Put it back where you found it.

HAKURYŌ.

How ? Is the owner of this cloak an angel of the sky ? Why, then, I will put it in safe keeping. It shall be a treasure in the land, a marvel to men unborn.[1] I will not give back your cloak.

ANGEL.

Oh pitiful ! How shall I cloakless tread
The wing-ways of the air, how climb
The sky, my home ?
Oh, give it back, in charity give it back.

HAKURYŌ.

No charity is in me, and your moan
Makes my heart resolute.
Look, I take your robe, hide it, and will not give
      it back.

(*Describing his own actions. Then he walks away.*)

ANGEL.

Like a bird without wings,
I would rise, but robeless

HAKURYŌ.

To the low earth you sink, an angel dwelling
In the dingy world.

ANGEL.

This way, that way.
Despair only.

HAKURYŌ.

But when she saw he was resolved to keep it . . .

ANGEL.

Strength failing.

[1] *Masse* here means, I think, "future generations," not "this degraded age."

HAKURYŌ.

Help none . . .

CHORUS.

Then on her coronet,
Jewelled as with the dew of tears,
The bright flowers drooped and faded.[1]
O piteous to see before the eyes,
Fivefold the signs of sickness
Corrupt an angel's form.

ANGEL.

I look into the plains of heaven,
The cloud-ways are hid in mist,
The path is lost.

CHORUS.

Oh, enviable clouds,
At your will wandering
For ever idle in the empty sky
That was my home !
Now fades and fades upon my ear
The voice of Kalavink,[2]
Daily accustomed song.
And you, oh you I envy,
Wild-geese clamorous
Down the sky-paths returning ;
And you, O seaward circling, shoreward sweeping
Swift seagulls of the bay :
Even the wind, because in heaven it blows,
The wind of Spring I envy.

HAKURYŌ.

Listen. Now that I have seen you in your sorrow,
I yield and would give you back your mantle.

ANGEL.

Oh, I am happy ! Give it me then !

---

[1] When an angel is about to die, the flowers of his crown wither,
his feather robe is stained with dust, sweat pours from under the
arm-pits, the eyelids tremble, he is tired of his place in heaven.

[2] The sacred bird of heaven.

HAKURYŌ.

Wait.   I have heard tell of the dances that are danced in heaven.   Dance for me now, and I will give back your robe.

ANGEL.

I am happy, happy.   Now I shall have wings and
      mount the sky again.
And for thanksgiving I bequeath
A dance of remembrance to the world,
Fit for the princes of men :
The dance-tune that makes to turn
The towers of the moon,
I will dance it here and as an heirloom leave it
To the sorrowful men of the world.
Give back my mantle, I cannot dance without it.
Say what you will, I must first have back the robe.

HAKURYŌ.

Not yet, for if I give back your robe, not a step would you dance, but fly with it straight to the sky.

ANGEL.

No, no.   Doubt is for mortals ;
In heaven is no deceit.

HAKURYŌ.

I am ashamed.   Look, I give back the robe.

(*He gives it to her and she takes it in both hands.*)

ANGEL.

The heavenly lady puts on her garment,
She dances the dance of the Rainbow Skirt, of the
      Robe of Feathers.

HAKURYŌ.

The sky-robe flutters ; it yields to the wind.

ANGEL.

Sleeve like a flower wet with rain . . .

HAKURYŌ.

The first dance is over.

ANGEL.

Shall I dance ?

CHORUS.

The dance of Suruga, with music of the East ?
Thus was it first danced.

(*The* ANGEL *dances, while the* CHORUS *sings the words
of the dance, an ancient Shintō chant.*)

" Why name we
Wide-stretched and everlasting
The sky of heaven ?
Two gods [1] there came of old
And built, upon ten sides shut in,
A measured world for men ;
But without limit arched they
The sky above, and named it
Wide-stretched and everlasting."

ANGEL.

Thus is the Moon-God's palace :
Its walls are fashioned
With an axe of jade.

CHORUS.

In white dress, black dress,
Thrice ten angels
In two ranks divided,
Thrice five for the waning,
Thrice five for nights of the waxing moon,
One heavenly lady on each night of the moon
Does service and fulfils
Her ritual task assigned.

ANGEL.

I too am of their number,
A moon-lady of heaven.

[1] Izanagi and Izanami.

CHORUS.

" Mine is the fruit of the moon-tree,[1] yet came I to
    the East incarnate,[2]
Dwelt with the people of Earth, and gave them
A gift of music, song-dance of Suruga.

Now upon earth trail the long mists of Spring ;
Who knows but in the valleys of the moon
The heavenly moon-tree puts her blossom on ?
The blossoms of her crown win back their glory :
It is the sign of Spring.
Not heaven is here, but beauty of the wind and sky.
Blow, blow, you wind, and build
Cloud-walls across the sky, lest the vision leave us
Of a maid divine !
This tint of springtime in the woods,
This colour on the headland,
Snow on the mountain,[3]
Moonlight on the clear shore,—
Which fairest ? Nay, each peerless
At the dawn of a Spring day.
Waves lapping, wind in the pine-trees whispering
Along the quiet shore. Say you, what cause
Has Heaven to be estranged
From us Earth-men ; are we not children of the Gods,
Within, without the jewelled temple wall,[4]
Born where no cloud dares dim the waiting moon,
Land of Sunrise ? "

ANGEL.

May our Lord's life
Last long as a great rock rubbed
Only by the rare trailing
Of an angel's feather-skirt.[5]

---

[1] The "Katsura" tree, a kind of laurel supposed to grow in the moon.
[2] Lit. "dividing my body," an expression used of Buddhist
divinities that detach a portion of their godhead and incarnate it
in some visible form.
[3] Fuji.   [4] The inner and outer temples at Ise.
[5] Quoting an ancient prayer for the Mikado.

Oh, marvellous music !
The Eastern song joined
To many instruments ;
Harp, zither, pan-pipes, flute,
Belly their notes beyond the lonely clouds.
The sunset stained with crimson light
From Mount Sumeru's side ; [1] *Meru*
For green, the islands floating on the sea ;
For whiteness whirled
A snow of blossom blasted
By the wild winds, a white cloud
Of sleeves waving.

(*Concluding the dance, she folds her hands and prays.*)

NAMU KIMYŌ GWATTEN-SHI.

To thee, O Monarch of the Moon,
Be glory and praise,
Thou son of Seishi Omnipotent ! [2]

CHORUS.

This is a dance of the East.

(*She dances three of the five parts of the dance called
" yo no Mai," the Prelude Dance.*)

ANGEL.

I am robed in sky, in the empty blue of heaven.

CHORUS.

Now she is robed in a garment of mist, of Spring
mist.

ANGEL.

Wonderful in perfume and colour, an angel's skirt,—
left, right, left, left, right.

(*Springing from side to side.*)

[1] Sumeru is the great mountain at the centre of the universe. Its
west side is of rubies, its south side of green stones, its east side of
white stones, etc.
[2] Called in Sanskrit Mahāsthāma-prāpta, third person of the Trinity √
sitting on Amida's right hand. The Moon-God is an emanation of
this deity.

The skirt swishes, the flowers nod, the feathery
  sleeves trail out and return, the dancing-sleeves.

(*She dances " Ha no Mai " the Broken Dance.*)

CHORUS.
  She has danced many dances,
  But not yet are they numbered,
  The dances of the East.
  And now she, whose beauty is as the young moon,
  Shines on us in the sky of midnight,
  The fifteenth night,
  With the beam of perfect fulfilment,
  The splendour of Truth.
  The vows [1] are fulfilled, and the land we live in
  Rich with the Seven Treasures
  By this dance rained down on us,
  The gift of Heaven.
  But, as the hours pass by,
  Sky-cloak of feathers fluttering, fluttering,
  Over the pine-woods of Mio,
  Past the Floating Islands, through the feet of the
      clouds she flies,
  Over the mountain of Ashitaka, the high peak of
      Fuji,
  Very faint her form,
  Mingled with the mists of heaven ;
  Now lost to sight.

[1] Of Buddha.

CHAPTER VI

TANIKŌ

IKENIYE

HATSUYUKI

HAKU RAKUTEN

NOTE ON TANIKŌ AND IKENIYE.

BOTH of these plays deal with the ruthless exactions of religion; in each the first part lends itself better to translation than the second. *Tanikō* is still played; but *Ikeniye*, though printed by both Ōwada and Haga, has probably not been staged for many centuries.

The pilgrims of *Tanikō* are *Yamabushi*, "mountaineers," to whom reference has been made on page 59. They called themselves *Shugenja*, "portentworkers," and claimed to be the knight-errants of Buddhism. But their conduct seems to have differed little from that of the *Sōhei* (armed monks) who poured down in hordes from Mount Hiyei to terrorize the inhabitants of the surrounding country. Some one in the *Genji Monogatari* is said to have "collected a crowd of evil-looking Yamabushi, desperate, stick-at-nothing fellows."

Ikeniye, the title of the second play, means " Pool Sacrifice," but also " Living Sacrifice," i.e. human sacrifice.

TANIKŌ

(The Valley-Hurling)

Part I

By Zenchiku

PERSONS

A Teacher.	A Young Boy.
The Boy's Mother.	Leader of the Pilgrims.
Pilgrims.	Chorus.

Teacher.

I am a teacher. I keep a school at one of the temples in the City. I have a pupil whose father is dead ; he has only his mother to look after him. Now I will go and say good-bye to them, for I am soon starting on a journey to the mountains. (*He knocks at the door of the house.*) May I come in ?

Boy.

Who is it ? Why, it is the Master who has come out to see us !

Teacher.

Why is it so long since you came to my classes at the temple ?

Boy.

I have not been able to come because my mother has been ill.

Teacher.

I had no idea of that. Please tell her at once that I am here.

Boy (*calling into the house*).

Mother, the Master is here.

MOTHER.

Ask him to come in.

BOY.

Please come in here.

TEACHER.

It is a long time since I was here. Your son says you have been ill. Are you better now ?

MOTHER.

Do not worry about my illness. It is of no consequence.

TEACHER.

I am glad to hear it. I have come to say good-bye, for I am soon starting on a ritual mountain-climbing.

MOTHER.

A mountain-climbing ? Yes, indeed ; I have heard that it is a dangerous ritual. Shall you take my child with you ?

TEACHER.

It is not a journey that a young child could make.

MOTHER.

Well,—I hope you will come back safely.

TEACHER.

I must go now.

BOY.

I have something to say.

TEACHER.

What is it ?

BOY.

I will go with you to the mountains.

TEACHER.

No, no. As I said to your mother, we are going on a difficult and dangerous excursion. You could not possibly come with us. Besides, how could you leave your mother when she is not well ? Stay here. It is in every way impossible that you should go with us.

BOY.

Because my mother is ill I will go with you to pray for her.

TEACHER.

I must speak to your mother again. (*He goes back into the inner room.*) I have come back,—your son says he is going to come with us. I told him he could not leave you when you were ill and that it would be a difficult and dangerous road. I said it was quite impossible for him to come. But he says he must come to pray for your health. What is to be done ?

MOTHER.

I have listened to your words. I do not doubt what the boy says,—that he would gladly go with you to the mountains ; (*to the* BOY) but since the day your father left us I have had none but you at my side. I have not had you out of mind or sight for as long a time as it takes a dewdrop to dry ! Give back the measure of my love. Let your love keep you with me.

BOY.

This is all as you say. . . . Yet nothing shall move me from my purpose. I must climb this difficult path and pray for your health in this life.

CHORUS.

They saw no plea could move him.
Then master and mother with one voice :
" Alas for such deep piety,
Deep as our heavy sighs."

The mother said,
" I have no strength left ;
If indeed it must be,
Go with the Master.
But swiftly, swiftly
Return from danger."

BOY.

Checking his heart which longed for swift return
At dawn towards the hills he dragged his feet.[1]

. . . . .

TEACHER.

We have climbed so fast that we have already
reached the first hut.   We will stay here a little while.

LEADER.

We obey.

BOY.

I have something to say.

TEACHER.

What is it ?

BOY.

I do not feel well.

TEACHER.

Stay !   Such things may not be said by those who
travel on errands like ours.   Perhaps you are tired
because you are not used to climbing.   Lie there and
rest.

LEADER.

They are saying that the young boy is ill with
climbing.   I must ask the Master about it.

PILGRIMS.

Do so.

---

[1] Here follows a long lyric passage describing their journey and
ascent.   The frequent occurrence of place-names and plays of word
on such names makes it impossible to translate.

LEADER.

I hear that this young boy is ill with climbing. What is the matter with him ? Are you anxious about him ?

TEACHER.

He is not feeling well, but there is nothing wrong with him. He is only tired with climbing.

LEADER.

So you are not troubled about him ?

(*A pause.*)

PILGRIM.

Listen, you pilgrims. Just now the Master said this boy was only tired with climbing. But now he is looking very strange. Ought we not to follow our Great Custom and hurl him into the valley ?

LEADER.

We ought to indeed. I must tell the Master. Sir, when I enquired before about the child you told me he was only tired with climbing ; but now he is looking very strange.

Though I say it with dread, there has been from ancient times a Great Custom that those who fail should be cast down. All the pilgrims are asking that he should be thrown into the valley.

TEACHER.

What, you would hurl this child into the valley ?

LEADER.

We would.

TEACHER.

It is a Mighty Custom. I cannot gainsay it. But I have great pity in my heart for that creature. I will tell him tenderly of this Great Custom.

LEADER.

Pray do so.

TEACHER.

Listen carefully to me. It has been the law from ancient times that if any pilgrim falls sick on such journeys as these he should be hurled into the valley, —done suddenly to death. If I could take your place, how gladly I would die. But now I cannot help you.

BOY.

I understand. I knew well that if I came on this journey I might lose my life.
Only at the thought
Of my dear mother,
How her tree of sorrow
For me must blossom
With flower of weeping,—
I am heavy-hearted.

CHORUS.

Then the pilgrims sighing
For the sad ways of the world
And the bitter ordinances of it,
Make ready for the hurling.
Foot to foot
They stood together
Heaving blindly,
None guiltier than his neighbour.
And clods of earth after
And flat stones they flung.[1]

[1] I have only summarized the last chorus. When the pilgrims reach the summit, they pray to their founder, En no Gyōja, and to the God Fudō that the boy may be restored to life. In answer to their prayers a Spirit appears carrying the boy in her arms. She lays him at the Priest's feet and vanishes again, treading the Invisible Pathway that En no Gyōja trod when he crossed from Mount Katsuragi to the Great Peak without descending into the valley.

IKENIYE
(THE POOL-SACRIFICE)

Part I

By SEAMI [1]

PERSONS

THE TRAVELLER.	THE INNKEEPER.
HIS WIFE.	THE PRIEST.
HIS DAUGHTER.	THE ACOLYTE.

CHORUS.

TRAVELLER.

I am a man who lives in the Capital. Maybe because of some great wrong I did in a former life . . . I have fallen into trouble and cannot go on living here.

I have a friend in the East country. Perhaps he would help me. I will take my wife and child and go at once to the ends of the East.

(*He travels to the East, singing as he goes a song about the places through which he passes.*)

We are come to the Inn. (*Knocks at the door.*) We are travellers. Pray give us shelter.

INNKEEPER.

Lodging, do you say? Come in with me. This way. Tell me, where have you come from?

TRAVELLER.

I come from the Capital, and I am going down to the East to visit my friend.

[1] The play is given in a list of Seami's works composed on the authority of his great-grandson, Kwanze Nagatoshi, in 1524. Ōwada gives it as anonymous.

INNKEEPER.

Listen. I am sorry. There is something I must tell you privately. Whoever passes this night at the Inn must go to-morrow to the drawing of lots at the sacrifice. I am sorry for it, but you would do best to leave the Inn before dawn. Tell no one what I have said, and mind you start early.

TRAVELLER.

If we may sleep here now we will gladly start at dawn.

(*They lie down and sleep in the open courtyard. After a while they rise and start on their journey.*)

Enter the PRIEST.

PRIEST.

Hey! where are you ?

Enter the ACOLYTE.

ACOLYTE.

Here I am.

PRIEST.

I hear that three travellers stayed at the Inn last night and have left before dawn. Go after them and stop them.

ACOLYTE.

I listen and obey. Hey, you travellers, go no further !

TRAVELLER.

Is it at us you are shouting ?

ACOLYTE.

Yes, indeed it is at you.

TRAVELLER.

And why should we stop ? Tell me the reason

ACOLYTE.

He is right. It is not to be wondered at that he should ask the reason. (*To the* TRAVELLER.) Listen. Each year at this place there is a sacrifice at the Pool. To-day is the festival of this holy rite, and we ask you to join in it.

TRAVELLER.

I understand you. But it is for those that live here, those that were born children of this Deity, to attend his worship. Must a wanderer go with you because he chances to lodge here for a night ?

(*He turns to go.*)

ACOLYTE.

No, no ! For all you say, this will not do.

PRIEST.

Ṣtay ! Sir, we do not wonder that you should think this strange. But listen to me. From ancient times till now no traveller has ever lodged this night of the year at the Inn of Yoshiwara without attending the sacrifice at the Pool. If you are in a hurry, come quickly to the sacrifice, and then with a blessing set out again on your journey.

TRAVELLER.

I understand you. But, as I have said, for such rites as these you should take men born in the place. . . . No, I still do not understand. Why should a fleeting traveller be summoned to this Pool-Sacrifice ?

PRIEST.

It is a Great Custom.

TRAVELLER.

That may be. I do not question that that is **your** rule. But I beg you, consider my case and excuse **me**.

PRIEST.

Would you be the first to break a Great Custom that has been observed since ancient times ?

TRAVELLER.

No, that is not what I meant. But if we are to discuss this matter, I must be plain with you. . . . I am a man of the Capital. Perhaps because of some ill deed done in a former life I have suffered many troubles. At last I could no longer build the pathway of my life, so I took my wife and child and set out to seek my friend who lives in the East. Pray let me go on my way.

PRIEST.

Indeed, indeed you have cause for distress. But from ancient times till now
Parents have been taken
And countless beyond all knowing
Wives and husbands parted.
Call this, if you will, the retribution of a former life. But now come with us quickly to the shores of the Holy Pool.

(*Describing his own actions.*)

So saying, the Priest and acolytes went forward.

WIFE and DAUGHTER.

And the wife and child, crying " Oh what shall we do ? " clutched at the father's sleeve.

TRAVELLER.

But the father could find no words to speak. He stood baffled, helpless. . . .

PRIEST.

They must not loiter. Divide them and drive them on !

ACOLYTE.

So he drove them before him and they walked like . . .

TRAVELLER.

If true comparison were made . . .

CHORUS.

Like guilty souls of the Dead
Driven to Judgment
By fiends reproachful ;
Whose hearts unknowing
Like dew in day-time
To nothing dwindle.
Like sheep to shambles
They walk weeping,
No step without a tear
Till to the Pool they come.

PRIEST.

Now we are come to the Pool, and by its edge are
ranged the Priest, the acolytes, the virgins and dancing-
boys.

CHORUS.

There is one doom-lot ;
Yet those that are thinking
" Will it be mine ? "
They are a hundred,
And many times a hundred.

PRIEST.

Embracing, clasping hands . . .

CHORUS.

Pale-faced

PRIEST.

Sinking at heart

CHORUS.

" On whom will it fall ? "
Not knowing, thick as snow,
White snow of winter fall their prayers
To their clan-gods, " Protect us " . . .
Palm pressed to palm.

PRIEST.

At last the Priest mounted the daïs, raised the lid of
the box and counted the lots to see that there was one
for each to take.

CHORUS.

Then all the people came forward
To draw their lots.
And each when he unfolded his lot
And found it was not the First,
How glad he was !
But the traveller's daughter,
Knowing her fate,
Fell weeping to the earth.

PRIEST.

Are there not three travellers ? They have only
drawn two lots. The First Lot is still undrawn. Tell
them that one of them must draw it.

ACOLYTE.

I listen and obey. Ho, you travellers, it is to you
I am speaking. There are three of you, and you have
only drawn two lots. The Priest says one of you must
draw the First Lot.

TRAVELLER.

We have all drawn.

ACOLYTE.

No, I am sure the young girl has not drawn her lot.
Look, here it is. Yes, and it is the Doom-lot !

WIFE.

The First Lot ! How terrible !

Hoping to rear you to womanhood, we wandered blindly from the City and came down to the unknown country of the East. For your sake we set our hearts on this sad journey. If you are taken, what will become of us ? How hideous !

DAUGHTER.

Do not sob so ! If you or my father had drawn this lot, what should I have done ? But now it has fallen to me, and it is hard for you to let me go.

TRAVELLER.

What brave words ! " If you or my father had drawn this lot . . ." There is great piety in that saying. (*To his* WIFE.) Come, do not sob so before all these people. We are both parents and must have like feelings. But from the time I set out to this holy lottery something told me that of the three of us one would be taken. Look ! I am not crying.

WIFE.

I thought as you did, yet . . .
It is too much ! Can it all be real ?

TRAVELLER.

The father said " I will not show weakness," yet while
    he was speaking bravely
Because she was his dear daughter
His secret tears
Could not be checked.

WIFE.

Is this a dream or is it real ?

       (*She clings to the daughter, wailing.*)

PRIEST.

Because the time had come
The Priest and his men
Stood waiting on the shore.

CHORUS.

They decked the boat with ribands
And upon a bed of water-herbs
They laid the maiden of the Pool.

PRIEST.

The Priest pulled the ribands
And spoke the words of prayer.

[In the second part of the play the dragon of the Pool is appeased
and the girl restored to life.]

HATSUYUKI

(EARLY SNOW)

By KOMPARU ZEMBŌ MOTOYASU (1453–1532)

PERSONS

EVENING MIST, a servant girl.
A LADY, the Abbot's daughter.
TWO NOBLE LADIES.
THE SOUL OF THE BIRD HATSUYUKI (" Early Snow ").
CHORUS.

SCENE : *The Great Temple at Izumo.*

SERVANT.

I am a servant at the Nyoroku Shrine in the Great
Temple of Izumo. My name is Evening Mist. You
must know that the Lord Abbot has a daughter, a
beautiful lady and gentle as can be. And she keeps a
tame bird that was given her a year ago, and because it
was a lovely white bird she called it Hatsuyuki, Early
Snow ; and she loves it dearly.

I have not seen the bird to-day. I think I will go
to the bird-cage and have a look at it.

(She goes to the cage.)

Mercy on us, the bird is not there ! Whatever shall
I say to my lady ? But I shall have to tell her. I think
I'll tell her now. Madam, madam, your dear Snow-bird
is not here !

LADY.

What is that you say ? Early Snow is not there ?
It cannot be true.

(She goes to the cage.)

It is true. Early Snow has gone! How can that
be ? How can it be that my pretty one that was so
tame should vanish and leave no trace ?

Oh bitterness of snows
That melt and disappear !
Now do I understand
The meaning of a midnight dream
That lately broke my rest.
A harbinger it was
Of Hatsuyuki's fate.

(She bursts into tears.)

CHORUS.

Though for such tears and sighs
There be no cause,
Yet came her grief so suddenly,
Her heart's fire is ablaze ;
And all the while
Never a moment are her long sleeves dry.
They say that written letters first were traced
By feet of birds in sand
Yet Hatsuyuki leaves no testament.

(They mourn.)

CHORUS (" *kuse* " *chant, irregular verse accompanied by
dancing*).

How sad to call to mind
When first it left the breeding-cage
So fair of form
And coloured white as snow.
We called it Hatsuyuki, " Year's First Snow."
And where our mistress walked
It followed like the shadow at her side.
But now alas ! it is a bird of parting [1]
Though not in Love's dark lane.

LADY.

There's no help now. *(She weeps bitterly.)*

---

[1] " Wakare no tori," the bird which warns lovers of the approach
of day.

CHORUS.

    Still there is one way left. Stop weeping, Lady,
    And turn your heart to him who vowed to hear.
    The Lord Amida, if a prayer be said—
    Who knows but he can bring
    Even a bird's soul into Paradise
    And set it on the Lotus Pedestal ? [1]

LADY.

    Evening Mist, are you not sad that Hatsuyuki has
gone ? . . . But we must not cry any more. Let us
call together the noble ladies of this place and for
seven days sit with them praying behind barred doors.
Go now and do my bidding.

(EVENING MIST *fetches the* NOBLE LADIES *of the place.*)

TWO NOBLE LADIES (*together*).

    A solemn Mass we sing
    A dirge for the Dead ;
    At this hour of heart-cleansing
    We beat on Buddha's gong.

                (*They pray.*)

    NAMU AMIDA BUTSU
    NAMU NYORAI
        Praise to Amida Buddha,
        Praise to Mida our Saviour !

(*The prayers and gong-beating last for some time
and form the central ballet of the play.*)

CHORUS (*the bird's soul appears as a white speck in
the sky*).

    Look ! Look ! A cloud in the clear mid-sky !
    But it is not a cloud.
    With pure white wings beating the air
    The Snow-bird comes !
    Flying towards our lady
    Lovingly he hovers,
    Dances before her.

           Turn it into a Buddha.

THE BIRD'S SOUL.

Drawn by the merit of your prayers and songs

CHORUS.

Straightway he was reborn in Paradise.
By the pond of Eight Virtues he walks abroad :
With the Phœnix and Fugan his playtime passing.
He lodges in the sevenfold summit of the trees of
  Heaven.
No hurt shall harm him
For ever and ever.

Now like the tasselled doves we loose
From battlements on holy days
A little while he flutters ;
Flutters a little while and then is gone
We know not where.

HAKU RAKUTEN

By SEAMI

INTRODUCTION

THE Chinese poet Po Chü-i, whom the Japanese call
Haku Rakuten, was born in 772 A.D. and died in 847.
His works enjoyed immense contemporary popularity
in China, Korea and Japan. In the second half of the
ninth century the composition of Chinese verse became
fashionable at the Japanese Court, and native forms
of poetry were for a time threatened with extinction.

The Nō play *Haku Rakuten* deals with this literary
peril. It was written at the end of the fourteenth
century, a time when Japanese art and literature
were again becoming subject to Chinese influence.
Painting and prose ultimately succumbed, but poetry
was saved.

Historically, Haku Rakuten never came to Japan.
But the danger of his influence was real and actual,
as may be deduced from reading the works of Sugawara
no Michizane, the greatest Japanese poet of the ninth
century. Michizane's slavish imitations of Po Chü-i
show an unparalleled example of literary prostration.
The plot of the play is as follows :

Rakuten is sent by the Emperor of China to " subdue "
Japan with his art. On arriving at the coast of Bizen,
he meets with two Japanese fishermen. One of them
is in reality the god of Japanese poetry, Sumiyoshi
no Kami. In the second act his identity is revealed.
He summons other gods, and a great dancing-scene
ensues. Finally the wind from their dancing-sleeves
blows the Chinese poet's ship back to his own country.

Seami, in his plays, frequently quotes Po Chü-i's poems ; and in his lament for the death of his son, Zemparu Motomasa, who died in 1432, he refers to the death of Po Chü-i's son, A-ts'ui.

PERSONS

RAKUTEN (a Chinese poet).
AN OLD FISHERMAN, SUMIYOSHI NO KAMI, who in Act II becomes the God of Japanese Poetry.
ANOTHER FISHERMAN.
CHORUS OF FISHERMEN.

SCENE : *The coast of Bizen in Japan.*

HAKU.

I am Haku Rakuten, a courtier of the Prince of China. There is a land in the East called Nippon.[1] Now, at my master's bidding, I am sent to that land to make proof of the wisdom of its people. I must travel over the paths of the sea.

I will row my boat towards the setting sun,
        The setting sun ;
And seek the country that lies to the far side
Over the wave-paths of the Eastern Sea.
        Far my boat shall go,
        My boat shall go,—
With the light of the setting sun in the waves of its wake
And a cloud like a banner shaking the void of the sky.
Now the moon rises, and on the margin of the sea
        A mountain I discern.
I am come to the land of Nippon,
        The land of Nippon.

So swiftly have I passed over the ways of the ocean that I am come already to the shores of Nippon. I will cast anchor here a little while. I would know what manner of land this may be.

---

[1] The fact that Haku is a foreigner is conventionally emphasized by his pronunciation of this word. The fishermen, when using the same word later on, called it " Nihon."

THE TWO FISHERMEN (*together*).

Dawn over the Sea of Tsukushi,
          Place of the Unknown Fire.
Only the moonlight—nothing else left !

THE OLD FISHERMAN.

    The great waters toss and toss ;
    The grey waves soak the sky.

THE TWO FISHERMEN.

    So was it when Han Rei [1] left the land of Etsu
    And rowed in a little boat
Over the misty waves of the Five Lakes.

How pleasant the sea looks !
From the beach of Matsura
Westward we watch the hill-less dawn.
A cloud, where the moon is setting,
Floats like a boat at sea,
          A boat at sea
That would anchor near us in the dawn.
Over the sea from the far side,
From China the journey of a ship's travel
Is a single night's sailing, they say.
And lo ! the moon has vanished !

HAKU.

I have borne with the billows of a thousand miles of
sea and come at last to the land of Nippon.   Here is a
little ship anchored near me.   An old fisherman is in
it.   Can this be indeed an inhabitant of Nippon ?

---

[1] The Chinese call him Fan Li. He lived in China in the fifth
century B.C.   Having rendered important services to the country
of Yüeh (Etsu), he went off with his mistress in a skiff, knowing that
if he remained in public life his popularity was bound to decline.
The Fishermen are vaguely groping towards the idea of " a Chinaman "
and a " boat."   They are not yet consciously aware of the arrival
of Rakuten.

OLD FISHERMAN.

Aye, so it is. I am an old fisher of Nihon. And your Honour, I think, is Haku Rakuten of China.

HAKU.

How strange ! No sooner am I come to this land than they call me by my name ! How can this be ?

SECOND FISHERMAN.

Although your Honour is a man of China, your name and fame have come before you.

HAKU.

Even though my name be known, yet that you should know my face is strange surely !

THE TWO FISHERMEN.

It was said everywhere in the Land of Sunrise that your Honour, Rakuten, would come to make trial of the wisdom of Nihon. And when, as we gazed westwards, we saw a boat coming in from the open sea, the hearts of us all thought in a twinkling, "This is he."

CHORUS.

" He has come, he has come."
So we cried when the boat came in
To the shore of Matsura,
The shore of Matsura.
Sailing in from the sea
Openly before us—
A Chinese ship
And a man from China,—
How could we fail to know you,
    Haku Rakuten ?
But your halting words tire us.
Listen as we will, we cannot understand
    Your foreign talk.
Come, our fishing-time is precious.
    Let us cast our hooks,
    Let us cast our hooks !

HAKU.

Stay ! Answer me one question.[1] Bring your boat closer and tell me, Fisherman, what is your pastime now in Nippon ?

FISHERMAN.

And in the land of China, pray how do your Honours disport yourselves ?

HAKU.

In China we play at making poetry.

FISHERMAN.

And in Nihon, may it please you, we venture on the sport of making " uta." [2]

HAKU.

And what are " uta " ?

FISHERMAN.

You in China make your poems and odes out of the Scriptures of India ; and we have made our " uta " out of the poems and odes of China. Since then our poetry is a blend of three lands, we have named it Yamato, the great Blend, and all our songs " Yamato Uta." But I think you question me only to mock an old man's simplicity.

HAKU.

No, truly ; that was not my purpose. But come, I will sing a Chinese poem about the scene before us.

" Green moss donned like a cloak
Lies on the shoulders of the rocks ;
White clouds drawn like a belt
Surround the flanks of the mountains."

How does that song please you ?

[1] Haku throughout omits the honorific turns of speech which civility demands. The Fishermen speak in elaborately deferential and honorific language. The writer wishes to portray Haku as an ill-bred foreigner.

[2] " Uta," i.e. the thirty-one syllable Japanese stanza.

FISHERMAN.

It is indeed a pleasant verse. In our tongue we should say the poem thus :

> *Koke-goromo*
> *Kitaru iwao wa*
> *Samonakute,*
> *Kinu kinu yama no*
> *Obi wo suru kana !*

HAKU.

How strange that a poor fisherman should put my verse into a sweet native measure ! Who can he be ?

FISHERMAN.

A poor man and unknown. But as for the making of " uta," it is not only men that make them. " For among things that live there is none that has not the gift of song." [1]

HAKU (*taking up the other's words as if hypnotized*).

" Among things that have life,—yes, and birds and insects—"

FISHERMAN.

They have sung Yamato songs.

HAKU.

In the land of Yamato . . .

FISHERMAN.

. . . many such have been sung.

CHORUS.

" The nightingale singing on the bush,
Even the frog that dwells in the pond——"

[1] Quotation from the Preface to the *Kokinshū* (" Collection of Songs Ancient and Modern "). The fact that Haku continues the quotation shows that he is under a sort of spell and makes it clear for the first time that his interlocutor is not an ordinary mortal. From this point onwards, in fact, the Fisherman gradually becomes a God.

I know not if it be in your Honour's land,
But in Nihon they sing the stanzas of the " uta."
And so it comes that an old man
Can sing the song you have heard,
A song of great Yamato.

CHORUS (*changing the chant*).

And as for the nightingale and the poem it made,—
They say that in the royal reign
Of the Emperor Kōren
In the land of Yamato, in the temple of High Heaven
A priest was dwelling.[1]
Each year at the season of Spring
There came a nightingale
To the plum-tree at his window.
And when he listened to its song
He heard it singing a verse :
   " *Sho-yō mei-chō rai*
       Fu-sō gem-bon sei."
And when he wrote down the characters,
Behold, it was an " uta "-song
Of thirty letters and one.
And the words of the song—

FISHERMAN.

Hatsu-haru no	Of Spring's beginning
Ashita goto ni wa	At each dawn
Kitaredomo	Though I come,

CHORUS.

Awade zo kaeru	Unmet I return
Moto no sumika ni.	To my old nest.

Thus first the nightingale,
And many birds and beasts thereto,
Sing " uta," like the songs of men.
And instances are many ;

---

[1] The priest's acolyte had died. The nightingale was the boy's
soul.

Many as the myriad pebbles that lie
On the shore of the sea of Ariso.
" For among things that live
There is none that has not the gift of song."

Truly the fisherman has the ways of Yamato in his
heart.   Truly, this custom is excellent.

FISHERMAN.

If we speak of the sports of Yamato and sing its
songs, we should show too what dances we use ; for
there are many kinds.

CHORUS.

Yes, there are the dances ; but there is no one to
dance.

FISHERMAN.

Though there be no dancer, yet even I—

CHORUS.

For drums—the beating of the waves.
For flutes—the song of the sea-dragon.
For dancer—this ancient man
Despite his furrowed brow
Standing on the furrowed sea
Floating on the green waves
Shall dance the Sea Green Dance.

FISHERMAN.
And the land of Reeds and Rushes . . .

CHORUS.
Ten thousand years our land inviolate !

[*The rest of the play is a kind of* "*ballet* " ; the words are merely
a commentary on the dances.]

Act II.

FISHERMAN (*transformed into* SUMIYOSHI NO KAMI, *the God of Poetry*).

Sea that is green with the shadow of the hills in the water !

Sea Green Dance, danced to the beating of the waves.

(*He dances the Sea Green Dance.*)

> Out of the wave-lands,
> Out of the fields of the Western Sea

CHORUS.

> He rises before us,
> The God of Sumiyoshi,
> The God of Sumiyoshi !

THE GOD.

> I rise before you
> The god—

CHORUS.

The God of Sumiyoshi whose strength is such
That he will not let you subdue us, O Rakuten !
So we bid you return to your home,
Swiftly over the waves of the shore !
First the God of Sumiyoshi came.
Now other gods [1] have come—

> Of Isé and Iwa-shimizu,
> Of Kamo and Kasuga,
> Of Ka-shima and Mi-shima,
> Of Suwa and Atsu-ta.

And the goddess of the Beautiful Island,
The daughter of Shakāra
King of the Dragons of the Sea—
Skimming the face of the waves
They have danced the Sea Green Dance.

[1] They do not appear on the stage.

And the King of the Eight Dragons—
With his Symphony of Eight Musics.
As they hovered over the void of the sea,
Moved in the dance, the sleeves of their dancing-
    dress
Stirred up a wind, a magic wind
That blew on the Chinese boat
And filled its sails
And sent it back again to the land of Han.
Truly, the God is wondrous ;
The God is wondrous, and thou, our Prince,
Mayest thou rule for many, many years
    Our Land Inviolate !

CHAPTER VII

SUMMARIES

SUMMARIES

OF the plays which are founded on the *Ise Monogatari* [1] the best known are *Izutsu* and *Kakitsubata*, both by Seami. *Izutsu* is founded on the episode which runs as follows :

Once upon a time a boy and a girl, children of country people, used to meet at a well and play there together. When they grew up they became a little shame-faced towards one another, but he could think of no other woman, nor she of any other man. He would not take the wife his parents had found for him, nor she the husband that her parents had found for her.

Then he sent her a poem which said :

" Oh, the well, the well !
    I who scarce topped the well-frame
    Am grown to manhood since we met."

And she to him :

"The two strands of my hair
    That once with yours I measured,
    Have passed my shoulder ;
    Who but you should put them up ? " [2]

So they wrote, and at last their desire was fulfilled. Now after a year or more had passed the girl's parents died, and they were left without sustenance. They could not go on living together ; the man went to and fro between her house and the town of Takayasu in Kawachi, while she stayed at home.

Now when he saw that she let him go gladly and showed no grief in her face, he thought it was because her heart had changed. And one day, instead of going

---

[1] The love-adventures of Narihira (825–880 A.D.) in 125 episodes, supposed to have been written by Narihira himself.

[2] The husband puts up the bride's hair.

to Kawachi, he hid behind the hedge and watched.
Then he heard the girl singing :

" The mountain of Tatsuta that rises
Steep as a wave of the sea when the wind blows
To-night my lord will be crossing all alone ! "

And he was moved by her song, and went no more to
Takayasu in Kawachi.

In the play a wandering priest meets with a village
girl, who turns out to be the ghost of the girl in this
story.   The text is woven out of the words of the *Ise
Monogatari*.

Kakitsubata is based on the eighth episode.   Narihira
and his companions come to a place called Yatsuhashi,
where, across an iris-covered swamp, zigzags a low
footpath of planks.

Narihira bids them compose an anagram on the
work *Kakitsubata*, " iris," and some one sings :

" *Ka*ra-goromo
Ki-tsutsu nare-ni-shi
*Tsu*ma shi areba
*Ba*ru-baru ki-nuru
*Ta*bi wo shi zo omou."

The first syllables of each line make, when read con-
secutively, the word *Kakitsubata*, and the poem, which
is a riddle with many meanings, may be translated :

"My lady's love
Sat close upon me like a coat well worn ;
And surely now
Her thoughts go after me down this long road ! "

" When he had done singing, they all wept over their
dried-rice till it grew soppy."

In the play, a priest comes to this place and learns
its story from a village-girl, who turns out to be the
" soul of the iris-flower."   At the end she disappears
into the Western Paradise.   " Even the souls of flowers
can attain to Buddhahood."

HANAKATAMI

(The Flower Basket)

By Kwanami; revised by Seami

Before he came to the throne, the Emperor Keitai [1]
loved the Lady Teruhi. On his accession he sent her
a letter of farewell and a basket of flowers. In the
play the messenger meets her on the road to her home;
she reads the letter, which in elaborately ceremonial
language announces the Emperor's accession and departure to the Capital.

Teruhi.
 The Spring of our love is passed ! Like a moon left
  lonely
 In the sky of dawn, back to the hills I go,
 To the home where once we dwelt.

  (*She slips quietly from the stage, carrying the basket
   and letter. In the next scene the* Emperor [2] *is
   carried on to the stage in a litter borne by two
   attendants. It is the coronation procession.
   Suddenly* Teruhi, *who has left her home dis-
   traught, wanders on to the stage followed by her
   maid, who carries the flower-basket and letter.*)

Teruhi (*speaking wildly*).
 Ho, you travellers ! Show me the road to the Capital !
  I am mad, you say ?
 Mad I may be ; but love bids me ask. O heartless
  ones ! why will they not answer me ?

[1] Reigned 507–531.
[2] In this play as in all the part of Emperor is played by a young
boy or " child-actor."

MAID.

Madam, from these creatures we shall get no answer. Yet there is a sign that will guide our steps to the City. Look, yonder the wild-geese are passing!

TERUHI.

Oh well-remembered! For southward ever
The wild-geese pass
Through the empty autumn sky; and southward lies
The city of my lord.

Then follows the "song of travel," during which Teruhi and her companion are supposed to be journeying from their home in Echizen to the Capital in Yamato. They halt at last on the *hashigakari*, announcing that they have "arrived at the City." Just as a courtier (who together with the boy-Emperor and the two litter-bearers represents the whole coronation procession) is calling: "Clear the way, clear the way! The Imperial procession is approaching," Teruhi's maid advances on to the stage and crosses the path of the procession. The courtier pushes her roughly back, and in doing so knocks the flower-basket to the ground.

MAID.

Oh, look what he has done! O madam, he has dashed your basket to the ground, the Prince's flower-basket!

TERUHI.

What! My lord's basket? He has dashed it to the ground? Oh hateful deed!

COURTIER.

Come, mad-woman! Why all this fuss about a basket? You call it your lord's basket; what lord can you mean?

TERUHI.

What lord should I mean but the lord of this land of Sunrise? Is there another?

Then he :
" This flower is her soul."
And still he lingered, tenderly
Touched with his hand the petals' hem.
Till in the flower's dress and on his own
The same dew fell.
But the flower, he thought,
Was angry with him, for often when he touched it
It drooped and turned aside.

Such is the story upon which the play is founded.
The poem is one by Bishop Henjō (816–890) :

O lady-flowers
That preen yourselves upon the autumn hill,
Even you that make so brave a show,
Last but " one while."

Hito toki, " one while," is the refrain of the play.
It was for " one while " that they lived together in
the Capital ; it is for " one while " that men are young,
that flowers blossom, that love lasts. In the first part
of the play an aged man hovering round a clump of
lady-flowers begs the priest not to pluck them. In
the second part this aged man turns into the soul of
the lover. The soul of the girl also appears, and both
are saved by the priest's prayers from that limbo (half
death, half life) where all must linger who die in the
coils of *shūshin*, " heart-attachment."

MATSUKAZE

By KWANAMI ; revised by SEAMI

LORD YUKIHIRA, brother of Narihira, was banished to
the lonely shore of Suma. While he lived there he
amused himself by helping two fisher-girls to carry
salt water from the sea to the salt-kilns on the shore.
Their names were Matsukaze and Murasame.

At this time he wrote two famous poems ; the first,
while he was crossing the mountains on his way to
Suma :

> " Through the traveller's dress
> The autumn wind blows with sudden chill.
> It is the shore-wind of Suma
> Blowing through the pass."

When he had lived a little while at Suma, he sent to
the Capital a poem which said :

> " If any should ask news,
> Tell him that upon the shore of Suma
> I drag the water-pails."

Long afterwards Prince Genji was banished to the
same place. The chapter of the *Genji Monogatari*
called " Suma " says :

Although the sea was some way off, yet when the
melancholy autumn wind came " blowing through the
pass " (the very wind of Yukihira's poem), the beating
of the waves on the shore seemed near indeed.

It is round these two poems and the prose passage
quoted above that the play is written.

A wandering priest comes to the shore of Suma and

sees a strange pine-tree standing alone. A " person
of the place " (in an interlude not printed in the usual
texts) tells him that the tree was planted in memory
of two fisher-girls, Matsukaze and Murasame, and asks
him to pray for them. While the priest prays it grows
late and he announces that he intends to ask for shelter
" in that salt-kiln." He goes to the " waki's pillar "
and waits there as if waiting for the master of the kiln
to return.

Meanwhile Matsukaze and Murasame come on to the
stage and perform the " water-carrying " dance which
culminates in the famous passage known as " The moon
in the water-pails."

CHORUS (*speaking for* MURASAME).
    There is a moon in my pail !

MATSUKAZE.
    Why, into my pail too a moon has crept !

> (*Looking up at the sky.*)
    One moon above . . .

CHORUS.
    Two imaged moons below,
    So through the night each carries
    A moon on her water-truck,
    Drowned at the bucket's brim.
    Forgotten, in toil on this salt sea-road,
    The sadness of this world where our souls cling !

Their work is over and they approach their hut,
i.e., the " *waki's* pillar," where the priest is sitting
waiting. After refusing for a long while to admit him
" because their hovel is too mean to receive him,"
they give him shelter, and after the usual questioning,
reveal their identities.

In the final ballet Matsukaze dresses in the " court-
hat and hunting cloak given her by Lord Yukihira "

and dances, among other dances, the " Broken Dance,"
which also figures in Hagoromo.

The " motif " of this part of the play is another
famous poem by Yukihira, that by which he is represented in the *Hyakuninisshu* or " Hundred Poems by
a Hundred Poets " ·

" When I am gone away,
　If I hear that like the pine-tree on Mount Inaba
　You are waiting for me,
　Even then I will come back to you."

There is a play of words between *matsu*, " wait," and
matsu, " pine-tree " ; Inaba, the name of a mountain
and *inaba*, " if I go away."

The play ends with the release of the girls' souls
from the *shūshin*, " heart-attachment," which holds them
to the earth.

See p.58

SHUNKWAN

By SEAMI

THE priest Shunkwan, together with Naritsune and Yasuyori, had plotted the overthrow of the Tairas. They were arrested and banished to Devil's Island on the shore of Satsuma.

Naritsune and Yasuyori were worshippers of the Gods of Kumano. They brought this worship with them to the place of their exile, constructing on the island an imitation of the road from Kyōto to Kumano with its ninety-nine roadside shrines. This "holy way" they decked with *nusa*, "paper-festoons," and carried out, as best they might, the Shintō ceremonies of the three shrines of Kumano.

When the play begins the two exiles are carrying out these rites. Having no albs [1] to wear, they put on the tattered hemp-smocks which they wore on their journey; having no rice to offer, they pour out a libation of sand.

Shunkwan, who had been abbot of the Zen [2] temple Hosshōji, holds aloof from these ceremonies. But when the worshippers return he comes to meet them carrying a bucket of water, which he tells them is the wine for their final libation. They look into the bucket and cry in disgust : *Ya ! Kore wa mizu nari !* "Why, it is water ! "

In a long lyrical dialogue which follows, Shunkwan, with the aid of many classical allusions, justifies the identification of chrysanthemum-water and wine.

---

[1] Ceremonial white vestments, *hakuye.*
[2] For "Zen" see Introduction, p. 58.

CHORUS (*speaking for* SHUNKWAN).

> Oh, endless days of banishment !
> How long shall I languish in this place,
> Where the time while a mountain dewdrop dries
> Seems longer than a thousand years ?
> A spring has gone ; a summer grown to age ;
> An autumn closed ; a winter come again,
> Marked only by the changing forms
> Of flowers and trees.
> Oh, longed-for time of old !
> Oh, recollection sweet whithersoever
> The mind travels ; City streets and cloisters now
> Seem Edens [1] garlanded
> With every flower of Spring.

Suddenly a boat appears carrying a stranger to the shore.
This is represented on the stage by an attendant carrying
the conventionalized Nō play " boat " on to the *hashigakari*. The envoy, whose departure from the Capital
forms the opening scene of the play—I have omitted
it in my summary—has been standing by the " Waki's
pillar." He now steps into the boat and announces
that a following wind is carrying him swiftly over the
sea. He leaves the boat, carrying a Proclamation in
his hand.

ENVOY.

> I bring an Act of Amnesty from the City.
> Here, read if for yourselves.

SHUNKWAN (*snatching the scroll*).

> Look, Yasuyori ! Look ! At last !

YASUYORI (*reading the scroll*).

> What is this ? What is this ?
> " Because of the pregnancy of Her Majesty the
> Empress, an amnesty is proclaimed throughout the
> land. All exiles are recalled from banishment, and,

---

[1] Lit. Kikenjō, one of the Buddhist paradises.

of those exiled on Devil's Island, to these two, Naritsune,
Lieutenant of Tamba and Yasuyori of the Taira clan,
free pardon is granted."

SHUNKWAN.

Why, you have forgotten to read Shunkwan's name !

YASUYORI.

Your name, alas, is not there.   Read the scroll.

SHUNKWAN (*scanning the scroll*).

This must be some scribe's mistake.

ENVOY.

No ;   they told me at the Capital to bring back
Yasuyori and Naritsune, but to leave Shunkwan upon
the island.

SHUNKWAN.

How can that be ?
One crime, one banishment ;
Yet I alone, when pardon
Like a mighty net is spread
To catch the drowning multitude, slip back
Into the vengeful deep !
When three dwelt here together,
How terrible the loneliness of these wild rocks !
Now one is left, to wither
Like a flower dropped on the shore.
Like a broken sea-weed branch
That no wave carries home.

Is not this island named
The Realm of Fiends, where I,
Damned but not dead walk the Black Road of
    Death ?
Yet shall the foulest fiend of Hell
Now weep for me whose wrong
Must needs move heaven and earth,

Wake angel's pity, rend
The hearts of men, turn even the hungry cries
Of the wild beasts and birds that haunt these
    rocks
To tender lamentation.

> (*He buries his face in his hands; then after a while
> begins reading the scroll again.*)

CHORUS.

He took the scroll that he had read before.
He opened it and looked.
His eyes, like a shuttle, travelled
To and fro, to and fro.
Yet, though he looked and looked,
No other names he saw
But Yasuyori's name and Naritsune's name.
Then thinking "There is a codicil, perhaps,"
Again he opens the scroll and looks.
Nowhere is the word Sōzu,[1] nowhere the word
    Shunkwan.

> (*The* ENVOY *then calls upon* NARITSUNE *and* YASU-
> YORI *to board the boat.* SHUNKWAN *clutches at*
> YASUYORI'S *sleeve and tries to follow him on
> board. The* ENVOY *pushes him back, calling to
> him to keep clear of the boat.*)

SHUNKWAN.

Wretch, have you not heard the saying :
"Be law, but not her servants, pitiless."
Bring me at least to the mainland. Have so much
    charity !

ENVOY.

But the sailor [2] knew no pity ;
He took his oar and struck. . . .

---

[1] Priest.   [2] Acted by a *kyōgen* or farce-character.

SHUNKWAN (*retreating a step*).
Nevertheless, leave me my life. . . .
Then he stood back and caught in both his hands
The anchor-rope and dragged . . .

ENVOY.
But the sailor cut the rope and pushed the boat
to sea.

SHUNKWAN.
He clasped his hands. He called, besought them—

ENVOY.
But though they heard him calling, they would not
carry him.

SHUNKWAN.
It was over ; he struggled no more.

CHORUS.
But left upon the beach, wildly he waved his sleeves,
Stricken as she [1] who on the shore
Of Matsura waved till she froze to stone.

ENVOY, NARITSUNE and YASUYORI (*together*).
Unhappy man, our hearts are not cold. When we
reach the City, we will plead unceasingly for your recall.
In a little while you shall return. Wait with a good
heart.

> (*Their voices grow fainter and fainter, as though
> the ship were moving away from the shore.*)

SHUNKWAN.
" Wait, wait," they cried, " Hope, wait ! "
But distance dimmed their cry,
And hope with their faint voices faded.
He checked his sobs, stood still and listened, listened—

> (SHUNKWAN *puts his hand to his ear and bends
> forward in the attitude of one straining to catch
> a distant sound.*)

---

[1] Sayohime who, when her husband sailed to Korea, stood waving on the cliff till she turned into stone.

THE THREE.

Shunkwan, Shunkwan, do you hear us ?

SHUNKWAN.

You will plead for me ?

THE THREE.

Yes, yes.   And then surely you will be summoned ...

SHUNKWAN.

Back to the City ?   Can you mean it ?

THE THREE.

Why, surely !

SHUNKWAN.

I hope ; yet while I hope . . .

CHORUS.

" Wait, wait, wait ! "
Dimmer grow the voices ; dimmer the ship, the wide
    waves
Pile up behind it.
The voices stop.   The ship, the men
Have vanished.   All is gone

> There is an ancient Kōwaka dance called Iō ga
> Shima, "Sulphur Island," another name for
> Devil's Island. It represents the piety of
> Naritsune and Yasuyori, and the amoral mysti-
> cism of the Zen abbot Shunkwan. Part of the
> text is as follows :

NARITSUNE.

This is the vow of the Holy One,
The God of Kumano :
" Whosoever of all mortal men
Shall turn his heart to me,
Though he be come to the utmost end of the desert,
To the furthest fold of the hills,
I will send a light to lead him ;

I will guide him on his way."
And we exiled on this far rock,
By daily honour to the Triple Shrine,
By supplication to Kumano's God,
Shall compass our return.
Shunkwan, how think you ?

SHUNKWAN.

Were it the Hill King of Hiyei,[1] I would not say
no. But as for this God of Kumano, I have no faith
in him. (*Describing the actions of* NARITSUNE *and*
YASUYORI.)

Then lonely, lonely these two to worship went;
On the wide sea they gazed,
Roamed on the rugged shore;
Searching ever for a semblance
Of the Three Holy Hills.
Now, where between high rocks
A long, clear river flowed;
Now where tree-tops soar
Summit on summit upward to the sky.
And there they planned to set
The Mother-Temple, Hall of Proven Truth;
And here the Daughter-Shrine,
The Treasury of Kan.
Then far to northward aiming
To a white cliff they came, where from the clouds
Swift waters tumbled down.
Then straightway they remembered
The Hill of Nachi, where the Dragon God,
Winged water-spirit, pants with stormy breath
And fills the woods with awe.
Here reverently they their Nachi set.

The Bonze Shunkwan mounted to a high place;
His eye wandered north, south, east and west.
A thousand, thousand concepts filled his heart.

[1] The headquarters of the Tendai sect of Buddhism.

Suddenly a black cloud rose before him,
A heavy cloak of cloud ;
And a great rock crashed and fell into the sea.
Then the great Bonze in his meditation remembered
An ancient song :
" The wind scattered a flower at Buddha's feet ;
A boulder fell and crushed the fish of the pool.
Neither has the wind merit, nor the boulder blame ;
They know not what they do."
" The Five Limbs are a loan," he cried, " that must
    be repaid ;
A mess of earth, water, air, fire.
And the heart—void, as the sky ; shapeless, sub-
    stanceless !
Being and non-being
Are but twin aspects of all component things.
And that which seems to be, soon is not.
But only contemplation is eternal."
So the priest : proudly pillowed
On unrepentance and commandments broke.

AMA
(THE FISHER-GIRL)

By SEAMI

FUJIWARA NO FUSAZAKI was the child of a fisher-girl.
He was taken from her in infancy and reared at the
Capital. When he grew to be a man he went to Shido
to look for her. On the shore he met with a fisher-girl
who, after speaking for some while with him, gave him
a letter, and at once vanished with the words : " I
am the ghost of the fisher-girl that was your mother."
The letter said :

Ten years and three have passed since my soul fled to the Yellow
Clod. Many days and months has the abacus told since the white
sand covered my bones. The Road of Death is dark, dark ; and
none has prayed for me.

I am your mother. Lighten, oh lighten, dear son, the great darkness
that has lain round me for thirteen years !

Then Fusazaki prayed for his mother's soul and she
appeared before him born again as a Blessed Dragon
Lady of Paradise, carrying in her hand the scroll of
the *Hokkekyō* (see Plate II), and danced the *Hayamai*,
the "swift dance," of thirteen movements. On the
Kongō stage the Dragon Lady is dressed as a man ;
for women have no place in Paradise.

TAKE NO YUKI

(SNOW ON THE BAMBOOS)

BY SEAMI

PERSONS

TONO-I.
HIS FIRST WIFE.
HIS SECOND WIFE.

TSUKIWAKA (his son by the first wife).
TSUKIWAKA'S SISTER.
A SERVANT.
CHORUS.

TONO-I.

My name is Tono-i. I live in the land of Echigo.
I had a wife; but for a trifling reason I parted from her
and put her to live in the House of the Tall Pines,
which is not far distant from here. We had two children;
and the girl I sent to live with her mother at the House
of the Tall Pines, but the boy, Tsukiwaka, I have here
with me, to be the heir of all my fortune.

And this being done, I brought a new wife to my
home. Now it happens that in pursuance of a binding
vow I must be absent for a while on pilgrimage to a
place not far away. I will now give orders for the
care of Tsukiwaka my son. Is my wife there?

SECOND WIFE.

What is it?

TONO-I.

I called you to tell you this : in pursuance of a vow
I must be absent on pilgrimage for two or three days.
While I am away, I beg you to tend my child Tsukiwaka
with loving care. Moreover I must tell you that the
snow falls very thick in these parts, and when it piles

up upon the bamboos that grow along the four walls
of the yard, it weighs them down and breaks them to
bits.

I don't know how it will be, but I fancy there is snow
in the air now. If it should chance to fall, pray order
my servants to brush it from the leaves of the bamboos.

SECOND WIFE.

What ? A pilgrimage, is it ? Why then go in peace,
and a blessing on your journey. I will not forget
about the snow on the bamboos. But as for Tsukiwaka,
there was no need for you to speak. Do you suppose
I would neglect him, however far away you went ?

TONO-I.

No, indeed. I spoke of it, because he is so very
young. . . .
But now I must be starting on my journey. (*He goes.*)

SECOND WIFE.

Listen, Tsukiwaka ! Your father has gone off on
a pilgrimage. Before he went, he said something to
me about you. ˙ " Tend Tsukiwaka with care," he said.
There was no need for him to speak. You must have
been telling him tales about me, saying I was not
kind to you or the like of that. You are a bad boy.
I am angry with you, very angry ! (*She turns away.*)

> TSUKIWAKA *then runs to his mother at the House of
> the Tall Pines. A lyric scene follows in which
> TSUKIWAKA and his mother (the CHORUS aiding)
> bewail their lot.*

> *Meanwhile the* SECOND WIFE *misses* TSUKIWAKA.

SECOND WIFE.

Where is Tsukiwaka ? What can have become of
him ? (*She calls for a servant.*) Where has Tsukiwaka
gone off to ?

SERVANT.

I have not the least idea.

SECOND WIFE.

Why, of course ! I have guessed. He took offence
at what I said to him just now and has gone off as usual
to the Tall Pines to blab to his mother. How tiresome !
Go and tell him that his father has come home and has
sent for him ; bring him back with you.

SERVANT.

I tremble and obey. (*He goes to the " hashigakari "
and speaks to* TSUKIWAKA *and the* FIRST WIFE.) The
master has come back and sent for you, Master Tsukiwaka ! Come back quickly !

FIRST WIFE.

What ? His father has sent for him ? What a pity ;
he comes here so seldom. But if your father has sent
for you, you must go to him. Come soon again to give
your mother comfort !

(*The* SERVANT *takes* TSUKIWAKA *back to the* SECOND
WIFE.)

SERVANT.

Madam, I have brought back Master Tsukiwaka.

SECOND WIFE.

What does this mean, Tsukiwaka ? Have you been
blabbing again at the House of the Tall Pines ? Listen !
Your father told me before he went away that if it
came on to snow, I was to tell some one to brush the
snow off the bamboos round the four walls of the yard.
It is snowing very heavily now. So be quick and
brush the snow off the bamboos. Come now, take off
your coat and do it in your shirt-sleeves.

(*The boy obeys. The* CHORUS *describes the " sweeping
of the bamboos." It grows colder and colder.*)

CHORUS.

The wind stabbed him, and as the night wore on,
The snow grew hard with frost ; he could not brush
  it away.
" I will go back," he thought, and pushed at the
  barred gate.
" Open ! " he cried, and hammered with his frozen
  hands.
None heard him ; his blows made no sound.
" Oh the cold, the cold ! I cannot bear it.
Help, help for Tsukiwaka ! "
Never blew wind more wildly !

(TSUKIWAKA *falls dead upon the snow.*)

*The servant finds him there and goes to the House
of the Tall Pines to inform the mother. A
scene of lament follows in which mother,
sister and chorus join. The father comes
home and hears the sound of weeping. When
he discovers the cause, he is reconciled with
the first wife (the second wife is not mentioned
again), and owing to their pious attitude, the
child returns to life.*

TORI-OI

By KONGŌ YAGORŌ

Bears a strong resemblance to *Take no Yuki.*
The date of the author is unknown.

A CERTAIN lord goes up to the city to settle a lawsuit,
leaving his steward in charge of his estate. In his
absence the steward grows overbearing in his manner
towards his mistress and her little son Hanawaka,
finally compelling them to take part in the arduous
labour of " bird-scaring," rowing up and down the river
among the rice-fields, driving away the birds that
attack the crop.

TANGO-MONOGURUI

By I-AMI

THERE are several plays which describe the fatal anger of a father on discovering that his child has no aptitude for learning. One of these, *Nakamitsu* or *Manjū*, has been translated by Chamberlain. The *Tango-Monogurui*, a similar play, has usually been ascribed to Seami, but Seami in his *Works* says that it is by a certain I-ami. The father comes on to the stage and, after the usual opening, announces that he has sent a messenger to fetch his son, whom he has put to school at a neighbouring temple. He wishes to see what progress the boy is making.

FATHER (*to his* SERVANT).

I sent some one to bring Master Hanamatsu back from the temple. Has he come yet?

SERVANT.

Yes, sir. He was here last night.

FATHER.

What? He came home last night, and I heard nothing about it?

SERVANT.

Last night he had drunk a little too much, so we thought it better not to say that he was here.

FATHER.

Oho! Last night he was tipsy, was he? Send him to me.

(*The* SERVANT *brings* HANAMATSU.)

Well, you have grown up mightily since I saw you last.

I sent for you to find out how your studies are progressing. How far have you got ?

HANAMATSU.

I have not learnt much of the difficult subjects. Nothing worth mentioning of the Sūtras or Shastras or moral books. I know a little of the graduses and Eight Collections of Poetry ; but in the Hokke Scripture I have not got to the Law-Master Chapter, and in the Gusha-shastra I have not got as far as the Seventh Book.

FATHER.

This is unthinkable ! He says he has not learnt anything worth mentioning. Pray, have you talents in any direction ?

SERVANT (*wishing to put in a good word for the boy*).

He's reckoned a wonderful hand at the chop-sticks and drum.[1]

FATHER (*angrily*).

Be quiet ! Is it your child I was talking of ?

SERVANT.

No, sir, you were speaking of Master Hanamatsu.

FATHER.

Now then, Hanamatsu. Is this true ? Very well then ; just listen quietly to me. These childish tricks— writing odes, capping verses and the like are not worth anything. They're no more important than playing ball or shooting toy darts. And as for the chop-sticks and drum—they are the sort of instruments street urchins play on under the Spear [2] at festival-time.

---

[1] The *sasara* (split bamboos rubbed together) and *yatsubachi*, "eight-sticks," a kind of vulgar drum.

[2] A sort of maypole set up at the Gion Festival.

But when I ask about your studies, you tell me that in
the Hokke you have not got to the Law-Master Chapter,
and in the Gusha-shāstra you have not reached the
Seventh Book. Might not the time you spent on the
chop-sticks have been better employed in studying the
Seventh Book ? Now then, don't excuse yourself ! Those
who talk most do least. But henceforth you are no son
of mine. Be off with you now !

(*The boy hesitates, bewildered.*)

Well, if you can't get started by yourself I must help you.

(*Seizes him by the arm and thrusts him off the stage.*)

In the next scene Hanamatsu enters accompanied by
a pious ship's captain, who relates that he found the
lad on the point of drowning himself, but rescued him,
and, taking him home, instructed him in the most
recondite branches of knowledge, for which he showed
uncommon aptitude ; now he is taking him back to
Tango to reconcile him with his father.

At Tango they learn that the father, stricken with
remorse, has become demented and is wandering over
the country in search of his son.

Coming to a chapel of Manjushrī, the captain persuades
the lad to read a service there, and announces to the
people that an eminent and learned divine is about to
expound the scriptures. Among the worshippers comes
an eccentric character whom the captain is at first
unwilling to admit.

MADMAN.

Even madmen can school themselves for a while.
I will not rave while the service is being read.

CAPTAIN.

So be it. Then sit down here and listen quietly.
(*To* HANAMATSU.) All the worshippers have come.
You had better begin the service at once.

HANAMATSU (*describing his own actions*).

Then because the hour of worship had come
The Doctor mounted the pulpit and struck the silence-
bell ;
Then reverently prayed :
Let us call on the Sacred Name of Shākyamuni, once
incarnate ;
On the Buddhas of the Past, the Present and the
Time to Come.
To thee we pray, Avalokita, Lord of the Ten Worlds ;
And all Spirits of Heaven and Earth we invoke.
Praised be the name of Amida Buddha !

MADMAN (*shouting excitedly*).

Amida ! Praise to Amida !

CAPTAIN.

There you go ! You promised to behave properly,
but now are disturbing [1] the whole congregation by
your ravings. I never heard such senseless shouting.

(*A lyrical dialogue follows full of poetical allusions,
from which it is apparent that the* MADMAN *is
crying to Amida to save a child's soul.*)

CAPTAIN.

Listen, Madman ! The Doctor heard you praying for
a child's soul. He wishes you to tell him your story.

*The father and son recognize one another. The
son flings himself down from the pulpit and
embraces his father. They go home together,
attributing their reunion to the intervention
of Manjushrī, the God of Wisdom.*

[1] Literally " waking."

IKKAKU SENNIN

(The One-horned Rishi)

A Rishi lived in the hills near Benares. Under strange
circumstances [1] a roe bore him a son whose form was
human, save that a single horn grew on his forehead,
and that he had stag's hoofs instead of feet. He was
given the name *Ekashringa*, " One-horn."

One day it was raining in the hills. Ekashringa
slipped and hurt himself, for his hoofs were ill-suited
to his human frame. He cursed the rain, and owing
to his great merit and piety his prayer was answered.
No rain fell for many months.

The King of Benares saw that the drought would soon
bring famine. He called together his counsellors, and
one of them told him the cause of the disaster. The
King published a proclamation promising the half of his
kingdom to any who could break the Rishi's spell.
Then the harlot Shāntā came to the King and said,
" I will bring you this Rishi riding him pickaback ! "

She set out for the mountains, carrying fruit and
wine. Having seduced the Rishi, she persuaded him
to follow her to Benares. Just outside the town she
lay down, saying that she was too tired to go a step
further. " Then I will carry you pickaback," said the
Rishi.

And so Shāntā fulfilled her promise.

In the Nō play (which is by Komparu Zembō Motoyasu
1453–1532) the Rishi has overpowered the Rain-dragons,

---

[1] " Il aperçut un cerf et une biche qui s'accouplaient. La passion
impure s'excita en lui. . . . La biche . . . se trouva grosse." Péri,
Les Femmes de Çakyamouni, p. 24.

and shut them up in a cave. Shāntā, a noble lady of
Benares, is sent to tempt him. The Rishi yields to
her and loses his magic power. There comes a mighty
rumbling from the cave.

CHORUS.

Down blows the mountain wind with a wild gust,
The sky grows dark,
The rock-cave quakes,
Huge boulders crash on every side ;
The dragons' forms appear.

IKKAKU.

Then the Rishi in great alarm—

CHORUS.

Then the Rishi in great alarm
Pursued them with a sharp sword.
And the Dragon King
Girt with the armour of wrath,
Waving a demon blade,
Fought with him for a little while.
But the Rishi had lost his magic.
Weaker and weaker he grew, till at last he lay upon
the ground.
Then the Dragon King joyfully
Pierced the dark clouds.
Thunder and lightning filled
The pools of Heaven, and fast
The great rain fell ; the wide floods were loosed.
Over the white waves flying,
The white waves that rise,
Homeward he hastens
To the Dragon City of the sea.

YAMAUBA

(THE DAME OF THE MOUNTAINS)

Revised by KOMPARU ZENCHIKU UJINOBU from an original by SEAMI

YAMAUBA is the fairy of the mountains, which have been under her care since the world began. She decks them with snow in winter, with blossoms in spring; her task carrying her eternally from hill to valley and valley to hill. She has grown very old. Wild white hair hangs down her shoulders; her face is very thin.

There was a courtesan of the Capital who made a dance representing the wanderings of Yamauba. It had such success that people called this courtesan "Yamauba," though her real name was Hyakuma.

Once when Hyakuma was travelling across the hills to Shinano to visit the Zenkō Temple, she lost her way, and took refuge in the hut of a "mountain-girl," who was none other than the real Yamauba.

In the second part of the play the aged fairy appears in her true form and tells the story of her eternal wanderings—"round and round, on and on, from hill to hill, from valley to valley." In spring decking the twigs with blossom, in autumn clothing the hills with moonlight, in winter shaking snow from the heavy clouds. "On and on, round and round, caught in the Wheel of Fate. . . . Striding to the hill-tops, sweeping through the valleys. . . ."

CHORUS.

On and on, from hill to hill.
Awhile our eyes behold her, but now
She is vanished over the hills,
Vanished we know not where.

The hill, says a commentator, is the Hill of Life, where men wander from incarnation to incarnation, never escaping from the Wheel of Life and Death.

HOTOKE NO HARA

By SEAMI

GIŌ was the mistress of Kiyomori (1118–1181), the greatest of the Tairas. One day there arrived at his camp a famous dancing-girl called Hotoke. Kiyomori was for sending her away ; but Giō, who had heard wonderful stories of Hotoke's beauty, was anxious to see her, and persuaded Kiyomori to let Hotoke dance before him.

Kiyomori fell in love with the dancer, and after a while Giō was dismissed. She became a nun, and with her mother and sister lived in a hut in the wilds of Sagano.

Hotoke, full of remorse at her rival's dismissal, found no pleasure in her new honours, and saying " It was I who brought her to this," fled in nun's clothing to the hut at Sagano. Here the four women lived together, singing ceaseless prayers to Buddha.

In the play the ghost of Hotoke appears to a " travelling priest," and tells the story, which is indeed a curious and arresting one.

MARI

(THE FOOTBALL)

A FOOTBALLER died at the Capital. When the news was brought to his wife, she became demented and performed a sort of football-mass for his soul. " The eight players in a game of football," she declared, " represent the eight chapters in the Hokke Scripture. If the four goal-posts are added the number obtained is twelve, which is the number of the Causes and Effects which govern life. Do not think of football as a secular game."

The play ends with a " football ballet."

The *Journal* of the great twelfth century footballer, Fujiwara no Narimichi, contains the following story : " I had brought together the best players of the time to assist me in celebrating the completion of my thousandth game. We set up two altars, and upon the one we placed our footballs, while on the other we arranged all kinds of offerings. Then, holding on to prayer-ribbons which we had tied to them, we worshipped the footballs.

That night I was sitting at home near the lamp, grinding my ink with the intention of recording the day's proceedings in my journal, when suddenly the football which I had dedicated came bouncing into the room followed by three children of about four years old. Their faces were human, but otherwise they looked like monkeys. "What horrid creatures," I thought, and asked them roughly who they were.

"We are the Football Sprites," they said. "And if you want to know our names—" So saying they lifted their hanging locks, and I saw that each of them had his name written on his forehead, as follows : Spring Willow Flower, Quiet Summer Wood, and Autumn Garden. Then they said, "Pray remember our names and deign to become our *Mi-mori*, ' Honourable Guardian.' Your success at *Mi-mari*, ' Honourable Football,' will then continually increase."

And so saying they disappeared.

TŌRU

By KWANAMI or SEAMI

TŌRU was a prince who built a great palace at Rokujō-kawara, near Kyōto. In its grounds was a counterfeit of the bay of Naniwa, which was filled and emptied twice a day in imitation of the tides. Labourers toiled up from the sea-shore, which was many miles distant, carrying pails of salt water.

In the play a priest passing through Rokujō-kawara meets an old man carrying salt-water pails. It is the ghost of Tōru. In the second part he rehearses the luxury and splendour of his life at the great palace Rokujō-kawara no In.

MAI-GURUMA [1]

(The Dance Waggons)

By Miyamasu (date unknown)

A man of Kamakura went for a year to the Capital
and fell in love with a girl there. When it was time
for him to return to Kamakura he took her with him.
But his parents did not like her, and one day when he
was not at home, they turned her out of the house.

Thinking that she would have gone towards the
Capital, the man set out in pursuit of her. At dusk
he came to a village. He was told that if he lodged
there he must take part next day in the waggon-
dancing, which was held in the sixth month of each
year in honour of the god Gion. He told them that he
was heart-sore and foot-sore, and could not dance.

Next day the villagers formed into two parties. The
first party mounted the waggon and danced the *Bijin-
zoroye*, a ballad about the twelve ladies whom Narihira
loved. The second party danced the ballad called
Tsumado, the story of which is :

Hosshō, Abbot of the Hiyeizan, was sitting late one
summer night by the Window of the Nine Perceptions,
near the Couch of the Ten Vehicles, in a room sprinkled
with the holy water of Yoga, washed by the moonlight
of the Three Mysteries. Suddenly there was a sound
of hammering on the double-doors. And when he
opened the doors and looked—why, there stood the
Chancellor Kwan, who had died on the twenty-fifth day
of the second month.

" Why have you come so late in the night, Chancellor
Kwan ? "

---

[1] Sometimes called *Bijin-zoroye* or *Bijin-zoroi*.

" When I lived in the world foul tongues slandered me. I am come to destroy my enemies with thunder. Only the Home of Meditation [1] shall be spared. But if you will make me one promise, I will not harm you. Swear that you will go no more to Court ! "

" I would not go, though they sent twice to fetch me. But if they sent a third time . . ."

Then Chancellor Kwan, with a strange look on his face, drew a pomegranate from his sleeve, put it between his lips, crunched it with his teeth, and spat it at the double-doors.

Suddenly the red pomegranate turned into fire ; a great flame flickered over the double-doors.

When the Abbot saw it, he twisted his fingers into the Gesture of Libation ; he recited the Water-Spell of the Letter Vam, and the flames died down.

And the double-doors still stand before the Abbot's cell, on the Hill of Hiyei.

When the two dances were over, the master of ceremonies called for a dance from one of those who had been watching. A girl stepped forward and said she would dance the " Dance of Tora Parting from Sukenari." Then they called across to the man who had lost his wife (he was over by the other waggon). " Come, you must dance now." " Forgive me, I cannot dance." " Indeed you must dance." " Then I will dance the ' Dance of Tora Parting from Sukenari.' "

" But this dance," said the master of ceremonies, " is to be danced by a girl on the other side. You must think of another dance."

MAN.

I know no other dance.

MASTER OF CEREMONIES.

Here's a pretty fix ! Ha, I have it ! Let's set the waggons side by side, and the two of them shall dance their dance together.

---

[1] The cell of the Zen priest.

When they step up on to the waggons, the man finds that his partner is the wife he was seeking for. They begin to dance the " Dance of Tora," but soon break off to exchange happy greetings. The plays ends with a great ballet of rejoicing.

There is one whole group of plays to which I have hitherto made no reference : those in which a mother seeks for her lost child. Mrs Stopes has translated *Sumidagawa*, and Mr Sansom, *Sakuragawa*. Another well-known play of this kind is *Miidera*, a description of which will be found in an appendix at the end of this book (p. 313).

A few other plays, such as *Nishikigi*, *Motomezuka*, and *Kinuta*, I have omitted for lack of space and because it did not seem to me that I could in any important way improve on existing versions of them.

CHAPTER VIII

KYŌGEN

KYŌGEN

(Farcical Interlude)

THE BIRD-CATCHER IN HELL [1]

(Esashi Jūō)

PERSONS

Yama, King of Hell.
Kiyoyori, The Bird-Catcher.
Demons.
Chorus.

Yama.

Yama the King of Hell comes forth to stand
At the Meeting of the Ways.[2]

> (*Shouting.*)

Yai, yai. Where are my minions ?

Demons.

Haa ! Here we are.

Yama.

If any sinners come along, set upon them and drive them off to Hell.

Demons.

We tremble and obey.

> (*Enter the bird-catcher*, Kiyoyori).

Kiyoyori.

" All men are sinners." What have I to fear
More than the rest ?

My name is Kiyoyori the Bird-Catcher. I was very well known on the Terrestrial Plane. But the span

---

[1] *Kyōgen Zenshū*, p. 541. This farce is a parody of such Nō-plays as *Ukai*.   [2] The Buddhist " Six Ways," *Rokudō*.

of my years came to its appointed close ; I was caught
in the Wind of Impermanence ; and here I am, marching
to the Sunless Land.

Without a pang
I leave the world where I was wont to dwell,
The Temporal World.
Whither, oh whither have my feet carried me ?
To the Six Ways already I have come.
Why, here I am already at the meeting of the Six Ways
of Existence.   I think on the whole I'll go to Heaven.

DEMON.

Haha !   That smells like a man.   Why, sure enough
here's a sinner coming.   We must report him.   (*To*
YAMA.)   Please, sir, here's the first sinner arrived
already !

YAMA.

Then bustle him to Hell at once.

DEMON.

I tremble and obey.   Listen, you sinner !
" Hell is ever at hand," [1] which is more than
Can be said of Heaven.   (*Seizing* KIYOYORI.)
Come on, now, come on !   (KIYOYORI *resists*.)
Yai, yai !
Let me tell you, you're showing a great
Deal more spirit than most sinners do.
What was your job when you were on the
Terrestrial Plane ?

KIYOYORI.

I was Kiyoyori, the famous bird-catcher.

DEMON.

Bird-catcher ?   That's bad.   Taking life from morning to night.   That's very serious, you know.   I am
afraid you will have to go to Hell.

[1] See *Ukai*, p. 169.

KIYOYORI.

Really, I don't consider I'm as bad as all that. I should be very much obliged if you would let me go to Heaven.

DEMON.

We must ask King Yama about this. (*To* YAMA.) Please sir— !

YAMA.

Well, what is it ?

DEMON.

It's like this.   The sinner says that on the Terrestrial Plane he was a well-known bird-catcher. Now that means taking life all the time ; it's a serious matter, and he certainly ought to go to Hell. But when we told him so, he said we'd entirely misjudged him.
What had we better do about it ?

YAMA.

You'd better send him to me.

DEMON.

Very well. (*To* KIYOYORI.)   Come along, King Yama says he'll see you himself.

KIYOYORI.

I'm coming.

DEMON.

Here's that sinner you sent for.

YAMA.

Listen to me, you sinner. I understand that when you were in the world you spent your whole time snaring birds. You are a very bad man and must go to Hell at once.

KIYOYORI.

That's all very well. But the birds I caught were sold to gentlemen to feed their falcons on ; so there was really no harm in it.

YAMA.

" Falcon " is another kind of bird, isn't it ?

KIYOYORI.

Yes, that's right.

YAMA.

Well then, I really don't see that there *was* much harm in it.

KIYOYORI.

I see you take my view. It was the falcons who were to blame, not I. That being so, I should be very much obliged if you would allow me to go straight to Heaven.

YAMA (*reciting in the Nō style*).

Then the great King of Hell—
Because, though on the Hill of Death
Many birds flew, he had not tasted one,
" Come, take your pole," he cried, and here and now
Give us a demonstration of your art.
Then go in peace.

KIYOYORI.

Nothing could be simpler.
I will catch a few birds and present them to you.
Then he took his pole, and crying
" To the hunt, to the hunt ! . . ."

CHORUS.

" To the bird-hunt," he cried,
And suddenly from the steep paths of the southern
    side of the Hill of Death
Many birds came flying.

Then swifter than sight his pole
Darted among them.
" I will roast them," he cried.
And when they were cooked,
" Please try one," and he offered them to the King.

YAMA (*greedily*).

Let me eat it, let me eat it.

(*Eats, smacking his lips.*)

Well !   I must say they taste uncommonly good !

KIYOYORI (*to the* DEMONS).

Perhaps you would like to try some ?

DEMONS.

Oh, thank you !   (*They eat greedily and snatch.*)   I
want that bit !   No, it's mine !   What a flavour !

YAMA.

I never tasted anything so nice.   You have given us
such a treat that I am going to send you back to the
world to go on bird-catching for another three years.

KIYOYORI.

I am very much obliged to you, I'm sure.

CHORUS.

You shall catch many birds,
Pheasant, pigeon, heron and stork.
They shall not elude you, but fall
Fast into the fatal snare.
So he, reprieved, turned back towards the World ;
But Yama, loth to see him go, bestowed
A jewelled crown, which Kiyoyori bore
Respectfully to the Terrestrial Plane,
There to begin his second span of life.

SHORT BIBLIOGRAPHY

EUROPEAN

B. H. Chamberlain : *The Classical Poetry of the Japanese*, 1880 (Rhymed paraphrases of *Sesshōseki*, *Kantan*, *Nakamitsu* and part of *Hagoromo* ; translations of the farces *Honekawa* and *Zazen*). The *Chrysanthemum*, 1882. Translation of *Hachi no Ki*.

F. W. K. Müller in *Festschrift f. Adolf Bastian*, pp. 513–537, *Ikkaku Sennin, eine mittelalterliche—Oper*, 1896.

Aston, History of *Japanese Literature*, 1899. Osman Edwards : *Japanese Plays and Playfellows*, 1901. (Refers to performances of *Shunkwan*, *Koi no Omoni*, *Aoi no Uye*, *Benkei in the Boat* and *Tsuchigumo*).

F. Brinkley, *Japan*, III. 21–60, 1901–2. (Translates *Ataka* and the farce *Sannin Katawa*).

F. Victor Dickins, *Japanese Texts*, 1906. (Text and Translation of *Takasago*).

K. Florenz, *Geschichte d. Japanischen Literatur*, 1906. (Translations of *Takasago* and *Benkei in the Boat* ; summaries of *Ataka*, *Mochizuki* and *Hanjo*. Translation of the farce *Hagi-Daimyō*).

N. Péri : *Etudes sur le drame lyrique japonais*, in *Bulletin de l'Ecole d'Extrême-Orient*, 1909–1913. (Includes translations of *Oimatsu*, *Atsumori*, *Ōhara Gokō*, *Sotoba Komachi* and *The Damask Drum*).

G. B. Sansom : Translations of *Ataka*, *Benkei in the Boat* and *Sakuragawa*.

H. L. Joly : Notes on masks, dances, etc., in *Transactions of Japan Society*, 1912.

M. Stopes : *Plays of Old Japan*, 1913. (Translations of *Motomezuka*, *Kagekiyo* and *Sumidagawa* ; summary of *Tamura*).

E. Fenollosa and Ezra Pound : *Noh or Accomplishment*, 1916. (Translations by E. F., adapted by E. P. Gives some account of about twenty plays. The versions of E. F. seem to have been fragmentary and inaccurate ; but wherever Mr. Pound had adequate material to work upon he has used it admirably).

See also general articles on the Japanese drama, such as A. Lloyd's in *Trans.* of *Asiatic Society of Japan*, 1908.

Yone Noguchi : *Twelve Kyōgen* (text and translation), 1911.

M. A. Hincks: *The Japanese Dance*, 32 pp., 1910.

JAPANESE

(Only a few important works are selected)

Kwadensho : the *Later Kwadensho* in 8 vols., first published c. 1600. (The British Museum possesses what is apparently an early eighteenth century reprint.)

Nō no Shiori : by Ōwada Tateki, 6 vols. (Description of the *modus operandi* of 91 plays), 1903.

Yōkyoku Hyōshaku : edited by Ōwada Tateki, 9 vols, 1907–8. Texts of about 270 plays, with commentary. Referred to by me as " Ōwada."

Nōgaku Daijiten : by Masada and Amaya, 2 vols. (Dictionary of Nō).

Seami Jūroku-bu Shū : *Works* of Seami, 1909.

Yōkyoku Sōsho : edited by Y. Haga and N. Sasaki, 3 vols. (Texts of about 500 plays with short notes. Referred to by me as " Haga ").

Zenchiku Shū : Works of Seami's son-in-law, 1917.

Kyōgen Zenshū : Complete Collection of Farces, 1910.

Jibyōshi Seigi : by Yamazaki Gakudō, 1915. (A study of Nō-rhythm).

Yōkyoku Kaisetsu : Nō-plays explained in colloquial, by K. Kawashima, 1913.

Magazines such as *Nōgaku Gwahō*, *Yōkyokukai*, etc.; picture postcards and albums of photographs such as *Nōgaku Mandai Kagami*, 1916.

Ryōjin Hisshō : Folk-songs collected in the 12th century and rediscovered in 1911.

APPENDIX I

MODERN NŌ AND LETTERS FROM JAPAN

THE fact that Nō did not disappear with the over-throw of the Shōgun in 1868 was almost solely due to the efforts of Umewaka Minoru (1828–1909), whose ancestors had for generations played *tsure* parts in the Kwanze theatre. When the Mikado was restored in 1868 Kiyotaka, head of the Kwanze line, was convinced than an art so intimately connected with the Shōgunate must perish with it, and fled to Shizuoka where the fallen Shōgun was living in retreat.

Minoru alone remained behind, built himself a theatre [1] (1869–70) and " manned his lonely rampart." When confidence was re-established the other " troupes " soon returned, so that henceforward five theatres existed, the four of earlier days and that of Umewaka as a fifth. Minoru was succeeded by his brilliant sons, Mansaburō and Rokurō, who in 1919 opened a new Umewaka theatre. As a compliment to the Umewaka family and a tribute to its services, actors of the three other " schools " took part in the opening ceremony, but the Kwanzes refused to do so. The dispute turns on the right to grant certificates of efficiency (*menjō*) which, according to the Kwanzes' claim, belongs only to Motoshige, the head of their school. Such certificates have, in fact, been issued successively by Minoru, his sons and the " renegade " Kwanze Tetsunojō, who sides with the Umewaka.

[1] Or, according to Fenollosa, bought a stage belonging to an ex-daimyō.

The validity of Minoru's certificates was, I believe, never disputed during his lifetime.

To complete this note on modern Nō I include the following extracts from letters written in 1916 by Mr Oswald Sickert to Mr Charles Ricketts. The sender and recipient of the letters both authorized me to use them, and for this permission I am deeply grateful. But I wish that Mr Sickert, whose memories of Nō must already be a little dimmed, had had the leisure to write a book of his own on the two dramatic arts that so deeply interested him in Japan, the Nō and the Kabuki.

" It's odd if people describe the Nō performance as a thing that is simple or unsophisticated or unelaborated. The poem, to begin with, is not simple ; but it has a lyrical slenderness which wouldn't, one would say, lead anybody to think of going such lengths as to distribute its recitation among a chorus and actors, thus requiring perhaps eleven men to say the words, with two or three drums and a flute added, and masks and costumes fit for a museum, and angelic properties, and special stages, and attendants to wipe, in this hot weather, the sweat from immovable hands and from under chins. The volume of what goes to a performance is large, but it's all cut down outwardly and bent inwards. As for the recitation, the first necessity is to eliminate direct expressiveness in the saying of the words. This seems obvious in the saying of any good poetry. The chorus chants (it's rather like a Gregorian chant), the actors intone. Both may come to singing, only not with any tune that might carry you off by itself. Yet, within the limitations of intoning, with some turns, the actor taking the women's parts will achieve a pitch of pathetic intensity beyond the reach of one who sings words to an air that has an existence of its own, or who recites with meaning. The Nō actor is not directly expressive, it's always the poem he is doing and throwing you back on.

" I suppose the mask may have originated in a priest's needing to impersonate an angel or a beautiful girl, or an evil spirit ; but its justification, as against make-up, is absolute for the Nō purpose. I saw in the same week *Funa Benkei*, adapted for the theatre, at the Imperial and on a Nō stage. At the theatre, the part of Shizuka, the mistress whom Yoshitsune the pursued young lord is persuaded to send away, was taken by Baikō. It was one of his nights, and all the evening, as three different women and a ghost, he was so that I shall not again ever so much care about a beautiful woman taken by a beautiful woman. But in the theatre version of *Funa Benkei*, Shizuka wore no mask, and when she pleaded, Baikō, of course, acted ; it was charming ; but Heaven knows what *words* he was saying—certainly he was not turning the mind of his audience in upon any masterpiece of words, rhythm and poetical fancy. He was acting the situation. The Nō performer, on the other hand, is intensifying the poet's fancy. From sight of the masks hung up alone, I had not imagined how well their mixture of vacancy and realism would do the trick. The masks are not wayward, not extravagant (even the devil's masks are realistic) ; but they are undoubtedly masks tied on with a band, and they effect the purpose of achieving an impassive countenance of a cast suited to the character—impassive save that, with a good actor and a mask of a beautiful woman that just hits off the balance between too much and too little physiognomy, I'd swear that at the right moments the mask is affected, its expression intensifies, it lives.

" The costumes are tremendous, elaborate, often priceless heirlooms ; but again they are not extravagant, ' on their own,' being all distinctly hieratic (as indeed is the whole performance, a feature historically deriving, maybe, from its original source among priests, but just what one would desiderate if one were creating a Nō performance out of the blue), because the hieratic helps to create and maintain a host of restrictions and conventions which good taste alone, even in Japan, could scarcely have preserved against the fatal erosion of reason.

"The masked actors of beautiful women are stuffed out and by some device increase the appearance of height, though all go in socks and apparently with bent knees. The great masked figure, gliding without lifting the heels, but with all the more appearance of swiftness, to the front of the stage, is the most ecstatic thing to sit under, and the most that a man can do to act what people mean by 'poetical,' something removed from reality but not remote, fascinating so that you fall in love with it, but more than you would care to trifle with. This movement occurs in the dances which come in some plays—I think always as dances by characters invited to dance—and which are the best moments for the stranger, since then alone does the rhythm of the drums become regular enough for him to recognize it. For that is really, I am sure, the bottom essential of the Nō representation —the rhythm marked by two drums. For quite long intervals nothing else occurs. No actor is on the stage, no word is uttered, but the sharp rap sounds with the thimbled finger as on a box and the stumpy little thud of the bare hands follows, or coincides, from the second drum and both players give a crooning whoop. In some way, which I can't catch, that rhythm surely plays into the measure of the recitation when it comes and into the movements of the actors when they come. You know how people everywhere will persist in justifying the admirable in an art on the ground of the beautiful ideas it presents. So my friends tell me the drum beats suggest the travelling of the pilgrim who is often the hinge of the episode. I feel like a Japanese who wants to know whether a sonnet has any particular number of lines, and any order for its rhymes and repeats, and gets disquisitions on Shakespeare's fancy which might also apply to a speech in blank verse. Anyway, it is ever so evident

that the musicians do something extremely difficult
and tricky. The same musicians don't seem to play
on through the three pieces which make a programme.
As they have no book (and don't even look at each
other), they must know the performance by heart,
and the stranger's attention is often called by a friend
to one or the other who is specially famous for his
skill. Some one tried to explain the relation between
the musicians and the actors by saying that a perpetual
sort of contest went on between them. Certainly
there seems to be in a Nō performance some common
goal which has to be strained for every time, immensely
practised though the performers are. During the dance
this drum rhythm speeds up to a felt time, and at
moments of great stress, as when an avenging ghost
swims on with a spear, a third drum, played with
sticks, comes in with rapid regular beats, louder and
softer. Sometimes when the beats are not so follow-
able, but anyway quicker in succession, I seem to make
out that they must be involving themselves in some
business of syncopation, or the catching up and out-
stripping of a slow beat by a quicker one. But the
ordinary beats are too far apart for me to feel any
rhythm yet.

"The best single moment I have seen was the dance
of thanks to the fisherman who returns to the divine
lady the Hagoromo, the robe without which even an
angel cannot fly. It seemed to me an example of the
excellent rule in art that, if a right thing is perhaps
rather dull or monotonous lasting five minutes, you
will not cure the defect by cutting the performance
to two and a half minutes; rather give it ten minutes.
If it's still perhaps rather dull, try twenty minutes
or an hour. This presupposes that your limitations
are right and that you *are* exploiting them. The thing
may seem dull at first because at first it is the limitations the spectator feels; but the more these are
exploited the less they are felt to be limitations, and
the more they become a medium. The divine lady

returned on her steps at great length and fully six times after I had thought I could not bear it another moment. She went on for twenty minutes, perhaps, or an hour or a night; I lost count of time; but I shall not recover from the longing she left when at last she floated backwards and under the fatal uplifted curtain. The movements, even in the dance, are very restricted if one tries to describe or relate them, but it may be true, as they say, that the Nō actor works at an intense and concentrated pitch of all his thoughts and energies, and this tells through his impassive face or mask and all his clothes and his slow movements. Certainly the longer I looked at the divine lady, the more she seemed to me to be in action, though sometimes the action, if indeed there, was so slight that it could only be that she had worked us up to the fine edge of noticing her breathing. There was only one memorable quick motion in the dance, the throwing of the stiff deep gauze sleeve over the head, over the crown with its lotus and bell tassels. My wife has no inclination to deceive herself with the fascination of what she can't explain, and she agreed that this was the most beautiful thing that had ever been seen.

"You will see the two drum players in many of the cards. With them sits the player on the fue, a transverse flute, who joins in at moments with what often is, if you take it down, the same phrase, though it sounds varied as the player is not often exactly on any note that you *can* take down. The dropping of the flute's note at the end of the phrase, which before always went up, is the nearest approach to the 'curtain' of the theatre. It is very touching. The poem has come to an end. The figures turn and walk off. . . .

"I have been to more Nō performances, always with increasing recognition of the importance attaching to the beat, a subject on which I have got some assur-

ance from an expert kindly directed to me by a friend.
From beginning to end, all the words of every Nō
play fit into an 8-beat measure, and a performer who
sat in the dark, tapping the measure while skilfully
weaving in the words, would give a Nō audience the
essential ground of its pleasure. If they are not
actually being followed on books, in which they are
printed as ticks alongside the text, the beats are going
on inside (often to the finger tips of) all the people
whom I notice to be regular attendants at Nō performances. I saw a play (not a good one) at the Kabukiza
in which a Nō master refuses a pupil a secret in his
art. For some reason the pupil attaches importance
to being shown the way in this difficult point. The
master's daughter takes poison and, in fulfilment of
her dying request, the master consents to show the
pupil. It was no subtlety of gesture, no matter of
voice or mask, that brought things to such straits.
The master knelt at his desk, and, beating with his
fan, began reciting a passage, showing how the words
were distributed in the beat.

" It is very seldom that every beat in the eight is
marked by a drum. I don't think this happens save
in those plays where the taiko (the real drum played
with sticks) takes part, generally in an important or
agitated dance. In the ordinary course, only certain
of the eight beats are marked by the two players on
the tsuzumi (one held on the knee, the other over the
shoulder). The Japanese get much more out of
subtleties of rhythm (or, rather, out of playing hide-
and-seek with one simple rhythm) than we do and
are correspondingly lax about the interval between
one note and another. I don't believe a European
would have thought of dividing the drum beats
between two instruments. It must be horribly tricky
to do. This division gives variety, for the big tsuzumi
yields a clack and the small yields something between
a whop and a thud.

" As for masks, one would have to see very many

performances, I fancy, and think a lot, before one
got on to any philosophy of their fascination and
effectiveness. I am always impressed by the realism,
the naturalness of the Nō mask. It is not fanciful
in any obvious sense. After a few performances, I
found I knew when a mask was a particularly good
one. My preferences turned out to be precious heirlooms two hundred years old. In one instance when,
for a reason I don't yet understand, Rokurō changed
his mask after death for another of the same cast,
I could not say why the first was better than the
second—certainly not for a pleasanter surface, for it
was shining like lacquer ; I noticed the features were
more pronounced. We were allowed the thrill of
being let into the room of the mirror, immediately
behind the curtain, and saw Rokurō have his mask
fitted and make his entry after a last touch by his
brother Mansaburō. These brothers are Umewaka,
belong to the Kwanze School, and have a stage of
their own. I am told that my preference for them
is natural to a beginner and that later one likes as
much, or better, the more masculine style of the
Hōshō. At present Nagashi (Matsumoto), the chief
performer of this school (which has a lovely stage and
a very aristocratic clientèle), seems to me like an
upright gentlemen who has well learned his lesson,
while Rokurō and Mansaburō are actors. Both brothers
have beautiful voices. The Hōshō people speak with
a thickness in the throat. But I know it is absurd
for me to feel critical about anything. Moreover,
Rokurō and Nagashi would not take the same parts.

" MIIDERA. A mother, crazed by the straying away
of her little boy, is advised by a neighbour any way
to go to Ōtsu, for there stands the temple of Mii which
she had seen in a dream.

" The priests of Miidera, with the little boy among
them, are out in the temple yard viewing the full
autumn moon. The attendant tolls the great bell,
whose lovely note wavers long over the lake below.

The mad mother appears on the scene, and, drawn to the bell, makes to toll it. The head priest forbids her. There follows an argument full of bell lore, and its effect on troubled hearts. She tolls the bell, and mother and son recognize each other.

"One of the cards I sent shows the mother tolling the bell. She comes on first in a red flowered robe, is advised by the neighbour and goes off. The priests come on. The sounding of the bell is the hinge of everything, a thing of great sentiment. As it is, in reality, one of the most touching things in the world, it seemed to me clever that there was no attempt to represent it. On the contrary, the action centred in the toller, a cheery old gossiper used to the job, who more or less spat on his hands and said Heave ho as he swung the imaginary horizontal beam. Only when he had done so, he continued his Heave ho in a kind of long echoing hum. Then he danced. The mad mother came on in another dress, very strange, light mauve gauze over white, no pattern, and the bough in her hand. Why, when the old man had already tolled, for one's imagination, a non-existent bell in the real way with a heavy beam, the mother should actually pull a coloured ribbon tied to an elaborate toy, it is hard to say. But it is right.

"I saw this taken by Mansaburō, who, like his brother Rokurō, has a beautiful voice. The singing is so unlike ours, that at first one feels nothing about it. But after three or four performances one notices, and I recognized the beauty of both these brothers' voices before I knew they were brothers, or, indeed, that they were noted in any way. In fact I was still in the state when I had not yet realized that one might come to discussing the merits of these players hidden in robes and masks as hotly as one discusses the qualities of the favourites on the ordinary theatre.

"I don't know if you know about the curtain. Every subsidiary detail of the performance possesses, I don't know how to say, but a solidity. It's there.

God knows how it came there ; but there it is, and it's not a contrivance, not an 'idea.' The entry to the stage, as you know, is by a narrow gallery, beside which three little pine-trees rise like milestones. This gallery ends with a single heavy curtain, which does not rise as ours do, or draw aside or fall as in the Japanese theatre. It sweeps back, only bellying a little. It is, in fact, as I saw when I was allowed behind, lifted by poles fixed to the bottom corners. The poles are raised rapidly by two men kneeling a good way behind. Suddenly the curtain blows back as by a wind, and the expected figure, whom you know must be coming or something, i.e. suspense is prepared by what has already happened, is framed in the opening, and there pauses an instant. I am speaking, not of the first entry, but of the second one, when the person who aroused the pilgrim-visitor's curiosity as a temple-sweeper or a water-carrier, and vanished, reappears as the great General or princely Prime Minister he once was. The stage-wait necessitated by the change of costume and mask is filled in by an interminable sayer of short lines, with the same number of feet, each line detached from the next as if the speaker were going from one afterthought to another. He is a bystander—perhaps a shepherd in one play and a fisherman in another — who knows something, and dilates on it to fill in time. The musicians lay aside their drums. Everybody just waits. Up sweeps the curtain, and with the re-entry of the revealed personage comes the intenser and quicker second part for which the slow first part was a preparation."

APPENDIX II

Some of the facts brought to light by the discovery of Seami's *Works* :—

(1) It had long been suspected that the current *Kwadensho* was not the work of Seami. The discovery of the real *Kwadensho* has made this certain.

(2) Traditional dates of Kwanami and Seami corrected.

(3) It was supposed that only the music of the plays was written by their nominal authors. The words were vaguely attributed to "Zen Priests." We now know that in most cases Kwanami and Seami played the triple part of author,[1] musical composer and actor.

(4) It was doubted whether in the fourteenth century Sarugaku had already become a serious dramatic performance. We now know that it then differed little (and in respect of seriousness not at all) from Nō as it exists to-day.

(5) It was supposed that the Chorus existed from the beginning. We now learn from Seami that it was a novelty in 1430. Its absence must have been the chief feature which distinguished the Sarugaku of the fourteenth century from the Nō of to-day.

(6) Numerous passages prove that Nō at its zenith was not an exclusively aristocratic art. The audiences were very varied.

(7) Seami gives details about the musical side of the plays as performed in the fourteenth century. These passages, as is confessed even by the great Nō-scholar, Suzuki Chōkō, could be discussed only by one trained in Nō-music.

---

[1] Or rather " arranger," for in many instances he adapted already existing Dengaku or Kōwaka.

INDEX

Shinto, 15, 27, 28, 113?,